Grade 1

Helen G. Cappleman

With grateful acknowledgment to the late Anne H. Adams,
the originator of *SUCCESS in Reading and Writing*.

GoodYearBooks

An Imprint of ScottForesman
A Division of HarperCollinsPublishers

Cover illustration by Emily Payne.
Cover design by Amy O'Brien Krupp.
Book design by Carolyn McHenry.

Good Year Books
are available for preschool through grade 6 and for every basic curriculum subject plus many enrichment areas. For more Good Year Books, contact your local bookseller or educational dealer. For a complete catalog with information about other Good Year Books, please write:

Good Year Books
Scott, Foresman and Company
1900 East Lake Avenue
Glenview, Illinois 60025

Cappleman, Helen G.
    Success in reading and writing. Grade 1 / Helen G. Cappleman. -- 2nd ed.
        p. cm.
    Includes index.
    ISBN 0-673-36001-6
    1. Reading (Primary)--United States—Handbooks, manuals, etc. 2. Language arts (Primary)—United States—Handbooks, manuals, etc. 3. Teaching—Aids and devices—Handbooks, manuals, etc.
I. Title. II. Title: Success in reading and writing. Grade one.
LB 1525.C24 1992
372.4—dc20   91-17023
                                                                                              CIP

This book is printed on paper that exceeds the 50% minimum recycled paper requirement specified by the Environmental Protection Agency.

▶ Preface

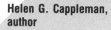

Helen G. Cappleman, author

SUCCESS in Reading and Writing is a student-centered integrated reading and writing program that is based on a belief in the capabilities of students and the professionalism of teachers. The instructional materials in this exciting program are library books and everyday materials, such as newspapers, magazines, and other materials from our print-rich world. Students of all abilities are routinely involved in individual and cooperative problem-solving activities that ask them to make decisions and take risks, without the necessity of placing them in ability groups. The flexible structure of the 180 lesson plans insures a balanced curriculum and a daily routine, but at the same time these lessons continually ask both teacher and student to make choices in the reading and writing taking place in the classroom.

Developed in the mid-1970s by the late Anne H. Adams, *SUCCESS in Reading and Writing* has stood the test of time. For more than twelve years in all kinds of settings, *SUCCESS in Reading and Writing* has proven that valuing literacy and thinking results in literate, thinking students and teachers.

This second edition of *SUCCESS in Reading and Writing* follows in its philosophy and intent the first edition. In the years since *SUCCESS in Reading and Writing* was first developed, we have learned much about process teaching and learning, and a great deal of what Dr. Adams knew instinctively has been researched and proven true. She was able, even then, to outline a structure that insured balanced teaching but was flexible enough that teachers could adapt it to their teaching styles, curricular demands, and, most importantly, their students.

Our goal with this new edition of *SUCCESS in Reading and Writing* was to make the philosophy of the program clearer and the program itself even easier to implement. Now the procedures are clearer; the Writing module has been updated; we have placed an even greater emphasis on the importance of students reading and otherwise experiencing good books; and we have provided more information assisting teachers in making decisions within the framework of *SUCCESS in Reading and Writing*. These decisions range from integrating content-area themes and incorporating more children's books throughout the curriculum to assessing and meeting the needs of all students.

Perhaps the most apparent change comes in the names of the modules. In an effort to make the module names consistent across all grade levels, Academic, Cultural Arts, and Current Events has been changed to Research; Language Experience to Writing; and Phonics/Spelling to Word Study.

The process of revision is ongoing. Learning about learning does not stop.

Acknowledgments

SUCCESS in Reading and Writing workshop leaders, who have helped shape SUCCESS as it has developed in classrooms across the country:

Mary Armstrong
Peggy Bahr
Jean Becker
Patti Bell
Jean Bernholz
Barbara Blackford
Jill Board
Elaine Bowie
Ann Bryan
Jacqueline Buckmaster
Helen Cappleman
Stacey Carmichael
Kathi Caulley
Betty Cramer
Donna Croft
Suzie Desilet
Bobbi Donnell
Marilyn Enger
Betty S. English
Sandra Fain
Debra Fetner
Neita Frank
Carol George
Randy Gill
Lynn Gori-Bjerkness
Letha Gressley
Andra Gwydir
Carol Hall
Mary Harris
Roberta Harrison

Becky Haseltine
Debby Head
Paula Hertel
Bridget Hill
Tina Hinchliff
Robbie Ivers
Connie John
Shae Johnson
Delores P. Jones
Joanne Jumper
Janice Keegan
Nancy Kerr
Dana Kersey
Annie Kinegak
Barbara Krieger
Esther Lee
Sue Lippincott
Lisa Lord
Kathy Malick
Judy Mansfield
Howard Martin
Judy Martin
Lila Martin
Nancy J. Mayhall
Becky Miller
Debbie I. Miller
Debby Miller
Paul Moller
Cinda Lee Moon
Avril Moore

Cam Newman
Kathy Newport
Ola Pickels
Libby Pollett
Karen Powell
Susan Quick
Donna Rea
Cathy Reasor
Patty Redland
Mary B. Reeves
Carole Reindl
Pat Reinheimer
Marilyn Renfro
Janice Reynolds
Marlene Rotter
Pat Scherler
Janet Schneider
Shirley T. Scruggs
Celeste Singletary
Kathleen Smith
Patty B. Smith
Pat Sumner
Pam Tate
Donnye Theerman
Shirley A. Thompson
Jean Weaver
Beth Whitford
Pat Wong
Michael Wong
Kristin Zeaser-Sydow

Special thanks to Jean Becker, Jean Weaver, Donnye Theerman, and Barbara Blackford for their helpful comments on the preliminary manuscript. Also, thanks to Betty Cramer, not only for her assistance in writing this book, but for her knowledge of children's literature and her illustrations. Thanks also to the wonderful teachers who gathered the students' artwork, particularly that art which related to specific lessons, and thanks to the students and their parents. Above all, thanks to my tolerant, loyal friends, most especially Nancy Duncan, who have heard nothing but "revision" for far too long.

▶ Art Acknowledgments

The following young artists have contributed to this edition of *SUCCESS in Reading and Writing*, Grade 1:

Charlie Hester, Springfield, Oregon
Chelsea Varnum, Yamhill, Oregon
Keegan Fogg, Yamhill, Oregon
Paterno Porter, Inman, South Carolina
Ben Weaver, Independence, Missouri
Cassie Slessman, Independence, Missouri
Erin Landauer, Yamhill, Oregon
Scott Bensing, Louisville, Kentucky
Adam Bungart, Independence, Missouri
Jennifer Toftdahl, Springfield, Oregon
Tyler Smith, Springfield, Missouri
Joey Bansen, Yamhill, Oregon
Nicholas Miller, Independence, Missouri
Amanda McAbee, Inman, South Carolina
Bryan Martorano, Springfield, Oregon
Michael Dominick, Independence, Missouri
Jenny Turek, Yamhill, Oregon
Kevin Wright, Louisville, Kentucky
Jake Carr, Springfield, Oregon
Ashley Westmoreland, Independence, Missouri
Sam Wyffles, Yamhill, Oregon
Abbie Chrisman, Springfield, Oregon
Jason Workman, Independence, Missouri
Bo Cappleman, Charlotte, North Carolina
Michael Gardner, Springfield, Missouri
Hannah Cornforth, Eugene, Oregon
Kristin M. Fischbach, Springfield, Missouri
Travis J. Shafer, Yamhill, Oregon

Angela Poland, Quitman, Georgia
Kirt Morris, Quitman, Georgia
Andrew Bartlett, Florissant, Missouri
Sarah Butts, Florissant, Missouri
Stephen Schuler, Florissant, Missouri
Dennis Polzel, Boring, Oregon
David Fornachon, Florissant, Missouri
Paul Casteel
Dustin Salta, Boring, Oregon
Krissy Risch
Noah Taylor, Boring, Oregon
Scott Taylor
Shawn Rose, Florissant, Missouri
Anna Branagan, Boring, Oregon
Ben Appling
Caroline Canfield, Yamhill, Oregon
Brian Melvin, Boring, Oregon
Matthew Brady
Joshua Neil, Eugene, Oregon
Tom Moore, Eugene, Oregon
Adam Burgh, Yamhill, Oregon
Brett Williams, Barney, Georgia
Kristen Condit
Teresa Ekberg, Eugene, Oregon
Ricky Seagrave, Springfield, Oregon
Ryan Westmoreland
Diana Davis
Sergio Tate, Cowpens, South Carolina
Steven Moore, Cowpens, South Carolina
Tiffanie Fox, Cowpens, South Carolina
Jordan Barrett, Cowpens, South Carolina
Brad Phillips, Cowpens, South Carolina
Trey Bogan, Cowpens, South Carolina

▶ Contents

Chapter 4   The Writing Module   54

Chapter 5   The Word Study Module   68

SuccesS
in Reading and Writing
Second Edition

Grade 1

Chapter 1 SUCCESS: The Basic Assumption

First grade is the time the world of a young child opens up to include the wonders of reading and writing, the joys of being able to explore the universe of books without depending on the schedule of an adult, the satisfaction of being self-sufficient, the confidence of being BIG!

SUCCESS in Reading and Writing is a proven way of teaching and learning that captures the excitement of the first-grader entering school. It is based on the belief that all children want to read, write, and learn. Equally important, SUCCESS teachers believe that all children, regardless of their past experiences or innate abilities, can become readers, writers, and learners. SUCCESS teachers love learning, and they experience true joy when they see young people unlock the mysteries of reading and writing.

Since its development in the late 1970s, SUCCESS has shown that all students can be successful learners. First proven in inner-city schools, it has also been used extensively in selective private schools. Students from comparatively language-poor environments, including students for whom English is a second language, have been able to capitalize on their experiences and succeed. Academically gifted students have had no ceiling placed on them. Those who did not function in the atmosphere of traditional schooling have been released to march to their own drummer and become competent students. By all measures, including standardized testing, SUCCESS has reinforced the fact that all students can learn.

▶ The SUCCESS Way of Teaching and Learning

Every day in every SUCCESS classroom, students read in books of their choice and have at least one book read to them. Every day every student has the opportunity to express his or her thoughts on paper through writing, drawing, or some combination of the two. Every day students explore real-life reading materials such as newspapers and magazines for information they can relate to the project proposed by the teacher. And every day the class generates a chart of words or groups of words from the students' vocabularies that have at least one of the characteristics proscribed by the teacher.

At all times the students are *actively* involved in their learning. They are totally engaged because every activity is meaningful to them. Each student chooses what to read and write. The words they study and the associations they make are their own. The language, experiences, and ideas of the individual students are the core of SUCCESS.

Each of the daily lessons contain activities which are called modules. Most activities last for thirty minutes; reading and being read to takes sixty minutes. Together the reading and writing instructional time totals 2 1/2 hours. These are the modules taught each day:

Chapter 1

Charlie Hester

1. Research
    a. The teacher introduces an activity; (5 minutes)
    b. students search and record what they find; (20 minutes)
    c. the students share what they learned. (5 minutes)

Students search through newspapers, magazines, content-area textbooks, library books, and functional reading materials for information they can associate directly or indirectly to the lesson's theme or topic.

2. Recreational Reading and Storytime
    a. The students read books they choose; (30 minutes)
    b. the teacher reads also or converses with students;
    c. the teacher reads a story or book aloud and the class discusses the book; (15-30 minutes)
    d. the students do an art or craft activity. (optional)

3. Writing
    a. The teacher leads a brief mini-lesson; (5 minutes)
    b. the students write; (20 minutes)
    c. the students share their writing. (5 minutes)

Students write on the topic introduced by the teacher, a topic of their own choosing, or continue writing on a previously begun topic.

4. Word Study
    a. The teacher leads chart-making; (15 minutes)
    b. the students write. (15 minutes)

The routine is the same each day. What changes is the students. They change in the types of books they read. They change in their understanding and appreciation of hearing books read. They change in what they write about and how they write it. They change in what they look for and what they find as they research printed materials. They change in their awareness and excitement about words, to say nothing about the change in their knowledge about how words work. They grow in their confidence and their willingness to take risks. Every day they become even better readers, writers, and learners.

The procedures remain basically the same all year. Students learn quickly that they can trust in that routine. They don't come to school wondering what the teacher has planned for them. They know the excitement of the day will come from exploring printed materials and from the new knowledge they discover. The procedures stay the same; it is the students, and what they know, that changes.

This book is a description of the philosophy behind the *SUCCESS in Reading and Writing* program, its components or modules, and how they work. Chapters 2 through 5 discuss each of the four modules. Chapter 6 addresses some of the daily details like evaluation, classroom management, and the materials needed. Following the chapters are the outlines of 180 flexible lesson plans, one for each day in a typical school year. Page 6 contains an example of a SUCCESS lesson format.

Specific topics, themes, letters, and books are suggested each day. They are just that: suggestions. Each of them is followed by the word *or* and a blank line. Teachers are encouraged to read the specific suggestions to decide if they are appropriate for their class that day. Many teachers opt to substitute topics that relate to a content-area theme the class is studying or emphasize a different reading or writing skill. Some teachers choose to make all of the lesson components relate to a book, theme, or current event. These modifications are important for teachers teaching their students, instead of trying to teach a program, and are central to the SUCCESS philosophy and procedures.

Although much about SUCCESS lessons *seems* the same, no two lessons will ever be the same. The experiences and personality of each teacher come through. The parts one teacher will emphasize will be diminished by another. The materials students use will vary from class to class, so the information they find will never be the same. But most importantly, the students are different in each class. No two groups think the same, act the same, or draw the same conclusions. Yet all can be right. There is rarely one single right answer, one single way of doing the task right. To be right in a SUCCESS lesson, the student has to be able to explain his or her reasoning logically. Those who can defend their ideas are right; those who cannot must try again.

My students get excited and turned on about learning. It's fun and not a chore. There are no absolute "right" answers. Everyone can be right, even giving different responses to one question.

Deatru R. Wages, teacher

Lesson **21**

Research

LEAD-IN
Teacher introduces the Project Idea.
Theme: Jobs or _____
Material: Magazines or _____
Reading Focus: Classification or

_____

SEARCH & RECORD
Project Idea: Individually, students cut or tear from magazines pictures or words related to the lesson's theme. They

paste or tape the pictures or words on their papers. Encourage discussion of findings with neighbors.
   Teachers check students for association of pictures/words with theme.

SHARING
Students discuss the items found that relate to the day's theme or _____.
   Papers are dated and filed.

Recreational Reading

For approximately 30 minutes all students read or look at books.

CONVERSATIONS
Check-In: Teacher moves among students having 2- to 3-minute conversations with as many individuals as possible. If appropriate, discuss main idea(s) and/or _____.

CLIPBOARD NOTES
Teacher notes who seeks meaning from books or _____.

BOOK SHARING
Each person tells another person something he or she has read about that day.

and Storytime

READ ALOUD
Owliver by Robert Kraus or _____
   Discuss *who* is in the story and *what* happened.

ACTIVITY (Optional)
Make an Owliver paper doll. Design a work costume for the job you would choose for Owliver.

Writing

MINI-LESSON
Teacher leads a 5- to 7-minute discussion about possible interpretations of the Writing Topic: Other Jobs in School or

_____.

COMPOSING
Each student writes (by drawing or developmental spelling) on
■ the lesson's topic
■ a personally chosen topic
■ a topic begun previously

SHARING
Papers are read to a classmate or the teacher, dated, and filed.

Word Study

CHART DEVELOPMENT
Spelling Emphasis: *v* and/or

_____

   On the chart the teacher writes any word clusters that contain the day's letter or _____.

WRITING
On their papers students write
■ their favorite words from the chart
■ other words/clusters/sentences that would be appropriate for the chart
Papers are dated and filed.

▶ Which Teachers Can Use SUCCESS?

All SUCCESS teachers are decision-making, literate people who believe students want to read, write, and learn.

They realize that the built-in rewards of literacy that adults enjoy are available to students—if teachers make decisions that allow students to be a part of a literary community at school.

They truly believe reading, writing, and learning are pleasurable, worthwhile, even essential for a satisfying life.

They are not adults who have "received" or "completed" an education; they are lifelong learners who are enthusiastic about sharing their ongoing education with younger learners.

They believe that reading, writing, and learning are so rewarding in themselves that the role of the teacher becomes one of facilitator, not director.

They are dissatisfied with meaningless, canned programs and want their classrooms to be based on literature and real-life situations, but they welcome a basic, flexible structure to guide their planning, so that they can save their time and energy for teaching, rather than preparing their own programs.

▶ The Big Decisions

Any teacher who sees himself or herself in the statements written about SUCCESS teachers will want to know more about what SUCCESS teachers do every day to carry out this language arts program. It is, after all, only a framework for instruction and any SUCCESS teacher will need to be making decisions constantly. What are those decisions all about?

DECIDING TO FOCUS ON STUDENTS

Because SUCCESS teachers believe students like to learn and are rewarded by what they learn, they choose to make instruction in a SUCCESS class student-centered. SUCCESS teachers choose to focus on the students they teach, on the learners who are in the process of developing their knowledge and abilities. Many of the other decisions teachers make spring out of what they learn from observing their students, the learners who are rewarded by their own reading and writing.

The emphasis is more on the processes of learning than on the products of the students' work or on what the contents of a particular textbook might be. The emphasis is on the person more than on the subject matter or skills. The students in SUCCESS classrooms are the center of the teaching.

SUCCESS teachers realize that they cannot give students full attention if either a textbook, a teacher's guide, or the teacher is the center of instruction in the class. Even many literature-based, whole language programs suffer from directing students' attention to the teacher to find out what is planned for them that day. SUCCESS teachers, on the other hand, have invited students to know exactly what to expect every day and to be active in anticipating and planning their own learning.

DECIDING TO DEVELOP A COMMUNITY OF LEARNERS

SUCCESS teachers think of their classes as communities of learners so that students can help each other and share what they are discovering. Motivation and an increased amount of thinking come along with all the talking and cooperating that is a daily part of the way the students work. There is little competition and little lonely work. There is a lot of explaining and suggesting. The words "What if we..." are heard often. Students consider many possible ways to go about their work and know that there is rarely only one right answer.

Because of the routine activities teachers lead, and the wealth of everyday reading materials in their classes, teachers don't have to ability-group the students to more nearly match a student's "level" with the demands of a particular textbook. Instead, with the structured, open-ended daily activities, students are expected to do the best work possible for them. In order to do so, they make choices. That students make choices about their own learning, rather than being governed by the choices made by teachers and textbook publishers, matters a lot.

Perhaps because of the community spirit in SUCCESS classes, SUCCESS students are willing to take risks as learners. Many choices are not only acceptable, but valuable; with the emphasis on process more than on product, students are not preoccupied with how they are judged by the teacher. Because of the cooperative approach to learning in a SUCCESS community, students do not feel threatened or afraid. How could they fear failure in SUCCESS classes? With the routine use of everyday reading materials, the initiative that teachers see students take is more likely to become a lifelong habit.

Chelsea Varnum

DECIDING ON A SCHEDULE

SUCCESS teachers are committed to a routine that will give students time they can count on for reading, for writing, and for seeking new information. Scheduling all of the SUCCESS modules and establishing the routines for the regular SUCCESS activities very quickly teaches students that every single day they will have sizeable periods of time for various literary endeavors. The teacher's decision about the schedule teaches the students what the priorities are: reading, writing, and learning new things must be the most valuable things in the school day. The structured schedule of time for the important things matters a great deal in a SUCCESS class.

The four modules do not need to be scheduled consecutively; content-area classes, lunch, recess, etc., can be interspersed among the SUCCESS modules. A SUCCESS teacher first needs to choose five thirty-minute periods when all, or most, of the students are in the class. (Recreational Reading & Storytime may be split into two thirty-minute blocks or taught in one sixty-minute block of time.) SUCCESS is intended for all first-graders, so the schedule should include the ones who go to resource classes for part of the day, the ones who leave for gifted and talented programs, and the ones who go to remedial classes. Different teachers also choose to teach the modules in various orders. One module may be taught first thing in the morning, for example, and the fourth one may not be scheduled until last thing in the day.

Ideally, teachers are able to integrate many content areas within the SUCCESS framework; in those cases, teachers will have time for the optional activity associated with Storytime, time to read additional books aloud to their students, and possibly extra time for writing.

What is important is that all four modules are presented every day. Ideally, the same schedule should be followed every day. Once the teacher has determined the schedule, he or she needs to post the names of the modules and the time each is taught by the classroom door. At the beginning of the year, the poster helps the teacher and the students get accustomed to the schedule. Before long, the schedule becomes second nature to everyone in the class, and the poster is then helpful to visitors.

Teachers who try to do "some" of SUCCESS as a supplement to another program will have trouble finding time for all of the modules. SUCCESS teachers do all four modules every day because they realize that the four different activities complement and reinforce each other.

Teachers who want to use the SUCCESS program, but who are required to use their district's adopted program, find it easiest to follow the four-module structure of SUCCESS and change the writing topics, skill foci, and other elements within the modules to incorporate those covered in the other program. Doing all four modules generally as they are written results in a complete language arts program; no reading groups, workbooks, spelling books, or language books need to be added. The objectives of these other materials are already covered in the SUC-

CESS lessons, plus they can easily be added or reviewed as often as the teacher deems necessary. They can also be introduced in the order that the other program introduces them. The teacher simply substitutes the objectives or specific skills instruction into the SUCCESS format.

DECIDING TO MAKE MORE DECISIONS

SUCCESS teachers have made three big decisions already:

1. to think of instruction as student-centered, not teacher or textbook-centered,

2. to create a community of learners, and

3. to create a framework of time that students depend on for their reading, writing, and learning.

Day by day, teachers decide what topics and materials to make available and when to include skills instruction or new information. They decide when it is appropriate to integrate content-area topics and when certain pieces of literature are important for the class. They decide when to ask questions and how to evaluate students' progress. Moment by moment, they decide when to pursue the teachable moments that constantly arise. Many of their decisions differ from year to year because they are learning from different students each year. Their decisions are not the same as those of other SUCCESS teachers because of the uniqueness of each teacher and class.

Keegan Fogg

▶ Is It Hard to Teach SUCCESS?

*M*y students gain the ability to think! The SUCCESS program allows for cooperative learning, which is so important in education. It is a well-balanced and total approach to learning to read and write!

Kristin Zeaser-Sydow, teacher

All these decisions! Why would anyone deliberately give up prepared assignments and a textbook teacher's guide? For the decision-making teacher, three things about SUCCESS make the teacher's work easier and more rewarding:

1. *Lesson plans for SUCCESS classes are virtually the same every day.* The teacher and the students learn the basic procedures for the four modules very quickly and everyone knows what to do next. Does this sameness of procedures make the SUCCESS classroom boring? No, because the topics, skills, and reading materials change a lot. Because the procedures are dependable, the exciting things in class are the new books people choose to read, the new information people learn and share, and the writing produced by the people.

Teachers don't spend time duplicating materials, checking papers, or listening to the same stories being read over and over. Nor do they spend long hours developing activities to accompany children's books.

2. *Individualizing instruction is easier.* SUCCESS has helped many students with special needs, both gifted students and students who have learning problems, because of the large amount of individualized instruction that takes place every day. Special needs are met partly because of all the choices students can make, but partly because the teacher is able to spend more time helping students in class.

During Recreational Reading, the teacher spends thirty minutes, or 100 percent of the time, responding to individual needs. In Storytime the teacher reads a book to the entire group and leads a discussion of the book and then helps students complete the activity. In the Writing module, after leading the mini-lesson, the teacher is available to give individual assistance for twenty-five minutes, including the time for sharing. In the Research module, after conducting the lead-in activity, the teacher is available to help individuals until time for sharing, for a total of twenty minutes. In the Word Study module, the teacher leads a class discussion for up to fifteen minutes, but he or she still has about fifteen minutes to help individuals afterwards.

Individual help is the main teaching that is done in SUCCESS; it isn't something that is squeezed in when the teacher has time. Neither is it something that embarrasses students who need extra help; everyone gets individual attention routinely. That is the SUCCESS teacher's job for at least 100 minutes every day in language arts class alone.

3. *It is easier to make all these decisions knowing that research supports SUCCESS.* The educational literature of the 1990s is filled with reports about how little time students actually read real books at school and how few minutes per day they write material longer than the fill-in-the-blank variety. Newspapers report alarming illiteracy rates and sad stories about poor teaching. That's the bad news; the good news in professional journals is information about literature-based instruction, whole language, cooperative learning, process writing, and many other ideas that are integral parts of SUCCESS.

The most convincing research is what each SUCCESS teacher is able to report about each of his or her students: how each student learns best, exactly what he or she is able to read and write, what his or her interests are, and so forth. Evidence from standardized test results has never been reported as a reason that a teacher stopped using SUCCESS; test results are always acceptable, and often outstanding. SUCCESS teachers believe that standardized test scores don't come close to showing all that their students have learned.

▶ The History of SUCCESS

Years before terms such as "whole language" and "cooperative learning" were used, SUCCESS was begun in 1976 by Anne H. Adams to provide an alternative to basal textbook instruction. At that time, it was popular to point out all the things that were wrong with basals, since the public was becoming aware of the growing illiteracy problem in the United States. When teachers attended professional conferences in those days, they heard speakers criticizing traditional reading instruction, but they didn't hear many suggestions of what might replace the basal.

Anne Adams, a Professor of Education at Duke University, joined the best of them in trying to persuade people that basals were certainly not solving the problem of illiteracy. She suggested that having students do one more skills worksheet just might do more harm than good. Most significantly, she gave teachers a structured, but flexible, daily plan to use instead of the basals. She gave some reasons that her ideas would work; and she reminded educators that teachers are professionals and should make lots of decisions every day about how to teach their students. She didn't have to give much of a rationale for SUCCESS; it was good enough to point out that the basal didn't work—that's what everyone said.

SUCCESS was used first in the late 1970s in the Durham City Schools in North Carolina. Students who had not been succeeding in learning to read and write were indeed successful in SUCCESS classes, and the word began to spread around the country. Anne Adams taught teachers in other states how to use SUCCESS, and more students benefited from this new way of organizing language arts instruction time. In 1980 Anne Adams died, before all of the original SUCCESS books were published. Even after her death, the work she had begun flourished because teachers told other teachers what was happening in their classrooms. The use of SUCCESS began to spread primarily because of what teachers said and because of how well their students were doing.

▶ SUCCESS in the 1990s

Now teachers can advocate SUCCESS because of all the things that are right about SUCCESS, not simply because of the perceived shortcomings of basals. Some of the old problems still exist in basal language arts materials, but many publishers have at least paid lip-service to some of the complaints of teachers. Some basals even incorporate a whole language approach. Many teachers have abandoned the basal anyway, and they have substituted instruction that centers around children's books, a welcome improvement.

Whatever the case may be with the major textbook programs of the 1990s and various forms of literature-based instruction, SUCCESS is still another way of organizing language arts instruction that helps students. After more than a decade and despite the unique nature of each teacher and group of students, SUCCESS classes exhibit certain common characteristics.

1. Students make many decisions, not only about the substance of their reading and writing, but also about who their partners and committee members will be.

2. Students read real-life materials, such as trade books, newspapers, and magazines. They write to communicate real thoughts about real topics so that others can read them.

3. Students understand that there is rarely just one right answer, and they know they can work with each other to solve problems and seek information; therefore, they are more willing to take risks as learners.

4. The teacher makes many decisions about topics, materials, skills, and about the social dynamics of students' sharing and working together.

5. The focus of the students, as well as the teacher, is more on the processes of learning than on the final products.

6. A daily routine of reading, writing, and learning time exists, allowing students extended periods of time for making choices about important things like what books to read and what types of writing to do.

7. A major emphasis of SUCCESS teachers is the importance of students' communicating with one another.

8. The teacher's role is to establish the framework within which students can read, write, and learn. Being a creative, energetic teacher in a SUCCESS classroom means being observant of the strengths and needs of the students and being open to the endless possibilities of what they might learn as literate people working together. A creative SUCCESS teacher learns much information from and with the students.

SUCCESS is not meant to be used by all teachers. It is recommended for teachers who appreciate the characteristics described above. Teachers must believe that reading and writing are wonderful and that students really do wish to join in the fun of learning and developing as literate human beings. It is one approach—one that puts a premium on teachers making decisions themselves and with their students. The next four chapters explain more details about this way of teaching by outlining each of the four modules. The last chapter, Chapter 6, is about the relatively minor decisions the teacher must make: how to get materials, how to evaluate; how to adapt SUCCESS to special situations; how to acquaint administrators, parents, and others with SUCCESS. The last half of the book contains the Lessons, which are 180 outlines of lesson plans that can be used in the framework of SUCCESS.

Chapter 2 The Research Module

The Research module is thirty minutes for students to explore a variety of everyday materials and search for information related to the assignment given by the teacher. The everyday materials include magazines, newspapers, content-area textbooks, library fiction and nonfiction books, and assorted other materials encountered in a literate world such as maps, catalogs, and telephone books. Students record the information they find by cutting and pasting, drawing and labeling, or writing using developmental spelling. Most often students work with a partner or in teams of three or four students.

The Research module is the most different of the SUCCESS modules. It is the messiest and noisiest. Beyond observing that the students seem to be intently busy and enjoying themselves, it is also the hardest for some teachers to determine what learning is occurring. Those teachers who give this module a chance, however, usually report that it becomes their favorite and their students' favorite.

▶ Rationale

Research seems an unlikely activity in a first-grade reading and writing program. How can first-graders do research? Let's consider what professional researchers do. First they identify a problem or topic they want to know more about. Then they search through related materials to uncover information. The information is not always obvious. Associations have to be made; conclusions have to be drawn; relationships have to be discovered which, perhaps, have never been seen by earlier researchers. While recording notes and certainly before publishing the conclusions, researchers usually discuss their ideas with a colleague. Often there are disagreements and compromises that need to be made. Finally, a report is prepared and presented to an audience of like-minded researchers.

This is the very process first-graders go through in every Research activity. A problem is presented by the teacher. The problem may be as literal as, "Find and cut out as many *Nn*'s or words containing *Nn* as you can from your newspaper." Or, it may be as abstract as "Look in your science textbooks to find examples of changes that have taken place or could take place." Research activities could be interpreted literally or more abstractly, depending on the perspective of the student. Regardless, there is not one right way to complete the task. Each individual will interpret it as he or she sees fit:

Teacher: Find in your magazines pictures of eyes or things you can associate with eyes. Cut them out and glue them on your paper. Be sure to show your neighbors what you have found and tell them why you think they relate to eyes.

Paterno Porter

Sam: How many do we cut out?

Teacher: I don't know. How many can you find?

Mary: I like to cut out both eyes—like a mask.

Andrea: Not me. I'm cutting out every eye by itself!

Billy: I'm cutting off the eyebrows because I only want their eyes. I think I'll cut off the eyelashes, too.

Sarah: I found some teddy bear eyes. Can we cut out animal eyes?

Teacher: Are they eyes? What do you think? It's up to you. Jermaine, why did you cut out these small bottles?

Jermaine: They look like my mother's bottles of eye make-up.

Melody: I'm not going to cut out his eyes. I want to cut out his whole face because I like the way he looks.

Teacher: What does his face have to do with eyes?

Melody: He has happy eyes. They are the first thing I see when I look at his face. I'm going to write "happy" beside his face.

Danielle: Hey, here is a picture of water. Tears are water that comes from eyes. I'm going to cut it out. Oh! Here is the word "blue." My eyes are blue, so I'm going to cut it out, too.

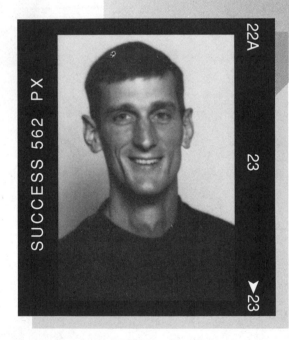

Both my six- and eight-year-old children have been taught reading with the SUCCESS program. They pick up literature ranging from newspapers, magazines, encyclopedias, and fact books as well as books on their reading level. SUCCESS has made my job as a parent—to stress reading and get both of them to enjoy reading rather than watching television all the time—more enjoyable.

Robert K. Beckwith, parent

Each young researcher is searching through a printed resource, locating information, making associations, discussing findings with others, and recording what he or she found by displaying the pictures and words on a piece of paper. Everyone is reading words and/or pictures. They are all thinking, associating, reasoning. They are justifying or explaining their ideas to a varied audience and preparing a presentation of their research findings.

No two finished products are the same for several reasons: No two researchers or research teams have exactly the same material. In the example above, everyone has a magazine, but many types of magazines are being used. Even if two students had the same magazine, the results would differ because no two people think alike. This module allows and encourages original thinking, indirect associations, and even "way out" ideas. The only requirement is that students must explain their thoughts clearly to anyone who asks. Wonderful things happen when nonconformity of thought is encouraged! Risk-taking, creativity, and individual uniqueness become the rule rather than the exception.

Critics and supporters of SUCCESS have stated that "anything goes" in this module. Both are wrong. Intentionally, there are many ways of approaching the task, many possibilities, many "right answers." But unlike the type of activity usually included in reading books and workbooks, it is not possible to guess or even cheat. Every conclusion has to be justified; all explanations must be clear to be right.

▶ Types of Lessons

There are six basic types of Research lessons. For the most part the material used determines the type of activity. There are lessons using newspapers, content-area textbooks, magazines, library books, and such functional reading materials as maps, menus, and forms. Near the end of the year there are several three- to seven-day series during which students write reports.

Each type of material is repeated for two days in a row. The same or a similar reading assignment is also repeated for two or three days, but the reading theme or topic and the materials are usually on a different phase. Therefore, the students look in different types of materials for the same type of information. See the Appendix for a table that shows how the materials and themes alternate in the Lessons.

▶ How to Lead a Research Lesson

Every Research module has three basic steps: Lead-In, Search & Record, and Sharing. (Specific suggestions for Research lessons are included in the Lessons section of this book.) In the Lead-In, the teacher introduces a reading focus, theme, and material. During the Search & Record step, students work individually or in teams to look through the resource, find information they can relate to the theme, and record their findings. The teacher circulates around the room discussing with many individuals or

Ben Weaver

teams what they have found and how it relates to the assignment. During the last few minutes of the module, students share with others what they have found and recorded.

PREPLANNING

The Lessons suggest a specific reading focus or skill, theme, and type of material. Each of these is followed by the word *or* and a blank line. The line is for teachers to record a different focus, theme, or type of material, if they choose to make a substitution. Instead of writing in their books, some teachers write this information in their plan books. Other teachers like having a year-by-year record of the actual lessons they have taught to their students. Regardless, prior to the lesson, teachers will decide whether to follow it as written or to change particular parts. One reason for changing the lesson components is to incorporate a content-area or literature theme. Another reason is to structure opportunities for the teacher to assess or teach a particular reading/writing skill or strategy. Teachers are encouraged to vary the Lessons.

Gathering a variety of materials Teachers have to gather a wide variety of materials to teach this module as it is described in the daily Lessons. Magazines, newspapers, content-area textbooks (math, science, and social studies), maps, telephone books, simple forms, art prints, and menus are all suggested materials. Students will experience many *types* of materials. Also, within each type, variety is strongly encouraged. For instance, if newspapers are the suggested material, teachers will not need a class set of newspapers. Nor will they choose a section or article and duplicate it for everyone to have a copy. Instead, collections of old newspapers are used. When math textbooks are the suggested material, students will seek information in first-, second-, third-, even fourth-grade math textbooks. Ideally, there will be more than one publisher's text at each grade level.

Why have a variety of materials? Conducting a lesson where every student has a different printed resource is unfamiliar and disconcerting for many teachers. Teachers are used to preparing questions (and answers) based on one material. The purpose for having many different resources is not to increase the teacher's frustration but rather to ensure that there are many "right answers" to any question asked. Thinking, even very divergent thinking, is encouraged. Obvious comparison of students is virtually impossible. Risk-taking is encouraged. The students think "What can I find?" rather that "What does the teacher have written in his book as the right answer?" Soon "Is this right?" is replaced by "Oh, look what I found. Bet you can't guess why I chose that."

Another frustrating, or at least new, factor for some teachers is that they cannot possibly be the audience for all ideas. They cannot possibly judge every thought as to its "correctness." Fellow students, partners, or teammates must decide whether the thinking is logical or misdirected.

> **Teacher:** Class, look in your magazines for *opposites*.
> **Lawrence:** Hey, look. Here's something that has an opposite.
> **Ben:** What? Aw, that doesn't either. That's a cartoon.
> **Lawrence:** I know that. But a person in a cartoon isn't real. Its opposite is a real person.
> **Ben:** Can we do that?
> **Lawrence:** Sure! All we have to do is be able to explain why we cut it out. We can do that.

Whenever the suggested material is not available, teachers need not skip the module, but instead substitute a different material and modify the reading assignment as needed.

LEAD-IN

At the beginning of the thirty-minute lesson, the teacher introduces the reading assignment, the materials to be used, and the size of the groups that will be working together. This step is very brief. The teacher says just enough to get the students started searching.

Modeling the procedure "What do I do if many of my students do not understand the assignment after a *very brief* explanation?" "What if we've never done that before? Don't I need to teach my students how to do it first?" These are good questions. They are often asked by caring, concerned teachers who want their students to succeed rather than fail. The answer most expect is, "Stop and teach" or "The first time you do a particular type of activity you need to demonstrate exactly how to do it." In SUCCESS that is not the answer. Nor is, "Let them sink or swim!"

Consider the following two scenarios about Lesson 102, in which students compare two art prints. One teacher decided that since his students had not compared art prints before, he needed to teach them how to compare them. He found four prints that have many similar characteristics. First, he displayed two of the prints so that all of his students could see them. On the chalkboard, he wrote the ideas the class generated in response to his questions under the headings ALIKE and DIFFERENT. Some of his questions were:

"How many people are in the first print? In the second print? Would you say they are close together or far apart? Which way are they looking? What are they doing?"

When he showed the class the other pair of prints and asked the teams to compare them, most of them recorded how many people were in the paintings, how close together they were, which way they were looking, and so forth. They followed the teacher's lead. They knew which answers were "right" and were hesitant to think beyond that.

The second teacher also had four art prints. He displayed all of them where everyone could see them and introduced the lesson this way:

> **Teacher:** Class, look at these pictures. Do you see anything about any two of them that is alike? What about them is different? Instead of telling me all you see, tell your partner. If your partner agrees with you, record what you decided under the headings ALIKE and DIFFERENT. Bill, you seem to have an idea. Tell me one thing you think is alike or different about these pictures.
>
> **Bill:** They all have people in them.
>
> **Teacher:** Great! You can write that under ALIKE. Now, everyone, see what you can find.

While the teacher circulated among the students, he saw several teams being successful, several that were finding interesting comparisons, but some teams that were struggling. Rather than telling the strugglers some things he saw, he interrupted the entire class and said:

"Excuse me, class. Let's discuss what you have concluded about the pictures. Jerry, you and Molly had some interesting observations. Tell the rest of us what you wrote down."

After calling on one or two other teams, the teacher challenged the entire class to see what else they could discover. Maybe they could find even more things to compare. The atmosphere the second teacher was trying to create was one where the students' ideas were more important than his. His students responded with such thoughts as "Oh, I see something else!" and "I bet nobody else thought of this!" The second teacher was able to help everyone be successful, without proscribing any limits.

Cassie Slessman

The ideas the students had were their own. This teacher empowered all of his students to generate original thoughts rather than use his ideas.

SEARCH & RECORD

Most of the thirty minutes allotted for this module are for students to look through the designated material to find information they can relate to the topic or theme and record what they find. (See page 23 for more information about the way students record information in each type of lesson.) Usually students work in teams of two to four students. For the cut-and-paste activities using newspapers and magazines, however, many students choose to work alone. In these cases, the teacher encourages students to discuss their findings with a neighbor before gluing or writing.

Working with a partner frees students to regard the assignment as a problem to be solved, or a puzzle, rather than a difficult task to be completed alone. The social, cooperative nature of process learning is enhanced, eliminating the test-like atmosphere of "do your own work." Since there is an unlimited number of "right answers," students are more willing to take risks. A personal challenge to succeed replaces competition for the best grade.

During this time students find as many things that relate to the assignment as possible. When students ask, "How many do we record?" teachers respond, "I don't know. How many can you find?" If a teacher spots individuals or teams that are not producing up to expectations, the teacher talks just to them, saying things like:

"Where are you going to look next?"

"Do you need a different resource? There are plenty over there on the table. Get another, if you want, or look in a different section of that resource."

"You two don't seem to be concentrating. Do I need to have you work with different partners?"

While students are searching and recording, the teacher is walking around the room, talking with students, making suggestions, listening to students' ideas or explanations of what they have recorded, and encouraging and stretching students to think. These lessons do not teach. Yes, students learn both problem-solving processes and the module's procedures, but mostly the lessons provide opportunities for teachers to find out how their students think, and time to observe students as they work with others to solve problems. They give teachers time to work with individuals, to assess strengths and weaknesses, to teach. Teachers who see this as a time when they can sit at their desks are missing the whole point of the module.

Teachers should carry a clipboard or have notepads available around the room for recording what they observe. They can record names of those who work well together and those who don't, parts of conversations overheard that indicate who the leaders are and who the followers are or how a team approached the task, even places in the classroom that students found to work. Whatever attracts the teacher's attention, either positively or negatively, should be recorded. Patterns will emerge over time that provide insight into ways to help students progress better and faster. Such observations are very useful for evaluation purposes, whether for giving grades or documenting the teacher's knowledge of a student to his or her parents during conferences.

SHARING

For the last three to six minutes students share what they have found with someone else. Occasionally, this is a whole-class discussion, where one student or team at a time reports something. One way many teachers bring closure to a magazine or newspaper activity is to have each student or team choose one item to display on a group chart or collage. As often as possible, teachers are encouraged to structure the sharing time so that more teams share in the same amount of time. For instance, if students work in pairs, they would report to another pair or everyone at their table. On other days two or three teams would meet together and compare findings.

After the sharing time is over, the papers are dated and filed in each student's Research folder. They become one of the records available to the teacher of the students' progress. At times, not everyone will have a paper to file in his or her individual folder, because teams will have had one recorder. In those cases, all team members' names should be written on the paper and it should be filed in one of the students' folders. (See

Chapter 6 for more information about how to use the folders for evaluation and for documentation of student progress.)

▶
Procedures for Each Type of Research Lesson

Although the basic steps of Lead-In, Search & Record, and Sharing are the same for all Research lessons, the internal procedures vary depending on the material used.

NEWSPAPER LESSONS

For most of the first half of the year, the newspaper lessons are essentially the same: students locate either the lower-case or upper-case form of the specified letter. Some students may choose to cut out words containing that letter. Still others may find pictures of objects whose written form contains the day's letter. Observing what students cut out is one way teachers can determine students' awareness of the concept of words and their realization of sound-symbol relationships. Given the chance, students, like all people, will show off just how much they know. Students who are aware of the concept of words are likely to cut out whole words, especially if they can read them. Students who recognize a letter-sound correspondence may find pictures of items whose written form contains the letter studied. *Requiring* students to cut out words or pictures instead of only cutting out letters will not increase their knowledge.

SUCCESS has made me organize myself so that I have become more effective. Therefore, my students are learning more. I enjoy it because they have fun and so do I!

Paula T. Simmons, teacher

CONTENT-AREA TEXTBOOKS

Math, science, and social studies textbooks are used alternately in the Research lessons. In these activities students work in partners or teams of three to find information they can associate with the reading topic or theme. Having a wide variety of levels of textbooks (for grades 1 to 4 and by several different publishers) is important for several reasons. First, the variety offers more opportunities for students to find information they can associate with the topic. Second, when there are many possible answers, students will be searching for what they can find, rather than trying to find the "right" answers. The focus will be on finding unique answers. Students whose thought processes tend to be less conventional will shine. Third, first-graders love to feel capable of "reading" an upper-grade textbook. And finally, first-grade textbooks frequently have very few words; when they are used, students are limited to pictures exclusively for information related to the theme.

Teachers can use nonfiction books to supplement content-area textbooks when teachers feel the need. These nonfiction books may relate directly to the reading topic, but that is not necessary. Students learn quickly to make indirect associations. They are challenged, for instance, to find information related to *jobs* in a book on *insects*.

Students discuss their findings with their teammates and record their conclusions on their papers. Sometimes they will draw pictures to display their ideas. Soon most will use developmental spelling or a combination of drawings and developmental spelling to summarize their ideas. At all times more will be discussed than is recorded. This is especially true at the beginning of the year.

For the first few weeks, many students will be uncomfortable working in groups, so the teacher or the whole class is usually the audience for students' ideas. Teachers usually walk around the class discussing with students what they have found and how their findings relate to the theme. Then the teacher assists students in recording an association they have made.

MAGAZINE LESSONS

Research lessons with magazines are usually cut-and-paste activities. A theme such as "things associated with money" or "soft, furry things" is included in the lesson. Students look for pictures and words they associate with the theme, cut them out, and paste them on their papers.

Even though students often choose to make their own finished product, discussion with other students is encouraged. "Show your neighbors what you have found and tell how it relates before you glue it on your paper. Be sure they agree that it relates to the theme," is always included in the assignment. Students are also given the option of writing their ideas beside some of the pictures they have pasted on their papers.

Teacher: Boys and girls, you may write what your "feet" are doing beside some of the feet you have glued on your paper.

Thomas: I already stopped cutting out pictures. I wanted to write about them.

Teacher: Diane, what are your feet doing?

Diane: They are dancing.

Teacher: Do you want to write "dancing feet" beside them?

Diane: No.

Teacher (walking away): OK, then see what else you can find in your magazine.

Diane: I think I *will* write "dancing feet."

Teacher: Jerry, what are your feet doing?

Jerry: These are resting and these are kicking a soccer ball.

Teacher: Are you going to write about one of them?

Jerry: Yes, I'm going to write "I can kick a soccer ball as far as this man. I like to play soccer."

LIBRARY BOOK LESSONS

For these lessons, students work in teams of two or three to search in any fiction or nonfiction library books for information they can relate to the reading topic or theme. As with the textbook lessons, recording of information will be in developmental spelling or drawing. Lively discussion is strongly encouraged.

An example of an assignment in the library book lessons may be something like, "Describe some of the characters in your library book. What is each character like? Draw and label the characters you find, or write in your own spelling what you think the characters are like. If you have not read the book before, just look at the pictures or read some of the story with your partner(s)."

FUNCTIONAL READING MATERIAL LESSONS

Beginning with Lesson 89, another type of material is included in the Research cycle. These are the types of materials used to function in everyday life: catalogs, maps, art prints, telephone books, menus, and forms. Each type of material is used for two consecutive days. The specific reading assignment is usually different for each of the two days. For example, the suggested material for both Lessons 95 and 96 is maps, but the reading assignment for Lesson 95 is "Locate rivers and lakes" and for Lesson 96 is "Locate big cities and little towns." Students work with partners or in small groups to find information related to the reading assignment. Only the catalog activities involve cutting and pasting, as a rule. For the other activities, drawing or developmental spelling is used for recording.

REPORT-MAKING LESSONS

Two types of report-making techniques are included in the Research lessons near the end of the year. (These techniques were originally developed by two veteran SUCCESS teachers, Debby Head and Libby Pollett, *SUCCESS Stories,* Winter 1989.) The first type is a *picture report.* The second is an *individual written report.* While some students do individual written reports, others may be making picture reports. Likewise, some students' first picture reports may include much writing.

Picture reports   Picture reports are designed for students who do not feel confident yet at expressing extended thoughts on a topic in writing. The format provides these students with a method for communicating lots of information, most of which is done through drawing pictures. Each day the teacher reads a book, shows a video or filmstrip, or gives a demonstration related to the general report topic. Each student draws one or more pictures of information he or she found interesting. Some students will label their pictures by drawing lines to pertinent parts of the picture. Others will write a sentence or two at the bottom of their pictures. Students who produce more than one picture may assemble their picture report into a booklet. Sharing the picture reports with some or all of the class accomplishes a publishing aspect to this report cycle.

Erin Landauer

Individual written reports The individual written report is somewhat more involved and is scheduled for five to seven days. Most often teachers also use the Writing module time for writing reports, especially when students edit or revise their reports. For written reports the teacher usually decides on the general topic. A topic is suggested in the Lessons, but many teachers substitute a lesson's topic with one related to a content-area theme the students are studying.

On the first day the class can decide on the subtopics to be covered and the order in which they will be presented in the finished reports. Booklets are made for notetaking purposes. There should be one page for each subtopic and usually a page for the opening and closing sections. Therefore, if three subtopics are included, the booklets would have five pages: Opening, Subtopic 1, Subtopic 2, Subtopic 3, and Closing.

Notetaking takes place on the next two to four days, depending on the number of subtopics. One subtopic is researched each day. Students are aware ahead of time which subtopic will be researched that day and will supplement the teacher's resources with information from home or the public library. Small groups search through the variety of materials available in the classroom. As the groups find information they think is pertinent, they volunteer that information to the teacher. The teacher records the information in notetaking form on a large sheet of chart paper. When a sufficient amount of information is on the class chart, each student *selects* the information he or she wants to write in the notetaking packet.

When the notetaking process is complete, students organize their notes by numbering the points they want to include in their report. As he or she writes the information, the student checks it off in the notetaking packet. All of the information that is recorded need not be included in the student's finished report. It is appropriate, however, for teachers to ask students why they deleted some information. Asking such questions helps teachers determine if students had reasons or forgot. It also gives students opportunities to explain their thought processes. The form of the written language (spelling, punctuation, handwriting, etc.) in these reports is far less important than the recording of thoughts.

Some students may be capable of revising the first draft of their report. Teachers can encourage peer editing, use of dictionaries after the rough draft is complete, and re-copying with more emphasis on handwriting if they feel such activities will encourage and excite rather than defeat and discourage. Other students may wish to illustrate their reports.

Finished reports should be widely published. Showing them to other classes or administrators, displaying them in the classroom to be read during Recreational Reading, having a program to which parents are invited, videotaping a program, or displaying the reports in the library are some of the many ways teachers can reward such monumental efforts of their first-graders.

▶ Materials

The list below details the materials that are needed to teach the Research module as suggested in the Lessons.

- collections of old and current newspapers
- collections of magazines
- a variety of science, social studies, and math textbooks
- fiction and nonfiction library books
- maps
- catalogs of any type
- telephone books (both white and yellow pages)
- menus
- art prints
- simple forms
- a manila file folder for each student and three to four boxes in which to store the folders
- scissors and glue

▶ Modifying the Research Module

Teachers should modify the Lessons to suit their needs and the needs of their students. However, teachers should have reasons for the changes they make. The most common reasons teachers give for changing what's in the Lessons include integrating content-area themes, integrating more literature, and teaching specific skills or strategies. Integrating any of these can be accomplished by simply making substitutions for one or more of the module components: the theme or topic, the material, or the specific reading/writing assignment.

Example 1:   Mr. Edward's class is studying magnets in science. On Lesson 53, which says to look in magazines for things relating to television, Mr. Edwards asks the students to find pictures of objects in their magazines to which magnets will and will not adhere.

Example 2:   Ms. McNeil has just read one of the books about babies in Lesson 27. She chooses to postpone or skip looking for words in math textbooks that contain j or k and has students look in math books (or a different type of material) for things related to babies.

Both teachers made a record of how they changed their lessons. One of them recorded the changes on the line provided in the manual. The other noted the change in the teacher's plan book. Keeping such a record helps teachers document exactly what their students have done over the year.

Teachers need to consider certain points in modifying this module. If the lesson is to maintain the normal qualities of a SUCCESS Research module, these characteristics need to remain:

- Students will use a variety of resources on any given day and a variety of types of materials over time.
- Whatever the reading/writing assignment, there will be many possible "right" answers.

■ This is never a "work quietly and do your own work" activity. It is a social, cooperative activity with much discussion.

■ Students are always responsible for explaining their answers to whomever asks. No answer is "right" unless it can be explained.

▶ Summary Chart

Preplanning:	Teacher decides to teach the Research module as suggested or to change the material, the group size, the reading/writing assignment, or the method of sharing.
Lead-in: 1–4 minutes	Teacher oversees the distribution of materials, introduces the reading/writing assignment, and helps students form the appropriate size groups.
Search & Record: 16–19 minutes	Students work together locating and recording information found; teacher converses with as many students as possible about what they have found.
Sharing: 5 minutes	Students show others some of what their team has found.

Chapter 3 The Recreational Reading & Storytime Module

The Recreational Reading & Storytime module provides sixty minutes for exploring books. Many different activities related to books take place in this hour. The module offers time for sustained silent reading and time to talk about books, as well as time for the teacher to read aloud to the class and, often, time for the students to complete an activity related to the book.

For approximately half of this module, students read in library books of their choice. While the students are reading (or being entertained exclusively by books), teachers either model by reading silently with the class or hold conversations with individual students about their books. During these conversations, teachers assess students' reading abilities, help students increase their command of the reading process, and convey to the students their personal love of books and reading.

The remaining thirty minutes of the module is for the teacher to read a particular book or type of book to the class and share mutual appreciation and understanding of the book through a group discussion. An optional activity related to the book is included in the lesson. Most often these activities are art or crafts that can be taken home.

▶ Rationale

SUCCESS teachers are educators who want students to love books, value reading, and become lifelong readers. When the school year begins, few first-graders are able to read independently or even look at pictures and text with the purpose of seeking a story or a message. Two factors are more important in learning to read than any and all instruction: 1) Students need many pleasurable experiences with books; and 2) they require time to explore books. These factors are essential for students to develop a purpose and desire for learning to read. Once they have those, they must discover for themselves the feeling of "I can!" Exploring books and getting a message from them builds that awareness and confidence more effectively than getting dozens of "Excellent!" comments from teachers on reading worksheets.* Students who want to be able to read and who believe they are *able* are well on their way to becoming independent readers.

During Storytime, students hear a book read aloud by the teacher and discuss it. The most common characteristic of children who read early is that they have been read to by their parents. Students who have not had the benefit of being read to need that experience in order to generate an awareness of what pleasures reading provides. Those who *have* been read to are eager to share their love of books with others, as well as to learn about new books. Whenever time allows, students complete a book-

*The most important *instructional* activity for teaching students how to read is teachers' reading aloud to students.

Scott Bensing

related art or craft activity that they can take home. The picture or object serves as a reminder of the book when telling Mom and Dad what they did at school.

Students also spend up to thirty minutes quietly exploring books each day. This time is not simply for rest and relaxation; students learn to read by reading. In addition, students who can count on thirty minutes every day to explore or read in books of their choice develop the habit of reading. Reading books for pleasure is a habit that many literate people never develop. Until a reader gets so lost in a book that he or she forgets the world around them, that reader will not choose to read for pleasure.

Individual conversations with students substitute for paper-and-pencil activities that are designed to test students' reading abilities. Not only can teachers learn more about students' basic reading skills through talking with students, teachers have the opportunity to determine how students are thinking and personalize their instruction to the student and the material he or she has chosen to read. Teachers can also ask questions that show students just how much meaning they can get out of a book, even though they cannot recite every word printed. Such questions build confidence, boost willingness to try, and guide students in how to get more and more of the writer's message as they spend time with books.

Through individual conversations teachers are able to assess strengths and weaknesses and to help individual students develop better reading strategies without the need for ability grouping. No one is labeled; no one is in the low group. Further, no one's time is wasted sitting in a reading group waiting a turn for the teacher's attention.

Many teachers are working hard to include more quality literature into their reading instruction. They have abandoned a basal reading program and are spending hours finding or developing activities for students to complete with library books. As entertaining and rewarding as the teachers' efforts might be, simply giving students a significant amount of time to read for pleasure in books of their choice is the most important way teachers can integrate more children's literature into their reading program. The students' pleasure comes from reading and talking about books with others, rather than from completing the teacher's activities.

This module can be divided into two parts. One part is Recreational Reading; the other part is Storytime. Some teachers do both parts together in one sixty-minute block of time. Others divide it into two thirty-minute blocks. Teachers who divide the module set a schedule for each part. The parts may be scheduled at any time of the day and in either order.

Recreational Reading

Recreational Reading includes time for students to read books and time for students to talk about what they have read, or Book Sharing. While the students are reading, the teacher reads, too, or has conversations with individual students, recording their strengths and weaknesses. The teacher also makes notes of general observations related to the students' reading behaviors.

PREPARATION

First-graders do not read independently for thirty minutes on the first day of school. In fact, they do this only after much time, effort, and preparation on the teacher's part. All teachers who have put forth this effort, however, agree it is well worth it.

Before beginning Recreational Reading, teachers need to do several things in preparation. First, teachers need to gather a large number of books. In addition to the extensive classroom libraries many teachers have collected, all teachers should check out thirty to fifty books from the school library. First-grade SUCCESS teachers usually select most of the books from the Easy or "Everybody" shelves of the library. They also choose several from the nonfiction section, the biography section, and even a few from the junior fiction shelves. By having these different types of books from the library in the classroom, teachers are helping students learn about all that is in a library. Every two to four weeks, the teacher should change the collection. Several schools have reported that when every teacher checks out fifty or even thirty books to take to their classrooms, the library's book supply is practically depleted. They solved their problem by teachers checking out fewer books and changing them more often.

Basal readers may be good additions to the Recreational Reading book collection. Newer basals, in particular, are often good anthologies of quality children's literature. Besides being additional sources of reading material, they can be helpful to the teacher for assessing students' strengths and weaknesses.

The second thing teachers need to do in preparation is to decide on their behavioral standards for the Recreational Reading module. Shall students be allowed to sit on the floor and under tables, or should they read at their seats? What about getting up to sharpen a pencil? (What do they need pencils for?) What about going to the restroom? Will students be allowed to exchange books once Recreational Reading begins? (Having students get three to five books before reading greatly reduces, but may not eliminate, the need to get up for more.) When setting standards, teachers should treat students like they want to be treated when reading for pleasure: Does an adult want anyone to tell her what to read? Does an adult want to be told he cannot get another book until he has finished the last one he checked out? But does an adult sometimes need or want suggestions when choosing a book, especially if the helper not only knows the reader, but also the books she might be interested in? The atmosphere during Recreational Reading time is that of a community of readers. Everyone values reading; everyone loves reading; everyone talks about books; everyone reads.

Before setting the rule that no one can leave his or her seat once Recreational Reading begins, please remember that the name of the module implies it should be a pleasurable time for everyone. Students who get up more often than seems necessary can be dealt with individually and quietly.

DISCUSSING STANDARDS

It is most important for students to understand and accept the behavioral standards of the Recreational Reading module. Teachers who discuss their expectations with their students prior to beginning the module are much more successful in achieving their goals. In fact, the more students can feel like the standards are set by them, the more ownership they have over the process and the more they adhere to the class procedures. One recommendation is to have as few "rules" as possible. Very general standards such as "Respect others," "Books are your only source of entertainment during Recreational Reading," and "Find a place and stay there unless you need to exchange your books" are usually easier to enforce. Teachers can then participate in the community as a fellow reader, not as the class constable.

Before setting the timer on the first day, be sure everyone knows what is expected, and how long the module will last. Even good readers will whisper to the teacher, "How much longer?" if not told in advance. Write the time or draw a clock on the board, representing the time Recreational Reading will be over. There should be no surprises!

STUDENTS SELECT BOOKS

Selecting one or two books can be time-consuming. If books are chosen too hurriedly, the reader is often dissatisfied with his or her choice and is soon ready to exchange a book for a different one. Teachers have developed several strategies for minimizing the time and dissatisfaction. Some

The Recreational Reading module works best for me. A priority for me is to instill in the children a love and dedication for reading on a regular basis. SUCCESS does this for me.

Carrie U. Bellamy, teacher

teachers have each student choose three to five books to take to a place and read. It actually takes less time to choose three to five books, and the student has more to look at or read before needing to exchange them for others. Other teachers place tubs of books at each table or in several strategic areas around the classroom. These teachers are careful to include a wide variety of books in each tub: fiction, nonfiction, old basal readers, wordless books—all kinds and levels. Still others schedule Recreational Reading after students have had free time. The students in those classrooms learn that one of their tasks during their free time was to get the books they wanted to read. One teacher said she always scheduled Recreational Reading immediately after recess. Her students were to place their Recreational Reading books on their desks before they left the classroom for recess. Talk about motivation to be speedy! As students become accustomed to the regular schedule, many will be prepared with plenty to read, regardless of when this module is scheduled.

STUDENTS READ BOOKS

Most teachers have found that it takes approximately four weeks of gradually increasing the Recreational Reading time before first-graders are able to read for thirty minutes. In the Lessons it is suggested that teachers begin with ten minutes the first week and increase the time five minutes each week. Before setting the timer each day, it is usually prudent to review the behavioral standards set by the class.

During these four weeks the teacher also reads silently for pleasure. If teachers walk around the room like a monitor instead of reading, the students will just watch the teacher and not read. But if the teacher reads, he or she can say, "Boys and girls, please don't bother me and I won't bother you. I'm going to be reading, too." Teachers are strongly encouraged to read books during this time. They may read novels written for adults (bring a book cover, if necessary) or children's literature. Those who try to use this time to complete paperwork notice that the students do not read. Modeling reading conveys a love of reading and respect for those who are reading. It creates an atmosphere of a community of readers. Teachers who work at their desks communicate to students that reading is not as important as paperwork.

DEVELOPING THE MODULE

Once the reading time has increased to approximately thirty minutes (after Lesson 20), the teacher begins to conduct conversations with students about what they are reading. During these conversations, teachers talk with students about what they are reading, help them develop more strategies for getting meaning from print, and assess students' reading strengths and weaknesses. Five types of conversations are described in the lessons. They are explained in detail on pages 36–47).

Teachers also keep two types of records during Recreational Reading, more general Clipboard Notes and specific notes from teacher-student conversations. The section on record-keeping describes each of these types of records, as well as suggestions of how to manage the process.

BOOK SHARING

When there are two to three minutes left in the Recreational Reading section of this module, the teacher interrupts the students' reading and has everyone turn to a neighbor and tell something he or she read about. Some of the discussion during this time might be:

"This book is neat. It doesn't have many words, but it's about two silly animals that get in trouble because they are showing off for each other."

"I've just read a little bit of this book. Already I know it is going to be good. This crazy lady is a maid and she gets everything mixed up!"

"I looked at these three books today. I like the pictures in this one the best and this one has a hole in every page."

"This is the book our teacher read to us yesterday. I like reading it by myself, because I can look at the pictures better."

"I read all of this book today. It is so funny! This girl grows antlers and nobody can get rid of them. Her mother keeps fainting. Let me read you this part! It's my favorite."

After each student has shared something about his or her book with another student, one or two students tell the entire class about their books. Using Jim Trelease's term from his *Read-Aloud Handbook* (Penguin, 1985), many teachers call this "giving a commercial" about a book. Some teachers even time the students. "Class, we have time for two fifteen-second commercials. Who would like to give a sales pitch for your book? OK, Andre, you have fifteen seconds. Nancy, you're next."

All first-graders, especially early in the school year, will not be able to read books word for word, but all can get something from the books they look at. Having a book sharing time each day familiarizes students with more books. It also gives the readers a purpose as they look at books. They approach the reading time with an expectation of getting meaning from their books and it brings closure to the activity.

▶
Conversations

There are five different types of conversations between teacher and student specified in the Recreational Reading section of the Lessons. The first type, "Getting Started," is included in Lessons 1–20. The purpose of this type is to get students acclimated to sitting relatively quietly with only books as the source of their entertainment. Beginning with Lesson 21, the other four types are rotated. The second type, "Check-In Conversations," is the most regularly repeated. It is a series of two- to three-minute conversations between the teacher and as many individuals as possible. The third type, "In-Depth Conversations," is a seven- to ten-minute conversation with three to four different individuals each day. In-Depth Conversations are included for a series of seven lessons twice each

Adam Bungart

nine weeks, once near mid-term and again near the end of each term. They can be very useful for mid-term evaluations, as well as determining what will be reported on grade cards. The fourth type, "Teacher Reads," is somewhat like the first type. On these days the teacher reads silently in a book of his or her choice. Teacher Reads conversations are every tenth day most of the year. After Lesson 100, they occur every twentieth day. The fifth type of conversation, "Small Group Conversations," occurs every tenth day beginning with Lesson 103.

As the need arises, teachers should schedule alternate types of conversations to those specified in the Lessons. The suggested schedule in the Lessons reminds teachers of the variety of activities that can occur. Many teachers find the variety well-balanced. Others prefer different schedules.

GETTING STARTED

Getting Started conversations are only found in the first twenty lessons while the reading time is being increased from ten to thirty minutes. In this type of lesson, the teacher reads while the students read. Teachers are encouraged to read books, ones written for adults or children. If students are encouraged to read books instead of magazines, newspapers, catalogs, and so forth, so should teachers.

Many teachers choose to talk with students for the last few minutes of the module. Those who exercise this option have found it important to notify students at the beginning of the reading time about what they will be doing. The teacher can converse with more students if he or she goes to the student's reading place, rather than having the student come to the teacher's desk. This type of conversation is very informal and should be similar to what any reader would discuss with another reader: "What are you reading? What is your book about? Who is this character (pointing to a picture)? What is happening in this picture?" Since these are the first twenty days of first grade, few students will be able to recite words. Asking them to do so would merely point out their inabilities. Instead, ask students to respond to a visual clue like a picture, or ask a general question, such as what their book is about. These are questions all students can answer, and they show the students what the teacher values. They also give students more direction when looking at their books.

CHECK-IN CONVERSATIONS

Check-In Conversations are the most commonly scheduled. They are brief two- to three-minute conversations between the teacher and one student. For a Check-In Conversation, the teacher goes to the student, asks permission or apologizes for interrupting the student's reading time, and then asks the student a couple of questions about the student's book. Asking permission to interrupt a reader or apologizing for doing so communicates the value teachers place on reading. Students learn that even though this adult really values reading, he or she is still a teacher, and

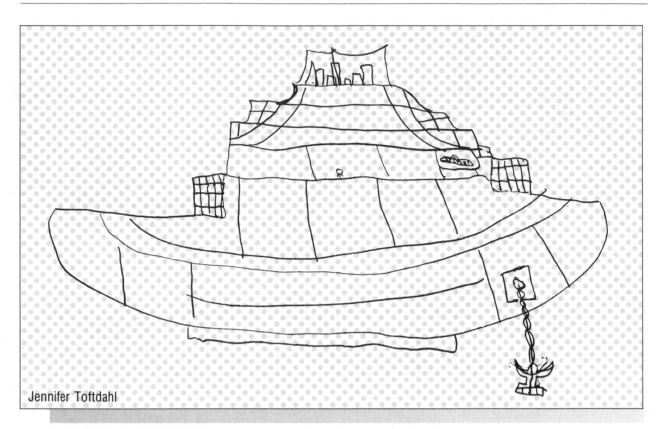

Jennifer Toftdahl

teachers have to know what is happening with students. They understand and do not hold being interrupted against the teacher.

Some teachers ask students to read to them during these conversations. There is nothing wrong with that, if it is helpful and rewarding to the student. Students who struggle to decode each word are reminded of their lack of ability. Students who are asked questions about their books that they are able to answer feel successful and are encouraged to learn more. If students are able to read the words on the page, they will let the teacher know. They will often volunteer to read and love doing it. Humans like to show off what they can do. They do not like being shown what they cannot do. The teacher's job during these conversations is to illuminate what students *can* do. That boosts confidence and students are ready to learn more.

Teachers going to students, rather than students coming to the teacher, means that more conversations are possible in thirty minutes. Most teachers hold seven to ten conversations on Check-In Conversation days. Obviously, having a conversation with a reader may disturb others nearby who are trying to read. This is not the problem it at first appears to be. Many students do not even notice the teacher after the first weeks of Recreational Reading conferences. Others benefit from overhearing the conversation and, as the teacher is walking away, he or she might hear someone whisper, "Can I have that book when you finish?"

Another reason these conversations are not particularly disruptive is they only last two to three minutes. On days when the conversation lasts longer (In-Depth Conversations), the teacher and conferee should be sitting away from those who are reading. Teachers who converse with students regularly for two to three minutes are amazed how much they learn about the reader's abilities, even when the reader does not "read" to them. It is not hard to discern how effectively students decode the print without having them say the words that are printed on the page. Those who know more about the story than is evident from the pictures have learned from the print, even if they cannot recite it verbatim.

Teachers are also amazed at how effectively they can teach new skills and strategies in two to three minutes. In a reading group someone else usually shouts out the answer to the teacher's question before the reader can think it through. That does not happen in individual conversations. When the focus of every aspect of the conversation is on the meaning of the story—on comprehension—even word-level skills are easily taught. Words become meaningful in the context of the story. They remain part of the whole, rather than each being a goal unto itself.

Included in the Lessons are elements of reading comprehension that are the suggested focus of a teacher's conversation with students. One element, such as main idea, details, prediction and inference, or comparison, is repeated for three consecutive days of Check-In Conversations. Two or more elements are suggested for each sequence of In-Depth Conversations. The main purpose of including them in the Lessons is to remind teachers to discuss all elements of reading with students, instead of asking the same type of question all of the time. Before the lesson, teachers should read what the suggested element is, decide if it is appropriate for the class in general, and, if it is not appropriate, change it. When conferring with students, the questions asked may reflect the suggested element or not, depending on the circumstances. At all times the conversations should be genuine, sincere conversations between two readers, not an oral test given by the teacher.

Sample questions   The following are sample questions that teachers can ask to evaluate and teach each of the elements of comprehension that are suggested in the Lessons:

Main Idea: What is your book about?

What is happening in this picture?

The title of your book is.... Why do you think the author named it that?

Detail: What is the character doing in this picture?

What is she holding?

This is the name of this character. Can you find it again?

Prediction/Inference: The title of your book is, ... What do you think it will be about? Why?

Let me read to you what it says on this page. What do you think will happen next?

Comparison: How are these characters alike? How are they different?

How are these two books alike? Different?

What changed from this picture to this one?

Cause and Effect: Look at the mess in this picture. What caused it to happen?

What is this character doing? What will happen when he does it?

Sequence: What happened at the beginning of the story? Then what happened?

How did your book end? How did it begin?

Let's talk about what is happening here. What happened before that?

Description: How would you describe this place? This character? This item?

It says here that someone is mean and evil. Which person do you think is being described? Which is quiet and shy?

Real and Make-Believe: Is this character real or make-believe?

What happened in this story that was magical? Could that happen in real life or only in stories?

Relate to Student's Experience: Has anything like this ever happened to you before?

Have you ever seen a place like this?

Does he remind you of anyone you know?

Can you do what she is doing?

Humor: Why did you laugh at that picture? What is funny?

Isn't this a silly story? Do you like to be silly? What do you do when you are acting silly?

What was funny about how she did that?

Is there a special word or group of words that made that funny?

When: When did that happen?

What time of day is it? Is it earlier or later in this picture?

What words tell when that happened?

Where: Where is this story taking place?

Show me some of the different places in your book.

Can you find any of the words that tell where they are?

Classification: What is this item? What else is like it?

How are all of these things alike?

Can you find all of the. . .?

Pronouns and Referents: Let me read this page. When I read "she," who did that mean?

Which of the words that you just read means all of the people in the story? Which just means Jim?

Connotations of Words Chosen by the Author: Why did the author use the word *sneaked* instead of *went*?

What word makes this especially funny? Silly? Scary?

Synonyms: Can you think of another word for this word?

What is another way of saying that?

Look at all the words that mean *said.* Let's see how many different ones we can find.

Opposites: What went up? What went down? What is the difference?

How would the story be different if he did just the opposite?

What word do you see that is the opposite for . . .?

Paraphrase: Tell me briefly what happened in your story.

Let me read this part to you. Now tell me in your own words what happened.

What is another way of saying that?

Problem-Solving: The characters in your book have a problem. What do you think they should do to solve the problem?

How did they figure out what to do?

What would you have done if you had been in the character's situation?

IN-DEPTH CONVERSATIONS

In-Depth Conversations are seven- to ten-minute conversations between the teacher and three to four students, one student at a time. These conversations are scheduled in the Lessons twice each nine-week grading period, once around mid-term and again near the end of the term. Teachers whose school's grading term is six weeks may want to rearrange the conversation schedule in the Lessons so that they will have two In-Depth Conversations each term. The longer nature of these conversations allows for more detailed evaluation and assessment, as well as more time to teach.

In-Depth Conversations are wonderful opportunities for teachers to communicate their love of books and reading to students. Although evaluation and specific instruction are often part of the conversation, the mood is one of two literate people sharing experiences with books.

Teacher: Thomas, what books have you brought?

Thomas: I brought *The Napping House* and this one. I don't know the name of it.

Teacher: You have brought two books that are among my favorites. Before you leave, be sure I tell you about some others by the same authors that I think you would like. We have some in the class and there are others in the library.

That one is *The Relatives Came* by Cynthia Rylant. Have you read any of it?

Thomas: I've read part of it. I looked at the pictures, mostly. Some people come to visit a family, and they sleep all over everywhere and play together. It looks like fun. But it also looks like a mess.

Teacher: Aren't these people funny? The people are the family's relatives, their grandparents, aunts and uncles, and cousins. Do you ever visit your relatives or have any of them ever visited you? Do any of your relatives look like these people?

Thomas: I have an uncle who is bald and has a big stomach like he does. Last summer we went to my grandmother's house. My cousins live near there, but they didn't stay with us.

Teacher: Would you like for me to read some of this to you? Choose a page or two that you want me to read. Then I'd like for you to tell me about *The Napping House*. Maybe you can read part of it to me or we'll read it together. It's a good book for reading together.

Usually, teachers schedule In-Depth Conversations with each student at least one day before, and they publish the order in which the conferences will be held. In that way, students have time to locate a book they have already read to bring to the conference. They also bring a book they are currently reading. Since this is a conversation between two readers, the teacher often brings a book, too, and he or she may talk to the student about that book. Knowing the order of the day's conversations allows those who have conversations scheduled that day to still have Recreational Reading. The student whose conversation is scheduled last, for instance, knows he or she has about twenty minutes to read. Students in SUCCESS classes prize their reading time!

THE TEACHER READS

Teachers modeling reading can be as important as their talking with students in terms of teaching students to read. For example, the students in one teacher's class learned a lesson one day that could not have been taught another way. The teacher was reading along with the class. It was amazingly quiet in the room that day, and the teacher became so involved in her book that she forgot where she was, read something funny, and laughed aloud. Her first-graders were truly awed by the fact that an adult, a teacher even, could be that entertained by a book!

Many teachers read for approximately twenty minutes and confer with students for the remainder of the module. Others read the entire time. A teacher reported that one day she was reading with her class when the timer went off. She squealed because she was right at the climax of her book, and she did not want to stop reading. When she explained her outburst to her class, they told her they wouldn't mind if she continued reading. They would read longer too. She thanked them, but said they had work to get done. The students volunteered a promise to hurry with the work, so maybe there would be extra time later in the day for her to finish her book. Teachers of SUCCESS must believe that they teach far more powerfully by what they do than by what they say.

SMALL-GROUP CONVERSATIONS

Small-Group Conversations are discussions about stories or other literature that a group of four to six students, with a variety of reading levels, have all read previously. The teacher decides what story a group of students is to read and makes an assignment several days in advance of the scheduled conversation. Since the Small-Group Conversations are regularly scheduled every tenth day, beginning with Lesson 103, it is easier for teachers to plan ahead and make assignments in advance.

Teachers may schedule one, two, or three conversations on each day, depending on their preference and their class. A teacher with a relatively independent group of accomplished readers may be able to hold three Small-Group Conversations. Teachers whose classes cannot be described that way may not be able to be away from the majority of the group for the entire thirty minutes. By the end of the year a few teachers have accomplished monitoring several simultaneous student-led discussion groups. During the student-led discussions, the teacher moves from group to group, interjecting a few thoughts about the group's book or asking a question of the group to keep the discussion going.

Multiple copies of special children's books are most often used for these conversations. Teachers who have limited collections of multiple copies of books can supplement with basal readers. As students and teachers become more accustomed to sharing decision-making, teachers may select either the book to be discussed or the make-up of the group. If the teacher selects the group, she may allow the group to choose from the collection of multiple copies of books. If the teacher selects the book, she may ask students to sign up if they would like to discuss that book with others.

RECORD-KEEPING

Like all SUCCESS modules, the teacher has many demands on his or her attention and time. During Recreational Reading he or she not only reads or talks with students about what they are reading, but the teacher

Tyler Smith

Joey Bansen

must observe the students' behavior, be aware of what each is reading, be able to recognize strengths and weaknesses without paper and pencil testing—and, above all, be alert to the infinite "teachable moments" that occur. Plus he or she has to keep records of observations. Sound overwhelming? It really isn't. It does require new habits of many teachers, though. Below is a description of several types of records that are related to Recreational Reading that can or should be kept. They were designed by teachers for teachers. Their intent is to be simple, quick, and effective. When thinking about the time required, realize that none of them requires teacher time after school. There are no tests to prepare or grade. Those activities are replaced by keeping short, precise, anecdotal records. (Chapter 6 includes more information about evaluation.)

Clipboard notes Clipboard notes are general observations about the whole class or specific students' behaviors during Recreational Reading. Samples of notes from teachers' clipboards:

"I don't remember so much movement last year"
"Darin is up again. Again! Again!!"
"Timmy seems to like 'Brown Bear.' Need to get more pattern books for him."
"Kevin has chosen to read under my desk. Need to watch to see if he's reading. Seems to be."
"Mood is surely different from three weeks ago. Didn't think it would ever happen."

Figure 3-1

Suggestions for Clipboard Notes Listed in the Lessons

who reads with whom
who studies or learns from pictures
who daydreams or watches the teacher
titles or types of books chosen
where students choose to read
who reads or attempts to read
who seems excited about books and reading
who is constantly seeking help decoding
    words
who reads a book previously read or
    introduced by the teacher
who moves lips or uses hand to guide their
    reading
who prefers what type of book
who is not an independent reader
who prefers which authors

who stays seated and who walks around
who gets up often
who seeks meaning from books
who re-reads the same book
who talks spontaneously about books
who recommends books to others
who seeks recommendations from others
who is searching for meaning
who reads books written by students or class
    books
who compares books by author, by topic, or
    by different versions of the same story
who continues to read the same book more
    than one day
which students read audibly

Figure 3-2

Sample Form for Clipboard Notes

Focus _____   Date _____

Class-General	Andrew	Barbara	Byron
Carrie	Charles	Colin	Daniel
Demetrius	Edward	Freida	Gavin
Harold	Henrietta	James	Juan
Kevin	Linda	Mark	Mary
Ned	Oprah	Patricia	Raoul
Robert	Samuel	Theodore	Will

A suggested focus for clipboard notes is included in the Lessons. Each suggestion repeats for three lessons. Like all suggestions of this nature in the Lessons, they are mostly reminders of different things for which to look. Figure 3-1 contains a list of the different suggestions that are included in the Lessons.

One teacher records her clipboard notes on a form (Figure 3-2) that has blocks the size of the smallest Post-It™ notes (1 3/4″ × 1 1/4″). In the blocks he or she writes the students' names in alphabetical order by first name. When something about a student attracts his or her attention, even if it isn't an earth-shattering discovery and whether or not it is related to the lesson's clipboard note suggestion, the teacher writes it on a Post-It™ and sticks it over that child's block. Some students have several notes at the end of a day, some have none. On the form for the next day, the teacher stars the names of students for which he or she made no observations today. That serves as a reminder to the teacher to notice those students. He or she then dates the Post-It™s and transfers them to a notebook page or folder for each student. Other teachers make similar forms, but record notes directly on the form. Still others use pages of address labels and peel off the labels and transfer them to the child's individual record.

Check-in conversation notes   Notes should also be made following Check-In Conversations. Whatever a teacher notices about each student is what he or she writes down. Most teachers try to record one strength and one weakness for each student. Many teachers use the same form they use for clipboard notes. Others use a form with more space for writing about each student, such as in Figure 3-3. Still

Figure 3-3

Sample of Conversation Notes Form

Comprehension Focus _____   **Date** _____

Student's Name	Comments

other teachers develop a checklist similar to the ones described in Chapter 6 that are used for recording notes gleaned from the student's folders.

In-depth conversation notes   Much more detailed information is recorded about each student after In-Depth Conversations. For example, a teacher might write the titles of the books the student brings, notes about the student's responses to comprehension questions, the student's opinions (such as which was his or her favorite book or character), and the suggestions the teacher made of books the student might like. The recording form may resemble a questionnaire. Another teacher's form may be, for the most part, a checklist of a broad range of reading skills, with additional space for anecdotal comments. Still other teachers may keep a notebook sectioned off with several pages for each student. Those teachers may be comfortable writing summary notes without a particular form.

RECORD OF BOOKS READ

In addition to the notations of book titles that teachers record on their clipboard notes, it is useful for students to keep a record of books they have read. Recording book titles, however, is not feasible at the beginning of the year; it would consume all of a student's reading time. Nor should the goal of Recreational Reading be to generate a long list of book titles. One teacher told of a conscientious first-grader who quietly selected her four books, returned to her desk, methodically and deliberately recorded the title of each, and without bothering a soul, returned the books to the shelf and got four more. She repeated that process without a hint of deceit or malice for the entire thirty minutes. Perhaps it is best to delay having students record book titles until it is meaningful. At that time they may also choose to record only those they want to *remember* they have read. Competition for the greatest number of books read usually runs counter to the mood and atmosphere intended for Recreational Reading.

AUDIO-TAPING CONVERSATIONS

One teacher, who felt all of her written records failed to convey completely the amazing growth of many of her students from the previous year, undertook a project that proved most worthwhile. She brought a thirty-minute cassette tape for each of her students and recorded one of the first conversations with each student. About midyear she recorded a second conversation on the same tape, and near the end of the year, a third. The students had an audio record to take home that reflected their enthusiasm as well as their increasing capabilities.

▶

Procedures for Storytime

During the Storytime part of this module, teachers read a story, poems, or a book aloud to the class and lead a discussion about the story. The discussion is a lively exchange between the teacher and students, which increases appreciation and understanding of the book. When time permits, the students complete an art or craft activity related to the selection.

READ ALOUD

Each day the teacher reads aloud to her students. The atmosphere is that of a community of literate people who love sharing books. A specific book or type of book is included in each Storytime section in the Lessons. Attempts were made to ensure quality and variety in the literature specified. The suggestions include both fiction and nonfiction. The Appendix contains a list of the books suggested for each Storytime lesson.

These books, like all of the topics in the SUCCESS Lessons, are mere suggestions. Often two or more books are listed because not all libraries will have all of the selections. Teachers who do not have access to a book that is listed simply choose another book. Sometimes they try to find another book that the art or craft activity will complement. Other times they substitute a different activity or elect to read and discuss the entire time and not do an activity.

Occasionally, teachers are asked to read two books and have the students compare them. At other times, the teacher reads one book more than once. Usually, that suggestion is made when the book has a rhythmic pattern. On the second reading the students "read" the repetitive parts with the teacher.

Read-aloud time should be a special time for the students and the teacher. The setting should be as relaxed and comfortable as possible. Many teachers gather their students around them. The students sit on the floor and the teacher sits on a stool or chair. Since most of the books that will be read to first-graders are picture books, students need to be in positions that make seeing the pictures possible.

DISCUSSION

The discussion is intended to be a natural part of the shared experience with the books. Most often it follows the reading, but occasionally a discussion preceding the reading is more appropriate. Always the mood is upbeat because people who love books are talking about a book they are enjoying together. The Lessons contain suggestions for a discussion focus. Following the direction of the discussion focus ensures that students will develop all kinds of listening and comprehension skills. Through listening to books and talking about them, students learn about reading and comprehending. They also learn more about writing that will affect their own compositions. They learn how stories are organized, what makes a story funny, how description affects understanding, why word choice is important, the effectiveness of a good title, and much, much more.

Many teachers try to have available additional books that are similar in content or form. For example, they bring in other books about the same subject, others that have rhythmic patterns, or others by the same author or illustrator. Sharing these with the class generates additional excitement about books and reading. In Recreational Reading, children tend to read books they have heard someone read or tell about. The more books they know about, the more effectively they will choose books during Recreational Reading and the sooner they will be reading independently.

Nicholas Miller

OPTIONAL ACTIVITY

An optional art or craft activity accompanies each book that is read during Storytime. The thirty minutes allotted to Storytime can easily be consumed by a relaxed reading of the book and a good discussion. Having students complete a creative activity is the teacher's choice. The activities are fun, but they should never detract from nor rush the enjoyment of the read-aloud book. Teachers are encouraged to embellish or diminish the activity each day to accommodate their schedule and art supplies. Integrating content-area themes into the modules may free time for the activity. It can also serve as the day's art or craft activity.

Art activities are defined here as those that students develop as they can and wish to. No two students' art projects will be identical. Craft activities are those whose primary purpose is to help students learn to follow directions. These finished products will be as alike as first-graders can make them. Art and craft activities are intended to result in creations that the students can take home to share with their families. Having the creation will also serve as a reminder of the book to which it was related.

Although most of the activities are take-home art or craft activities, occasionally the activity is a class project, such as a class book to which each student contributes at least one page. Making a class book could substitute for the Writing module on a day when time is tight. Class books stay at school. If additional class books are written during the Writing module or as math activities (story problem books), teachers will have enough class books for each student to have one to take home at the end of the year. Until then, the books become part of the Recreational Reading collection. Other activities that do not usually result in take-home objects are dramatic projects. If students make props for their drama, those may go home, at the teacher's discretion.

▶ Other Issues

BOOKS ON TAPES AND RECORDS

There is certainly more than one way students can have pleasurable experiences with books. Books on tapes and records can also be worthwhile additions to the Recreational Reading & Storytime module. Recorded books add a different dimension to students' exploration of books. Many teachers set up a listening center during Recreational Reading for a small number of students. All students should be included in the rotation through this center, not just those who are not yet independent readers. For example, one teacher has a cassette tape recorder and a record player set up each day. One student listens to each machine. All of the students are on the schedule for each machine, but readers have the option of listening or passing up their opportunity. Listening centers should never replace quiet time with books for any student.

Likewise, sometimes teachers opt to play a tape or record instead of reading aloud that day during the Storytime part of the module. This is a valuable option, but it also should not replace the teacher's reading aloud most of the time. A special bond forms between the teacher and the students when the teacher reads aloud. No professional reader conveys a personal excitement of books like the child's own teacher.

READING NON-BOOKS

There is a wonderful argument for letting students read *any* material during Recreational Reading. "I don't care what they read, as long as they read!" Consider, however, that reading books is largely a habit, and habits take time to form. Further, many adults read magazines, newspapers, and catalogs, but have never developed the habit of

Amanda McAbee

reading books. Recreational Reading can provide the time needed for developing not only an appreciation of books, but also the habit of choosing books to occupy leisure time. Some teachers select one day each week that students may read anything in print. Be careful that the message is not, "Boys and girls, you don't have to read books today, so you do not have to work as hard today. You can have more fun because you may read anything." Simply scheduling this option on Friday can give that message, without even a comment from the teacher.

MAKING GOOD USE OF THE BASAL READER

*O*ur classroom is a comfortable place where students learn to make decisions, take risks, care and share with their peers every day. Their enthusiasm and excitement for learning becomes contagious and I, as the teacher, thrill at how learning takes place.

Jean Becker, teacher

In addition to expanding the class collection of reading materials for Recreational Reading, basal readers can be useful for teachers. A major advantage is that their contents are limited, so teachers can be familiar with all of the stories in them. It is often easier to have a conversation with a reader about a story that the teacher knows. Until teachers expand their own awareness of the literature their students are reading, the basal can fill a void. This is only appropriate if the basal contains well-written, predictable literature. Since SUCCESS teachers are always expanding their knowledge of good children's literature, this use of the basal usually diminishes after a while.

Another advantage of having basals in the classroom is that multiple copies of stories are readily available. During the second half of the year, Small-Group Conversations are scheduled during Recreational Reading. Assuming that the basals contain good literature, they can be the source of some of the stories discussed in the Small-Group Conversations.

A third use of basal readers is for evaluation. It is often important for teachers to compare their students with what other first-graders are doing. The first year a teacher uses the SUCCESS program, having students read from a basal may boost the teacher's own confidence. In situations where most other teachers in a building or school district are using basals, SUCCESS teachers may have students read from basals during In-Depth Conversations or periodically take end-of-basal tests. If teachers discover a weakness in their students through these evaluations, they can then modify a component of a SUCCESS module to focus on that skill or strategy. Students can be taught what they need to learn using SUCCESS teaching strategies that are based on their vocabulary and real-life materials.

A word of caution. SUCCESS students may not be able to read some of the pre-primers as early as students in basal classrooms. Those students have spent weeks drilling on a relatively small number of words. SUCCESS students have been exposed to hundreds of words without having to memorize any of them. SUCCESS students also expect stories to make sense. They expect that their knowledge of language will be a help in predicting what words are written on a page. Pre-primers that do not make sense or are not written in predictable language will be difficult for SUCCESS students, especially early in the year. As they expand their knowledge of the reading process and develop strategies for reading all types of materials, they will be able to read even unpredictable stories with ease.

▶ What Can Be Taught in Recreational Reading & Storytime?

Recreational Reading & Storytime provide unlimited opportunities for teachers to teach whatever reading and writing strategies their students need. There is time to work with individuals, large groups, and small groups. Good literature is the model for writing. Meaningful stories are the vehicle for developing word analysis and comprehension skills. Teachers can work one-on-one with an individual, helping him in the context of what he is currently reading. Or a group can discuss and discover how authors communicate effectively. All of this can be accomplished without the need for ability grouping!

Content-area themes or literature studies may also be incorporated into this module. Teachers may gather several books related to a topic the class is studying in science or social studies for students to read during Recreational Reading. These books could be displayed in a special way or "auctioned off" at the beginning of the module. The teacher's Read-Aloud selection could be one of these books. Other teachers want their classes to be familiar with many different authors and illustrators. In addition to the "Get to Know the Author/Illustrator" series in the Lessons, these teachers focus on other authors or illustrators by scheduling a series of days in their honor.

▶ Decisions, Decisions, Decisions

Every SUCCESS module provides numerous opportunities for teachers and their students to make decisions. Both are active participants in learning. Below are some of the decisions each of them makes during Recreational Reading & Storytime.

TEACHER DECISIONS

1. Do I hold the type of conversation suggested in the Lessons or do I substitute a different type? Or do I do one type for half of the module and a different type the other half?

2. With which students shall I have conversations?

3. Shall I ask questions related to the suggested comprehension element or is that appropriate today with this student?

4. What shall I record on my clipboard as general observations and what shall I write about each student with whom I confer?

5. What style of record form shall I use?

6. Do I feel good about where my students are sitting and how they are behaving or does a change need to be made?

7. What did I learn about each student today?

8. Shall I read the suggested book or another?

9. When should I exchange the collection of books I got from the library and get others?

10. Do we have time to do the activity suggested? Should I modify it because of time or available materials? Do I have a better idea?

11. Is the discussion suggestion one I feel comfortable with or should I change it?

12. Do I want to integrate a content-area topic into this module? Or into another module so there will be more time for Recreational Reading and all parts of Storytime?

STUDENT DECISIONS

1. What book shall I read read today?

2. How many books should I get to look at?

3. Where shall I sit?

4. Do I want to read alone or ask someone to read with me?

5. With whom shall I share my book at the end of the module?

6. Do I want to record this book so I will remember I have read it?

7. Do I want to read every word or look at the pictures?

8. Do I want to participate orally in the discussion about the Read Aloud book?

9. How do I want to develop my art or craft activity?

▶ Summary Chart

RECREATIONAL READING

Before Beginning:	Teacher gathers a large collection and variety of books, decides about behavioral standards, and discusses expectations with the students.
Students Read Books:	Students read books. Teacher either reads too or holds individual conversations with students. Teachers record observations.
Book Share:	Each students tells someone about the books he or she has read that day.

STORYTIME

Preplanning:	Teacher selects a book to read aloud and, if the students will complete an activity, gathers the necessary materials.
Read Aloud:	Teacher reads a book(s) to the class and leads a discussion about the book.
Activity (Optional):	Students complete an art or craft take-home activity, make a class book, or act out parts of the story.

Chapter 4 — The Writing Module

In SUCCESS classrooms at least thirty minutes each day is devoted to students writing original compositions. From scribbles to short stories, from pictures to poetry, students express themselves on paper during the Writing module. Although a general topic is introduced almost every day, students always are encouraged to write on topics of their choice. The mode of their writing varies, based on the student's message and capabilities. First-grade writers begin to develop a sense of writing for an audience and proudly publish writings throughout the year.

▶ Basic Principles

The writing process and how students develop as writers have been studied extensively in recent years and exciting conclusions have been reached. The works of Lucy Calkins, Donald Graves, Nancy Atwell, and others have greatly influenced this edition of *SUCCESS in Reading and Writing*. Below are some of the principles defined by current researchers in the field of process writing on which the Writing module is based.

STUDENTS NEED TIME FOR WRITING

Writing helps human beings define themselves. College students paint the campus boulder or overpass, school-aged children write countless notes to friends, younger children scribble on dirty trucks or bedroom walls. People have a need to record their thoughts, serious or otherwise. The more often a person writes his or her thoughts, the more effectively those thoughts will be communicated to the reader. The SUCCESS Writing module ensures that the students have at least thirty minutes every day that they can write on any subject they choose. This is time students can always depend on having. Developing as a writer takes time, a consistent and an extended amount of time. Nothing improves writing skill like writing regularly.

STUDENTS NEED OPPORTUNITIES TO SHARE THEIR WRITING

Before any daily writing is filed in a student's writing folder, that student reads it to a fellow student. Sharing their writing helps first-graders learn that writing is for the purpose of communicating and recording ideas. When the listeners give their attention and respond favorably to another student's writing, writers recognize that others are interested in their thoughts. Also, they realize that everyone does not think exactly as they do.

STUDENTS MUST "PUBLISH" SOME OF THEIR WORK

Publishing compositions is just as important for first-graders as it is for any other writers. Publishing helps students realize the completion of the writing process—from rough draft to final copy. It also gives purpose for

Chapter 4

Bryan Martorano

improving writing form, spelling, and handwriting. When others see and comment on a person's writing, the writer is reinforced. If the readers are able to get the author's message, the reinforcement is positive, and the writer will want to continue writing. If the reader asks questions because he or she does not understand what the writer is trying to say, the writer can see where the composition needs to be revised to get the message across. If the confusion is the result of a lack of sufficient detail, the writer can add more to his or her writing (or illustration). If it is due to spelling or punctuation, the writer may begin to recognize the need for a standard form.

In the first-grade SUCCESS program, only two of the numerous steps involved in publishing are emphasized. The first is that all compositions are not published. Most compositions are rough drafts that will not be seen by the general public. Only certain papers are published. Without this experience, students do not develop an understanding of the difference between rough drafts and polished copies, which is essential to writing growth in subsequent years. Secondly, the writer is the person who determines which papers are special. Allowing the writer to choose favorites, the one he or she wants to publish, encourages personal involvement in what others read. Standard grammar, punctuation conventions, and standard spelling only exist to make accurate communication through writing possible. When a student selects a favorite composition, he or she is more interested in others being able to get the true message.

EDITING MUST BE EMPHASIZED APPROPRIATELY

In the first-grade Writing module, editing for perfect written form is relatively unimportant. However, teachers constantly interact with students and help them improve their use of standard written language form. Each time a teacher talks with a student, he or she points out one aspect of the writing that could be improved and one aspect that deserves praise. Rarely, if ever, would a teacher edit a student's paper to perfect form. Whenever a student chooses a composition to be displayed, that student is given the opportunity to add or change anything about the composition, including completing an illustration.

THE TEACHER LEADS A BRIEF MINI-LESSON

Each Writing module begins with a brief mini-lesson. During this time the teacher leads a discussion about writing. Most often the mini-lesson includes the introduction of a possible topic. Most lessons suggest a broad writing topic and the class brainstorms possible interpretations of the topic. Occasionally, teachers write a limited number of selected words or groups of words on the chalkboard that represent some of the ideas discussed. Also, teachers sometimes opt to talk about elements of writing during the mini-lesson. This discussion is brief and may relate to the discussion focus from Storytime (sequence, description, titles, humor, etc.) or be a reminder of aspects of standard form, such as capitalization, quotation marks, or final punctuation.

WRITING SKILLS ARE TAUGHT IN THE CONTEXT OF STUDENTS' WRITING

During the Composing time of the Writing module, teachers converse with individual students about the content and form of their writings. Every instructional comment relates directly to the student's current writing. As the teacher circulates among the students while they are writing, he or she talks with as many students as possible. In each conversation the teacher isolates one or two items the student could improve and one or two strengths of the writing. Teaching occurs through praise, as well as constructive critical comments. All of the teacher's comments are in the context of their immediate application in the students' writings.

An important writing skill that first-graders are learning is the process of spelling. In SUCCESS, spelling is recognized as a developmental process. Students progress naturally through developmental stages as they learn about the way words are spelled. Instead of basing students' learning to spell on having them memorize a list of words each week, students in SUCCESS learn to spell primarily through regular, daily attempts at communicating with others in writing. Spelling, like other skills related to writing, progresses developmentally through the context of their real, meaningful writing. Although consistent use of standard spelling happens slowly, it takes on a purpose as students attempt to communicate their thoughts to others.

Joyce proudly held out her paper for the teacher to read. "You read it," she replied when the teacher asked Joyce if she would like to read it.

"Mi store is abt a sjufewit," the paper began. The teacher had no trouble reading, "My story is about a," but she had no idea about the next word. "I'm sorry, Joyce, tell me this word, please. I'm not sure what it is and I want to hear your whole story."

"Dinosaur," Joyce said. "I didn't know how to spell it."

"Oh, yes. Do you know why I had trouble reading that word? Listen as I say 'dinosaur-r-r-r.' What do you hear at the end of *dinosaur*?"

"*R*," answered Joyce.

"That's right, Joyce. If you just add an *r* at the end, it will be much clearer that the word is *dinosaur*.

"Yeah, I see," sighed Joyce, as she confidently wrote the additional letter.

Even though Joyce's spelling of *dinosaur* was far from the standard spelling, she was encouraged to continue writing. Her anxiety about her ability to spell would have been increased if the teacher had spelled every letter in *dinosaur*, much less in every word. Instead, the teacher conveyed the message that Joyce should listen to sounds she hears in words as she tries to spell. Totally standard spelling is not necessary at this point for communication to occur.

STUDENTS CONSIDER THEIR AUDIENCE

Through reading their writings to others and regularly publishing their work, students learn that the teacher is not their only audience. Students also have opportunities to write for specialized audiences. They make birthday or holiday cards for their parents and friends. They write letters and send them. They write lists of materials needed and outline plans for group projects that are duplicated for each group member. When compositions are displayed outside the classroom, students in other grade levels read them. First-graders learn from the beginning that writing is for communicating ideas. It is not simply for completing assignments for the teacher to grade.

WRITING MODELS HELP STUDENTS

The students' exposure to books in the Recreational Reading & Storytime module relates directly to their growth as writers. Books they hear the teacher read or that they explore on their own become models for their writing. As they read books they see how pictures and words interact to tell stories. One student proudly presented her book about a loose tooth to a visitor. She explained that she had written only a few words on each page and drawn a related picture on each because, "That's the way they do it in my books. The authors of my books only wrote a word or two on each page, so that's what I did."

The Read-Aloud part of Storytime and the discussions that follow help students recognize the important elements of literature. Their compositions will begin to have beginnings, middles, and ends. Their stories will

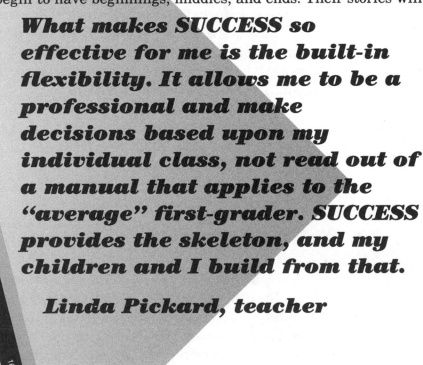

What makes SUCCESS so effective for me is the built-in flexibility. It allows me to be a professional and make decisions based upon my individual class, not read out of a manual that applies to the "average" first-grader. SUCCESS provides the skeleton, and my children and I build from that.

Linda Pickard, teacher

often follow the same patterns as those that students hear or read in books. Further, teachers will frequently see that students use words or phrases from favorite stories in their own compositions. Beyond "Once upon a time" and "They lived happily ever after," students will have animals "trip, trap, trip, trap" over "rickety bridge(s)" or accuse characters of "just talking silly talk."

STUDENTS MAINTAIN WRITING FOLDERS

Virtually all of the compositions written during the Writing module are filed in each student's writing folder. As soon as possible, students should learn how to date and file their own papers. Many teachers use special stickers or color coding to help students recognize their personal folders. Students will look back through their papers regularly to choose a special one to be displayed. Occasionally, some teachers encourage students to read from their writing folders during Recreational Reading. Not only are the folders a collection students are proud of, they are extremely valuable to the teacher for evaluation and assessment and parent conferences.

STUDENTS HAVE CHOICES IN WRITING TOPICS AND WRITING SCHEDULES

A different writing topic is included in each Writing lesson for most of the year. That does not mean that everyone will write on the teacher's topic each day. Nor does it mean that every composition will be begun and completed in one thirty-minute Writing module. Every day each student has the choice of writing on the topic introduced by the teacher (which may differ from the topic suggested in the Lesson), writing on a different topic, or continuing to write on a topic begun previously.

▶ Procedures for the Writing Module

There are three parts to each Writing module. For the first few minutes the teacher leads a brief discussion of a possible topic and, occasionally, a reminder of a writing element of which writers need to be aware. The majority of the Writing module is the Composing time. Students write and teachers assist in the writing process by talking with individuals about their plans or products. At the end of each daily module, students share their writing with at least one other student before filing their papers in their Writing folders.

PREPLANNING

When planning for the Lessons, teachers are encouraged to read the suggestions given and consciously decide to use or change them, as fits their classes and themselves. The suggestions include writing topics and a publishing schedule. Teachers either choose to follow the suggestions, modify them somewhat, or substitute entirely different ones. For example, Lesson 37 suggests that students write about "holidays." One teacher might discuss several holidays and encourage his students to write about any one of them. Another might discuss only Halloween because that holiday is forthcoming. She might add a brief discussion about how to write a title. A third teacher may choose to de-emphasize the students' preoccupation with Halloween and introduce a topic related to a content-area topic the class is studying.

WRITING TOPICS

There is considerable debate in the professional literature on teaching writing about whether teachers should introduce writing topics or whether all topics should be selected by each student. Much of this debate has developed because many writing topics have limited students. Some topics are very narrow, and students sense that there is one "right" way to develop them. These writing topics are reminiscent of essay-test questions. They often create anxiety, rather than helping students experience the freedom of writing one's thoughts. Other topics require a type of writing with which all students are not comfortable. One teacher, for instance, always introduces fantasy topics which require writing make-believe. Another teacher only introduces descriptive paragraphs. This type of assignment restricts both the writing style and the length of a student's composition. Still other teachers restrict most of their writing assignments to nonfiction, and functional writing, such as a list of procedures or simply retelling what they have read or studied. Students who write clear, precise directions would develop great confidence in themselves as writers if they were in this sort of class. However, if they were in another class, they might develop an entirely different image of themselves as writers.

Teachers who choose to introduce topics should keep several factors in mind:

1. *Make the topics broad.* During the mini-lesson students should be encouraged to think of all different ways they could develop this topic. Some students may write fiction stories. Others may write a dialogue or play. Still others may relate a true experience they had that the topic discussion reminded them of.

2. *Suggest topics that help students realize how much they know to write about.* The group discussions stimulate students to write about topics they had not thought of. Sometimes when students write only on self-selected topics, they tend to write about the same things over and over.

3. *Recommend topics that relate to experiences students have had or thought about.* These experiences can be things the students have done with their family or friends, subjects they have studied, or books they have read. Students who like to write fantasy can turn any topic into a make-believe story. Others can retell an event as it happened. Pragmatists can write instructions for someone else to duplicate the experience they had.

4. *Try to resist limiting the amount or style of a student's composition.* Instead of introducing a topic such as, "Write a paragraph about . . ." or "Write some sentences about . . ." or "Write a dialogue between two . . .,"

Michael Dominick

teachers who just say, "Write about . . ." free students to do it their way. During conversations between the teacher and one writer, the teacher might suggest the addition of some dialogue or he might help a student see where her writing could be divided into more than one paragraph. Those suggestions are helpful to the developing writer, rather than being restrictive.

5. *Let students have the option of writing on the topic or writing on a different topic of their choice.* Regardless of how well the topic follows the guidelines above, there will always be students who will use their writing time more productively and develop more as writers if they are free to write on the topic of most importance to them on that day.

Most often the writing topic suggested in the SUCCESS Lessons is related either to that lesson's Research project or the Read-Aloud book in Storytime. All topics are intentionally broad. Different teachers and students can interpret them as they choose. Usually they relate directly to a type of experience all students have had. Teachers are encouraged to broaden the topics they feel are more restrictive, rather than narrow the broader ones.

MINI-LESSON

The primary purpose of the mini-lesson is to stimulate students to write. The discussion is intended to help students feel, "I can write about that!" Instead of feeling constrained by an *assignment,* students should feel freedom to express their thoughts on a given subject. Second, mini-lessons can help students become more knowledgeable about the process of writing and conventions of written language.

During the mini-lesson, for four to six minutes the teacher leads a brief discussion about various interpretations of the writing topic. The teacher builds interest and awareness in the broad topic and then quickly releases students to put their thoughts on paper. As students volunteer thoughts related to the topic, the teacher may write words or groups of words on the chalkboard that represent some of the ideas discussed. These words are more for reminding students of some possible points they could include if they run out of ideas, rather than for showing students how to spell the words. Students should not feel limited by the words, nor should they be dependent on them for spelling. Whether or not to write words on the chalkboard depends on the teacher and the class. Some teachers, for instance, have noted that the more words they write on the board, the more times they are asked, "Which word is . . .?" Some have also noticed that some students write only about ideas recorded on the board. If the words become a hindrance to free expression of ideas, teachers might consider reducing their emphasis on this part of the procedure. Students who are not stimulated to write about the topic introduced by the teacher are encouraged to write on any topic of their choice. Keeping a personal list of potential writing topics expedites students' choosing alternative topics.

Students' personal list of writing topics   Lessons 1–159 include a different writing topic for each day. The suggested topics usually relate to one of the other modules in that lesson. Beginning with Lesson 160, there is not a suggested topic. On Lesson 160 students brainstorm topics on which they might write during the remaining twenty lessons. Their writing for Lesson 160 is to select topics from the class's discussion and make their own list of potential topics. The list of topics may be stapled to the student's writing folder, so it is readily available to the student. Some students may begin to compile a list of potential topics long before Lesson 160. Regardless of when it is begun, students will regularly add to their list as ideas come to them. On any day that a student is not interested in the topic that the teacher introduces, he or she can check the list and choose a topic from it. By Lesson 160 most every student should be able to maintain a list of topics. For the remainder of the year, their personal lists will be the source for the students' writing topics.

COMPOSING

For close to twenty minutes students express their thoughts on paper. At different times of the year, and for different students, that means they will draw pictures, scribble zigzag lines or other letter-like symbols, or write lengthy stories. Many students will do combinations of these for most of the year.

Drawing is an important way young writers rehearse what they want to write about. Many teachers report watching students refer back to their picture and then add to their writing. It is also possible for them to get more ideas on paper satisfactorily through drawing. Students who very diligently write pages full of word-like combinations of letters are often not able to remember what they wrote. Doing a drawing before or after writing helps them remember what their writing says, even days later.

While the students are writing, the teacher circulates around the room helping students grow as writers. Some students have difficulty getting started writing. Others feel they are finished when they have written little more than one sentence. Basic conventions of punctuation and capitalization, as well as handwriting, can be taught effectively in one-on-one conversations while students are involved in their compositions. Most students are anxious about spelling. For some it is a barrier to writing anything; others are concerned that all of their words be "spelled the right way." Without interrupting those who are actively involved in composing, the teacher is very busy doing whatever he or she can to help as many students as possible. The teacher may initiate a conversation by saying:

"Can't you think of what to write about? If you weren't excited about what we talked about during the mini-lesson, you may write about something else. What about your stickball game last night? I heard you won, but I'd like to know more about the game. Perhaps you will write about it."

"Oh, what an interesting picture! Read it to me, please. Would you like to write some words about your picture? I will write what you say or you can write it."

"Have you finished? Will you read or tell me about your composition? May I point out one thing that will make others be able to read this better? When you write the word *I*, it should always be capitalized. I am most impressed that you used the word *giggled* instead of *laughed*. I can just hear him doing that. What happened after you two got so silly and giggly? Did his mother say anything? Perhaps you would write what happened next."

*T*he Language Experience module [now the Writing module] has helped first-grade students learn to write easier than any other method. The total class instruction is what makes SUCCESS effective for me.

Lillian Sheets, teacher

Students also ask teachers for help during this module. For example, here are some conversations frequently initiated by students during this module and examples of responses by teachers:

Sean: I can't write.
Teacher: What would you like to say? Maybe I can help.
Sean: I want to say, "ride my bike." That's what I do after school.
Teacher: What do you think "ride" starts with?
That's right, write *r*. What do you hear next? You might hear the name of a letter.
Great, write *i*. And at the end?
Exactly, *d*. I thought you didn't know how to write that word! Keep going. You write "my bike" and I'll come back later and help you some more, if you need for me to. I hope you'll draw a picture of you on your bicycle.

Jeanie: I want to write about my cousin's visit yesterday. We played store. It was great. We made play money and everything, but I don't know how to spell all of the words.
Teacher: Try not to worry about spelling. If you want to just write one or two letters for each word, that's fine. But remember to leave a space between each word, so that it'll be easier to read later. Then you'll be able to tell more about what you did. What you have to say is much more important than worrying about spelling all of the words now. Besides, it's your story! Spell the words your way, too. I like the way you capitalized your cousin's name.

The content of teachers' writing conferences with students is not limited by an artificial first-grade "curriculum." It is limited only by the students and what they are attempting to communicate. Teachers are encouraged to teach each student one or at the most two things during each conversation. Whatever the teacher calls the student's attention to should relate directly to his or her writing. Teachers are also encouraged to point out one aspect of the student's writing that deserves praise. The comments need to be very specific, genuine, and directly related to the student's writing.

Spelling   The majority of the concerns of first-grade writers revolve around spelling. The teacher's most difficult job is to get across to all students that the objective is to write ideas, without being constrained by spelling. That does not mean that spelling is not important—spelling is extremely important! Studies of developmental spelling have proven that students' writing meaningful thoughts regularly—thoughts that they want others to read—is the most effective way for teaching or learning spelling. The teacher's difficult task is to help students feel free to write, without worrying about spelling.

The SUCCESS approach to spelling has many components, each of which complements the others. They are all important. If a teacher incorporates all of them into his or her spelling program, without adding anything else, students will develop as good spellers. They will understand the process by which letters are put together in English to make words. The major components of the SUCCESS process approach to spelling are:

1. Each individual writes daily.

2. Every two to three weeks papers are published, even if words are not spelled correctly. Students *almost always* choose the papers to be published.

3. Teachers make students feel confident as spellers through conversations while they are in the process of writing, even when their spelling is not standard.

4. Students are exposed every day to many books and other materials that contain models of standard spelling in a context that is meaningful to students.

5. Words from the students' own vocabularies (which are inherently meaningful) are discussed each day in Word Study. Students become excited about words and comfortable with letter patterns, sound patterns, and structural patterns within words.

SHARING

During the last four to six minutes of the Writing module, each student reads or tells about his or her composition to another student or a small group of students. By having students share with a small group instead of reading it to the entire class, more students are able to share in the same amount of time. Many first-graders are more comfortable reading to a smaller audience. Smaller audiences are also more likely to listen to the reader and are, therefore, more able to respond genuinely.

All compositions are dated and filed. Students who wish to continue writing on the same topic a second day may place their papers in a "To Be Continued" box the teacher has created, instead of their Writing folder. The compositions become a wonderful resource for teachers to use for evaluation and conferring with parents about students' progress. (Chapter 6 discusses specific strategies for using writing papers to assess students' progress.)

Most papers will stay at school for the entire school year. On the last day of school, students will take home a marvelous record of their growth

Jenny Turek

as a writer during the first grade. The compositions will also serve as a diary of the year. But there are appropriate exceptions to keeping all papers described in Chapter 6. The *only* time suggested to send all papers home is at the end of the year.

In addition to the small collections of writing, many teachers send home an occasional composition. Teachers are cautioned to make sure this practice does not alter the complexion of the Writing folder contents. For instance, if teachers send home all of the "best" papers, their evaluation will be affected. Likewise, if they keep only the "best" papers, the student's folder is no longer a complete record of his or her progress.

PUBLISHING

Publishing, or making writing available for "the public" to read, is essential to the completion of the writing process. Writers of all ages and abilities need to experience the total process. Of the many components involved in publishing, first-grade writing instruction in SUCCESS focuses primarily on the notion that all writing is not published. Writers choose their favorite compositions to share with others; what is published should be the writer's choice.

From Lesson 30 on, each student looks through his or her writing folder and chooses one composition he or she wants the teacher to display or otherwise publish. This is recommended every fifteenth lesson. The student is given the opportunity of adding to the composition or completing an illustration before its being published. If the student says something like, "But that isn't how that word is spelled," the teacher might suggest that the student read over the composition to see if there are other things to change. Until students notice non-standard form in their writing, the teacher's pointing it out will be anxiety-producing rather than instructive. Teachers who decide there is much that they would like to do before the paper is displayed may use the composing time that day or the subsequent day to prepare their papers for publication. Published first-graders' papers will not be in perfect written language form.

Publishing does not need to be elaborate or time-consuming unless the teacher chooses for it to be. There are obvious times that publishing may involve more time and effort on everyone's part, such as collections of the "best" stories from the year to give Mother for Mother's Day. Generally, publishing will entail displaying each student's paper on a bulletin board or in the hall. Other relatively simple ways to publish papers include making class books or individual's books, sending home the original (and keeping a duplicate copy in the Writing folder), or sharing the compositions with another class.

▶ Modifying the Writing Module

Only one part of the Writing module is not flexible, and it should not be changed: students should express their thoughts daily about a variety of topics and in a variety of ways. Creating a group experience story that all students copy may be appropriate for some teachers, but it is not the intent of the SUCCESS Writing module. Having students copy a page out of their handwriting book may have a place in some other teachers' classrooms, but that is not what SUCCESS promotes as writing. As long as students are expressing themselves on paper for an extended amount of time (scribbles and pictures included), they are working within the framework of the intent of this module.

Teachers should adapt this module to meet special needs and purposes. Many teachers abandon the suggested writing topic and replace it with a topic that relates to a subject the class is discussing in a content area. Some teachers suggest students write about, or in the manner of, books they have read. Occasionally, a teacher may feel the need or desire to emphasize a particular writing form, such as a thank-you letter, riddles, or poetry. They may focus on the writing form during the mini-lesson and suggest that students who are not in the middle of a previously begun composition might write in the form suggested. Even if some students do not write in that form that day, they have heard the mini-lesson and the information may be useful to them in a composition some day.

Another common way many SUCCESS teachers modify the Writing module is to follow more closely the writer's workshop described by Calkins, Graves, and others. In a writer's workshop, topics are rarely suggested to the entire class. Students almost always write on self-selected topics. A second difference is that students would not all publish papers on the same schedule. This modification more often affects classes beyond grade one when students do more editing and revising of their first drafts.

Decisions, Decisions, Decisions

Every module in *SUCCESS in Reading and Writing* involves both teachers and students making decisions. Below is a list of some of the choices. An occasional review of this list of questions occasionally reminds teachers about the flexible structure inherent in the SUCCESS program. The teacher should adapt the program to the class and to his or her interests. Likewise, allowing the students to make the decisions helps them feel ownership in their own learning.

TEACHER DECISIONS

1. Should I introduce the topic suggested in the Lesson? Should I introduce a topic at all?

2. Should the topic be related to a book I have read to the class, a topic we are studying in science, social studies, or another content area, or an event that affects the class?

3. Should I call the class's attention to an element of good composition, such as making an interesting title or description? Should I remind them about an aspect of written language form, such as capitalization?

4. Whom should I talk with today and what shall I help each person with? What shall I praise?

5. When and how should we publish compositions?

STUDENT DECISIONS

1. What topic shall I write about? Or shall I add to a composition I began yesterday?

2. How shall I develop my composition? What shall I say and how shall I say it?

3. Shall I illustrate my idea before or after writing about it?

4. Whom shall I read my composition to?

5. Which composition would I like to have published?

▶ Summary Chart

Preplanning:	Teacher decides on the writing topic (if any) and if there is to be an additional topic for the mini-lesson.
Mini-Lesson: 4–6 minutes	Teacher leads a discussion of possible interpretations of the writing topic and writes a few words or groups of words on the chalkboard that represent some of the ideas.
Composing: 20 minutes	Students write on the topic introduced, a topic of their choice, or continue writing on a previously begun topic. Teachers confer with as many students as possible without interrupting their writing.
Sharing: 4–6 minutes	Each student reads his or her composition to another student or a small group of students.

Chapter 5 The Word Study Module

The Word Study module is thirty minutes for students to explore letters, words, and sentences in the meaningful context of their own vocabularies. Students volunteer words, groups of words, or sentences that meet at least one of the lesson's criteria. As the teacher records the students' ideas on a large chart, the class talks about how letters are put together to form words and how words are combined to produce sentences or longer units of discourse. Vocabulary concepts, relationships among words, phonics, spelling, and handwriting are also discussed. Although the discussion is led by the teacher, it is far from teacher-centered. The center is the student and the student's vocabulary.

During the first part of the daily module, the teacher develops the chart. After that, students copy their favorite words from the chart or write other words they didn't get to have written on the class chart, and the teacher works with individuals. The charts, which are displayed around the room, become a diary of the class's interests and experiences throughout the year. Any visitor will sense the pride and ownership of the students for them. Students will take visitors by the hand and show them "their" words, words that they volunteered perhaps weeks ago.

"That's my word. And that's my friend's word."

"I can read this sentence. It says, 'Tyrone got a new green bicycle for his birthday.' Tyrone is my best friend."

Every part of this module engenders an excitement for words and for how our alphabetic system works. For thirty minutes students are given the chance to realize how much they know about words and to show off that knowledge. The charts become a published record of their ideas and knowledge and a source of pride.

▶ Rationale

The new knowledge that students gain through the chart development and the writing time is unlimited. The number of "teachable moments" that arise as students volunteer words is more than any teacher can (or should) expand on. In addition to those predicated by the suggested lesson criteria, teachers pre-arrange discussion topics and specific skills instruction by modifying the criteria or otherwise making sure that certain items appear on the chart. Following is a discussion of some of the divisions of language study that are taught at least partially through the Word Study module.

PHONICS

A working knowledge of phonics is important for all readers and writers. The SUCCESS program recognizes the importance of phonics and tries to develop students' knowledge in a variety of ways, many of which occur during the Word Study module.

Kevin Wright

Most phonics instruction is void of meaning because abstract, meaningless sounds are taught in isolation. Since meaningless learning is not likely to transfer to other settings, the SUCCESS approach is intended to be as meaningful as phonics instruction can be for these reasons:

a. The words written on the Word Study chart are volunteered by students and come from the students' vocabularies, which insures their being meaningful.

b. The letter patterns are studied in realistic and, therefore, meaningful situations. In the "real world," letter patterns occur at all places in words. The reader must examine the letters around a pattern to determine the sound represented by that pattern. In Word Study, words are charted if the letter pattern is present anywhere in the word. They are not restricted to a particular position (beginning, middle, or end), nor must they represent one particular sound. For instance, if the letter pattern is *c* (Lesson 2), students may volunteer *c*at, pi*c*nic, *C*hristmas, s*c*hool, *c*hur*c*h, pa*c*k, and *C*harlotte. Vocabulary is not controlled so that a letter pattern represents the same sound each time.

Teachers decide how much to discuss sounds. Teachers who choose to discuss sounds complete the chart first and then ask students to compare the sounds represented by the lesson's letter pattern. Instead of making a chart of the *ed* "sound," they make a chart of words with the letter pattern *ed*. Then they discuss the different sounds *ed* represents in words. Some teachers also label sounds, such as short and long vowel sounds, if they feel it increases the students' understanding.

c. The sound patterns being learned are always discussed in the context of words. Saying sounds in isolation is meaningless and should be avoided. When talking about the sound the letter *b* usually makes, a SUCCESS teacher would say, "the sound heard at the beginning of *ball*, the beginning and middle of *baby*, or the end of *cab*."

d. If sound-symbol relationships are discussed as described above, students will begin to generalize or discover graphophonic rules. First-graders cannot always articulate the generalities they have discovered, but they will apply them. The increasing knowledge will be evident in their compositions, as well as in the words they volunteer for Word Study charts.

SPELLING

In the American culture spelling ability is also associated with intelligence. Though this notion has been proven wrong (there is no correlation between spelling ability and I.Q.), this mistaken idea dies hard. Great thoughts may go unheeded if they are written with a misspelled word or two. To say that spelling is not important would not only be a mistake, but a disservice to all learners.

The SUCCESS approach to spelling has many components, each of which complements the others. Learning to spell is a part of every module. Teachers who appropriately address spelling in all of the modules, without adding any other instruction or testing time, will have students who develop as good spellers. Their students will understand the process by which letters are put together in English to make words. The major components of the SUCCESS approach to spelling are:

1. Each individual writes daily during the Writing module.

2. Every two to three weeks each student chooses a composition to be displayed. The purpose for standard spellings becomes apparent as students want others to be able to read what they have written.

3. Teachers make students feel confident as spellers through their conversations while the students are in the process of writing, even when their spelling is not standard.

4. Students are exposed every day to many books and other materials during Recreational Reading and Research which contain models of standard spelling in a context that is meaningful to the students.

5. During the Word Study module, students have numerous opportunities to discover how the English spelling system works. As the class discusses the words volunteered from their spoken vocabulary, they begin to discover the patterns and conventions of written English. Students are particularly interested in the words because they are *their* words. They feel a sense of ownership and excitement which transfers to a willingness to challenge themselves.

As students choose words to copy during the writing portion of the module, they select the longest, most interesting words that they can read to write on their papers. Often teachers hear students boast that they can spell the words or observe them trying to write the words without looking at the chart. Students also attempt to spell words that were not written on the chart. Students become excited about words and comfortable with letter patterns, sound patterns, and structural patterns within words.

HANDWRITING

If teaching handwriting can be meaningful, it is in this instructional format. Instead of being an isolated lesson focusing on the formation of one or two letters, students are learning to form parts of *their* words.

The handwriting instruction is in three forms. First, the teacher introduces or reviews the letter or letter combination. The teacher demonstrates how the letters are formed. Time is given for students to practice the letters, if the teacher feels it is needed. Second, the teacher models the proper formation of the letters each time a word is written on a chart. Finally, there is considerable time given for teachers to assess and assist individuals' handwriting while they are writing.

STRUCTURAL ANALYSIS

Starting with Lesson 91, the lessons include a structural criterion, such as a specified number of syllables. The intent is for students to realize words can be broken down into smaller parts, thereby making spelling of them easier. It is not necessary for first-graders to learn all of the complex rules of syllabication and other elements of structural analysis.

When students discover that words can be broken down, they are much more willing to attempt to spell longer, more interesting words. Minimally, they are less intimidated by "big" words.

In addition to syllabication, other aspects of structural analysis are discussed frequently. For instance, teachers may call attention to any compound word or any word that has a prefix or suffix any time one is written on the chart.

SENTENCE STRUCTURE

Understanding exactly what makes a sentence is difficult for beginning writers. Students learn this concept in several ways in the SUCCESS Word Study module. One of the most effective ways is the concentration on groups of words that are not sentences. In the Word Study module, *word clusters* (any two or more words that are not a sentence) are written on the chart for much of the first half of the year. By concentrating on what is *not* a sentence, students learn what a sentence *is*.

Students become very familiar with groups of words that could be a part of a sentence. Often the teacher will extract the cluster from the student's sentence. They learn about descriptive phrases, prepositional phrases, verbs and adverbs, and the like, all of which make sentences more interesting and complex. This knowledge transfers very effectively to their writing in the Writing module, as well as the sentence writing later in this chapter on Word Study. Their sentences are often so involved that only three or four can possibly be written on the chart!

By springtime students already have so much knowledge of how to generate interesting sentences that teachers are able to set additional challenges for the class. For example:

"Today, let's not have any of our sentences start alike. See if we can start only one sentence with *the* and one with *I*."

"Try to include very interesting verbs in our sentences today."

Students who have written word clusters for close to sixty lessons find these challenges fun rather than difficult.

VOCABULARY DEVELOPMENT

The Word Study module provides opportunities for the class to discuss the meanings of words. Since the words written on the chart are volunteered by students, they are at least somewhat familiar to someone in the class. Therefore, the discussion of the meanings of words goes beyond simple definitions. The class may discuss the multiple meanings, alternate forms of words (because of different suffixes), connotations and denotations, homonyms, homographs, synonyms, opposites, or whatever else the teacher deems appropriate. A word of caution: Try not to tell students anything they can tell the class themselves. The teacher should ask many more questions than tell answers. In other words, lecturing about words or concepts is not an effective way of generating interest and increasing knowledge.

I strongly believe in it. The students in my room give words and word phrases that prove to me their vocabulary is much broader than I expected—even students who are slower. SUCCESS stimulates the minds of my students and develops creative thinking!

Waltrina White Barnett, teacher

SUCCESS 562 PX
SUCCESS 562 PX
SUCCESS 562 PX

Teacher: Our letter today is the *u*. Can anyone think of a word with a *u* in it?

Melanie: *Mutant*. Teenage Mutant Ninja Turtles.

Teacher: That does have a *u* in it. Since we are writing word clusters, shall I write all of what you said?

Mark: Hey, *turtles* has a *u* in it, too!

Teacher: How about that! I'll underline that *u*, also. Tell me about these turtles. Why are they called "mutant?"

John: They aren't like other turtles. They can walk on two legs and sing, and do all kinds of things, like fight bad guys.

Teacher: How did they get this way?

Kate: They got into some radioactive water in the sewer where they lived and that made them change.

Teacher: In real life other things, plants and animals, are sometimes described as mutant. Does anyone have any idea what a mutant plant would look like?

Sherri: Could they walk and talk?

Teacher: Only in the movies. How could a real plant mutate? That's what we call it when something becomes a mutant. What do you think *mutant* or *mutate* means?

DICTIONARY SKILLS

It is not uncommon for students to volunteer words that the teacher is not sure how to spell. Teachers can take wonderful advantage of these times to model the solution literate adults have: the dictionary. They can talk through the process of looking up a word. Before long the students will be competent users of the dictionary without any other direct teaching. For that reason alone, any teacher who realizes he or she has not looked up a word in front of the class in the past week or so might want to pretend he or she does not know how to spell a word and open the dictionary.

DEVELOPING CONFIDENCE IN STUDENTS

The Word Study module helps students develop confidence as learners. They feel competent and in charge. In this module students feel in control of what is written on the chart. It is *their* chart, not the teacher's nor anyone else's. There are so many possible words that could go on the chart that students are willing to try. Thinking of a word that meets more than one of the day's criteria or has the letter in it more than once is so exciting that students practically jump out of their seats.

What they write on their papers during the second half of each module is also chosen by the student. Obviously, the teacher offers encouragement and guidance, but over and over is heard,

"I'm going to write, *Tyrannosaurus Rex*."

"I'm going to copy the whole chart!"

"Not me, I'm thinking of all different words."

▶ How to Lead a Word Study Lesson

There are two parts to each Word Study module. The first is Chart Development; the second is Writing. Below are guidelines for teaching the Word Study module.

PREPLANNING

Each lesson's Word Study module suggests a letter or combination of letters and gives a suggestion for what teachers should record on the chart: words, word clusters, or sentences. When planning the Word Study module, teachers read what is suggested in the lessons. They then make a conscious decision to follow the suggestions or change them. Guidelines for changing the module are found in the section entitled "Modifying the Word Study Module" (page 84). After deciding on the criteria for the chart, the teacher lists in a planbook several items that could be written on the chart. These are helpful later for keeping the module pace moving rapidly. If students cannot think of something that meets one of the criteria, the teacher can offer hints or write one of the items from the list.

CHART DEVELOPMENT

At the beginning of the module, the teacher tapes a piece of large chart paper to the chalkboard and labels it with the lesson number or the date and the day's letter. See both the Appendix and Figure 5-1 for the letter patterns and other criteria suggested in the Lessons.

Most teachers then begin with a brief handwriting lesson. They demonstrate the formation of the letter and have the students practice it by writing the letter in the air, writing it with their fingers on their desks or their neighbor's back, or attempting to write it on their papers. Not much time is devoted to this whole group instruction because the teacher will have time later in the module to help individuals as they write the words from the chart.

For the next twelve to fifteen minutes, the teacher writes words, word clusters, or sentences (depending on the lesson) on the chart. Each entry is volunteered by a student and has at least one word that meets one or more of the day's criteria. This activity is fast-paced, without being

Figure 5-1

Overview of Other Elements of the Word Study Chart Development

Lesson Numbers	Examples Written on the Chart	Lesson Numbers	Syllabication Emphasis
1–20	single words	1–90	no emphasis
21–80	word clusters	91–130	2 syllables
81–125	sentences	131–165	3 syllables
126–180	teacher's choice	166–175	4 syllables
		176–180	5 syllables

rushed. A quick pace keeps everyone's attention better, plus it gives more students the opportunity to participate.

Student participation   There are several ways students can partici-pate. First, they can volunteer items for the chart. Second, they can elab-orate on what is said by the original volunteer. For instance, they can add a descriptive word or enhance a sentence, provided the originator does not object. Each student should feel ownership over his or her word and only share that ownership if he or she is willing. Third, students can read parts of the chart as a review. At all times the atmosphere is encour-aging of success. Questions a teacher might ask that involve students without putting them on the spot include:

"Who will read this word?"
"What word do you want to read?"
"Boys, will you read this word? Girls, how about this one?"
"Mike, do you want to read a word? Which one?"

Everyone in the class should be involved in the chart development. That does not mean that everyone will volunteer a word for the chart. Quite the contrary. One word per student is usually too many words for a chart. Plus, it is too predictable. Involving all students is a difficult task for the teacher. It takes tremendous energy, alertness, and quick think-ing. Teachers in this module often have as big a management problem with the overeager child, the one who has all the answers and shouts them out, as with the less verbal child. No teacher wants to punish a child for being enthusiastic and knowledgeable, but that child ought not be allowed to dominate the entire discussion. Many teachers praise this type of child by remarking about how many words he or she is able to think of, but ask that he or she let other students also get their words on the chart. One teacher had the domineering child be the "judge." She had him verify that words met at least one of the criteria or that they were spelled correctly. This made him feel important, acknowledged his capa-bilities, but allowed others to participate.

Keeping the shy child involved without calling on him or her is diffi-cult. Ways teachers deal with this include having lots of eye contact with all students, especially those who are less verbal; including the shy stu-dent often in a group of students who are asked to reread parts of the chart ("Will this table read the last sentence on our chart?"); asking the student to verify a statement made by another ("Robert said we need to put a question mark at the end of this sentence. Do you agree?"); or let-ting the student be the arbiter ("Jackie wants us to write 'scary pumpkin' and Sarah said 'funny-looking pumpkin.' Which shall I write on the chart?"). Some teachers report that they whisper the letter for tomorrow's chart to a student who has not participated lately ("Tomorrow our letter will be *r*. See if you can think of a word tonight that I could write on our chart tomorrow. I miss having your words on the chart. But don't tell

Erin Landauer

anyone what the letter is. That's our secret!"). All of the effort that it takes to maintain a low-risk, accepting environment always pays off. Before long, even the most reluctant students will think of an entry that they cannot bear to leave unrecognized. The look of pride and self-satisfaction on a student's face make all the teacher's restraint worthwhile.

Charts for Lessons 1 to 32   All of the lower-case letters are introduced in the first thirty-two lessons. One new letter is introduced each day for four days in a row. The fifth day is a Review Lesson. Lesson 1 introduces the letter *b*. Lesson 2 follows with the letter *c*. The sequence continues until all of the consonants are introduced. Then the vowels are introduced (see the Appendix). Using *b* first and following it with the remainder of the consonants before introducing the vowels is arbitrary. Although this sequence has proved satisfactory for many teachers, other teachers start with *a* and follow the usual alphabet sequence. Still others have introduced them by their formation, grouping those with similar writing strokes. Regardless of the sequence, the teaching strategies of this module are applicable. The letters are only an organizational tool. The object is to learn letters in conjunction with their function in real words.

In these initial lessons the teacher lists words volunteered by the students that contain the letter of the day. There is no magic number of words to put on a chart. The amount of discussion about each word will determine how many can be written in the time allotted, approximately fifteen minutes. If at the end of the time there are only five words on the chart, there has probably been more discussion than necessary; if there are fifty words, there has been too little discussion. The following is a typical interaction between a teacher and students for Lesson 3, where the focus is on words containing the letter *d*.

Teacher: Can anyone think of a word that has a *d* anywhere in the word? OK, Jamie?

Jamie: *Dog* has a *d*.

Teacher: You are right. I'll tell you the names of the letters and you say the letters as I write them: *d-o-g*. I'll underline the *d* since it is our special letter today. Jamie, do you have a dog?

Jamie: No, but Eric does. He lives next to me.

Teacher: Let's all read our first word: *dog*. Who can think of another word with a *d*? Yes, Sandra?

Sandra: Daddy.

Teacher: Class, watch as I write *daddy*. Say the letters as I say and write them. What do you notice about *daddy*?

Mike: It has three *d*'s.

Teacher: It sure does. Who would like to read our first word? Our second word? What is another word we can write up here?

Ben: *Rudder*. We have a sailboat and it has a rudder.

Below is an example of a chart from Lessons 1 to 32.

Example of Chart for Letter f

foot	fall	food
fix	fig	family
after	before	football
muffin	giraffe	half
funny	fish	fifteen
fat	farm	find
four	free	fruit

Charts for Lessons 33 to 58 Lessons 33 to 58 introduce the upper-case letters. Most days one capital letter is presented in each lesson. Two capital letters are presented when one of the letters has few words that begin with the capital form, such as *X* and *Z*. Every word that is volunteered does not always require the capital form of the Spelling Emphasis. Call particular attention to those letters that are supposed to be capitalized, and discuss why the others are not capitalized. Below is an example of a chart on capital letters.

Example of Chart for Capital Letter F

Fred Flintstone	my sister Frieda
Frosty the Snowman	with my father, Bill
Frankenstein monster	the state of Florida
the month of February	Father's Day
freaky Freddie	Friday the Thirteenth
Fat Albert	

Charts for Lessons 59 to 180 In Lessons 59 to 180, the Spelling Emphasis is a two- to three-letter cluster. These letter clusters may occur in any position in a word and may represent more than one sound pattern. Beginning with Lesson 91 there is a second emphasis, a particular number of syllables. Students are challenged to think of words that contain the Spelling Emphasis or a word with the specified number of syllables. They do not have to think of words that meet both criteria, although they are likely to try. Teachers still chart words that contain the letter but do not have the specified number of syllables and vice versa. Students will be especially excited when they are able to volunteer words with both emphases, so occasionally the Spelling Emphasis returns to a single letter. This makes it easier for students to think of words that have the specified number of syllables, as well as the Spelling Emphasis. Below are examples of these kinds of charts from Lessons 59 to 180.

Example of Chart for the Letters ou and Words with two Syllables

Billy the Kid was an **ou**tlaw.
The gun made a very l**ou**d noise.
Don't play in the water f**ou**ntain!
My sister and I went m**ou**ntain.
His ice cream fell on the gr**ou**nd.
Mother fusses at me when I p**ou**t.

Example of Chart for the Letters bi and Words with Three Syllables

My new **bi**cycle is red.
The giant baby wore a **bi**b.
That is an am**bi**tious project!
A rabbit has **bi**g ears.
Daddy got a **bi**ll for his new golf clubs.
This food tastes **bi**tter.

WRITING

The second half of each Word Study module is Writing. During this time students write things of their choice that are related to the chart. Some students practice writing the letters of the Spelling Emphasis. Most students begin by copying their favorite words from the chart. Others write words they thought of that met the criteria but that they did not get to have written on the chart. A few students will write sentences long before sentences are emphasized.

The assignment given to the class by the teacher is very open-ended: "Students, for the next fifteen minutes, I want you to practice your hand-writing. Copy your favorite words from the chart and then other words you remember. Or if you thought of some words that could go on our chart, write those on your paper. Spell them the way you think they might be spelled." Encouraging students to write words they like will ensure that they are copying meaningful words, rather than meaningless geometric shapes. Students who say, "I want to write 'balloon' " or "I'm going to write 'abracadabra' " are reading *and* writing words. Students who are copying words they cannot read are merely copying.

Resisting the temptation to require students to write a minimum number of words is very difficult for some teachers. But doing so only causes problems; it does not solve them. Teachers who respond to the question, "How many do we write?" by saying "I don't know. How many can you write?" open up a world of possibilities for students. There are no limits. Teachers who respond with a number often get only that number. Then they have to deal with the students who say they are through. If a student is not working up to the teacher's expectations, all the teacher has to do is tell *that student* he or she still has time and more is expected.

While the students are writing things related to the chart, the teacher is also busy. This is not a time to sit down. Instead, it is a time to teach individuals. The teacher moves from student to student helping that stu-

SUCCESS builds confidence and self-esteem in each child. Each child is able to leave first grade feeling good about that they're doing. SUCCESS promotes ownership of the curriculum in the children.

Becky Haseltine, teacher

dent with whatever he or she needs help. With some students, the teacher will work on handwriting. Other students will want a word spelled that is not on the chart. The teacher takes this opportunity to help that student develop confidence and independence in developmental spelling. For some that means simply saying, "Guess and go." For other students, saying that only increases anxiety and is counterproductive. Teachers should ask most students to read one or more words they have written. This is also a time for the teacher to talk to individuals who did not participate verbally in the chart development. Going to them and asking what they have written, what they are going to write, and if they can think of a word that could have been written on the chart gives these more reticent students the opportunity to express ideas without speaking in front of the entire class. Do not forget the eager students who were discouraged from adding more words to the chart. Go to them and ask what some of the words are that they were thinking. Help them write some of them on their paper. Teachers who do not use this time to teach and assess are missing important teaching opportunities—ones integral to the SUCCESS teaching strategy.

DATING AND FILING PAPERS

The papers produced during the Writing time of the Word Study module are dated and filed in each student's Word Study folder. The papers stay at school and become part of the longitudinal record teachers have of students' progress. Chapter 6 discusses ideas on filing efficiently.

EVALUATION

The Word Study papers are a source of important information about each student. Teachers should look at these papers and those in the two other folders (Writing and Research) at least once a week and make notes about the strengths and weaknesses they notice. These observations are the basis for modifying lesson components when a weakness is widespread among the students. They become the focus of conversations between an individual student and the teacher: "I've noticed you make beautiful m's but you have trouble writing s's. Let me help you. Also, take this word home and study it. I want you to learn how to spell it." And, of course, they are important documentation for the grades teachers assign. For instance, these papers are the best source for a handwriting grade.

▶ Glossary of Word Study Terms

WORD CLUSTERS

Word clusters are simply two or more related words that are not a sentence. The purposes for writing word clusters instead of single words or sentences are 1) more words are written on the chart; 2) there is more apparent meaning, a written context, associated with a word cluster than with a single word; 3) students learn what is not a sentence and, therefore, develop more understanding of what a sentence is; and 4) as stu-

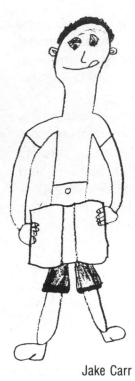

Jake Carr

dents learn about the parts of sentences, such as description, prepositional phrases, and adverbial clauses, and the sentences they generate in their compositions and later for the Word Study chart are much more interesting and complex.

The concept of a word cluster is rather difficult for students to understand at first. Teachers have found that the best way of teaching them is through example. Ask for a single word with the letter of the day. Then ask questions that elicit descriptive words. These can be added to the initial word to make it a cluster. If a student volunteers a complete sentence, extract a part of the sentence. Say something like, "We're writing word clusters on our chart today. May I just write this part?"

During the word cluster sequence (Lessons 21 to 80), teachers often write single words or complete sentences. What is written is ultimately up to the teacher. She or he must decide what is the most meaningful thing to write. Likewise, the teacher will write clusters on early charts where the emphasis is single words and single words or clusters or on charts when sentences are suggested.

LETTER CLUSTERS

Letter clusters are any combination of two or more letters. Some letter clusters have labels, such as blends and digraphs. In SUCCESS all types of letter combinations are studied, not just those that have names.

REVIEW LESSONS

Review lessons are conducted in the same manner as other lessons with two exceptions. First, the lesson focuses on two letters instead of one. Second, both of these letters will have been the focus of earlier lessons, so charts from those introductory lessons should be displayed in the room. Call the class's attention to the earlier charts and attempt to reread them. The students are likely not to remember all that is written on the chart. (If they remember very little of what is on the chart, make a note to discuss words more and read back over the chart more in introductory lessons.) If the chart is no longer hanging in a place that can be seen easily, the class can look at any other charts to find words with either of the letters.

MULTI-SYLLABLE WORDS

Beginning with Lesson 91 there is an added emphasis, multi-syllable words. The multi-syllable words do not have to contain the letter combination, just as the words that contain the letter cluster do not have to have the specified number of syllables. The teacher may call special attention, however, to words that meet more than one criterion. Some classes call these "double whammy" words. Thinking of a "double whammy" word is exciting enough. Teachers do not need to require them. If students can possibly think of one, they will. Although some adjustment has been made in the letter clusters to enhance the possibility of "double whammies," requiring all entries to meet both criteria makes the chart difficult. That means some students will not be able to participate. Before ending the Chart Development time, there should be at least one word with the letter cluster and one word with the specified number of syllables on the chart. Any more than one can be considered a bonus!

When syllables are first added as a second criteria, some teachers do not mention syllables until the chart is otherwise complete. They then have the students see if they can find any words on the chart that have two parts, or syllables. If they have difficulty, the teacher can choose one and have the class repeat it. Teachers may have students clap the syllables, hold their hand under their chin and count the number of times their chins move, or any other technique that helps students hear the syllables. Being able to hear that a word can be broken down into smaller parts is the only purpose in SUCCESS for introducing syllables to first-graders. This program does not recommend that you attempt to teach rules for separating syllables.

TEACHER'S CHOICE

Teacher's Choice, as it applies to the suggested Word Study lessons, refers to what is written on the chart. Up to Lesson 126, there is a suggestion for whether teachers should write single words, word clusters, or sentences. Beginning with Lesson 126, it is the teacher's choice. By this time of the year, teachers recognize skills or strategies on which their students need more instruction. If the teacher decides the class needs attention called to the past form of verbs, he or she may choose to elicit and chart a list of present-tense verbs from the students and make a second column on the chart of the past form. The following day he or she may write sentences, all of which are written in the past tense. Another day the chart may be filled with a group paragraph.

▶ Special Consider-ations

WRONG RESPONSES

Students may volunteer words that do not meet any of the criteria. For example, if a student volunteers the word "lamp" when the only criterion is the letter *t*, it would not be written on the chart. Instead, the teacher would write the word on the chalkboard, acknowledging that it is a very good word, but the teacher would have the student who said the word note that it did not have a *t* in it. The teacher ought not press the point or embarrass the student. If the same thing were to occur later, the teacher has another option. He or she would still write the word on the chalkboard and let the student see that it did not have the letter in it. But then he or she could ask if the student could think of a word cluster that would include "lamp" that also had the day's letter in it. For instance, if it were Lesson 22 the student might say *white lamp*, because the letter for that day is *w*. *White lamp* would then be written on the chart.

INAPPROPRIATE RESPONSES

Even first-graders know words that would not be appropriate displayed on a chart in a school classroom. In the event that a student gives an off-color word, or any word that the teacher is uncomfortable writing on the chart, it is best for the teacher to simply and calmly say, "I don't think that is appropriate for our chart. Can you think of another?"

Not all teachers find the same words inappropriate. One teacher had chosen to write the word *rape* on a Word Study chart. A group of visitors came into the classroom later in the day and noticed the word on the chart. Without hesitation, the teacher explained her reasoning. She said, "Under most circumstances I doubt I would write that word on a chart. But that word was volunteered by a little boy whose babysitter, a young woman he is very close to, had recently been raped. He was very disturbed about it, and I chose to acknowledge his (and her) pain rather than ignoring it. All we discussed was how unpleasant and wrong it was." Not a one of the visitors questioned the teacher's judgment. They might have made other choices themselves, but they supported her decision without exception.

POSSIBLE TEACHER MISTAKES

All teachers make mistakes on the chart. Teachers who are poor spellers are encouraged to keep a dictionary handy and use it often. When in doubt, look it up. It is a good model for students. Not all mistakes are caught before they are written on the chart. Teachers have devised ingenious ways to cover up their goofs. Some use white chalk. Others use white address labels and call them Band-Aids®. Post-It™ tape, one-inch-wide paper tape, is wonderful for covering even large mistakes.

Charts with errors on them cause bad public relations for the teacher and this method of teaching. Some wise teachers have paired up to check each other's charts. Even the best spellers write words incorrectly or fail to punctuate sentences properly. Find a colleague who is willing to read your charts weekly and to spot nonstandard English. Then make a big deal of it with your class the next day. Let them see that everyone makes mistakes. The important thing is to correct mistakes when found.

MATERIALS

The materials needed to teach the Word Study module are:

1. One sheet of large chart paper per day. The chart paper should be approximately 24″ x 36″ and may be lined or unlined, depending on the teacher's preference.

2. Wide-point felt markers. Darker colors are recommended. Red and orange can be used to highlight special features like the Spelling Emphasis, but some people find it difficult to read an entire chart written in one of these colors. Charts should be easily readable from a distance.

3. Masking tape and other things for hanging charts. Numerous Word Study charts are usually displayed around a SUCCESS classroom. Masking tape can be used to tape charts to walls, bookcases, and so forth. Many teachers string wire from corner to corner around the room and hang charts by taping over the wire or using clothespins. Others have organized PTA projects to purchase cork strips or soft wood strips onto which charts can be stapled.

4. A chart rack. After twenty to thirty days many teachers run out of room for displaying charts. At that time, they are encouraged to take down the oldest chart, tape or staple it to a coat hanger, and hang it on the chart stand like on a closet rod. Charts hung this way are easier to use than if they were hung on the chart stand the way it was designed.

ROOM ARRANGEMENT AND CHART VISIBILITY

The arrangement of the classroom can greatly affect the success of a Word Study lesson. All students need to be able to see the chart. Some teachers like to have their students sitting on the floor in front of the chart. Others prefer to avoid the transition from chart development to writing and have their students sit at their seats. Either works well. The important factor is that students are able to see to participate in the chart's development, as well as able to see comfortably when copying the chart.

Teachers also need to ensure that the chart is visible from a distance. Students are actually more able to see the relatively small writing on the chart for two reasons. They know what is written on it, and they are emotionally involved in its contents. If the teacher prepared the chart the night before and said, "Boys and girls, copy the chart," doing so would be almost impossible for many of them. Regardless, teachers should do all they can to make sure the chart is visible. The choice of markers affects the readability. Some colors are hard to read; others fade out when the sun hits them (remember, these charts are displayed in the room). A few teachers like to decorate their charts with illustrations or by using colored paper. Such variations are wonderful, unless they detract from the students' being able to read them later.

DISPLAYING CHARTS

A teacher may ask, "Is it really necessary for me to hang all of those charts? Doesn't the room look messy?" Having the most recent charts visible around the room is integral to the SUCCESS program. The charts are the publication of students' words and ideas from the Word Study module. Each student is proud to have them around the room, especially the ones that have *his* or *her* word on them. One student remarked, "At school we live in a dictionary!" And the thing that makes that dictionary special is that the words are the class's words.

Regularly displaying as many charts as possible and rotating old charts with new ones *is* important.

"Will the class really look at the charts?" The more a teacher calls the students' attention to the charts, the more they will use them. Teachers should encourage students to refer to the charts for spelling during the Writing module. Base "sponge" activities on the charts:

"Who can find a word that rhymes with *more* on a chart."

"Turn to the person in line beside you and read a sentence off any chart."

"I'm thinking of a word that is on a chart that has three syllables and is an animal. What is it? Now you give a clue for us."

Provide several pointers or "magic wands" around the room for students to use when reading charts to a friend. Include as a free-time activity option "playing school" with the charts. This is a favorite of many first-graders. With only a little encouragement from the teacher, the charts will be well used. When the charts are central to the class, getting one's ideas on a chart will become even more rewarding.

▶
Modifying the Word Study Module

In SUCCESS teachers have ultimate control over what is taught. Within each module are places where teachers are encouraged to make modifications that are appropriate for their students.

The Word Study module is the place for incorporating more teacher-directed lessons. If there are elements of written language that students are having difficulty with, they should be taught here. District curriculum objectives can also be covered here. Like all Word Study modules, however, the students and their language always remain the focal point of this module.

There are two elements that should remain consistent:

1. Virtually all things written on the day's chart come from the students. Teachers do not prepare the charts ahead of time. Nor do teachers provide all of the words or other material for the chart.

2. Whatever the criteria for the chart, there should be many "right answers."

EXAMPLES OF MODIFICATIONS

Example 1　Ms. Thompson was the only teacher in her school that was using SUCCESS. So that her students were being taught the same handwriting skills as the other classes, she decided to introduce the letters in the order suggested by the handwriting program. She introduced a new letter each day, but on the fifth day, she reviewed the first two, as is done in the SUCCESS Lessons. After all of the letters, both upper- and lower-case, were introduced, she followed the SUCCESS letter cluster sequence.

Example 2   Ms. Roberts noticed her students were not adding the suffixes *-ed* and *-ing* to verbs properly. She chose to ignore the letter clusters specified in the Lessons. She also decided to list words instead of word clusters. From the students she solicited *verbs*. On the chart she wrote the present-tense form of the verbs given by the students. Then the class discussed how to add either *-ed* or *-ing* to the present form. Ms. Roberts wrote the form with one of the suffixes on the chart in a second column.

Example 3   Mr. Blackburn's class was studying the seasons in science. Yesterday they discussed autumn, and he read a book about autumn to them. As a review, Mr. Blackburn used the Word Study time to chart things the students volunteered that they see or do in autumn. Some of the entries on the chart were: red and yellow leaves; cool weather; time to rake; sweaters and long pants; and squirrels gathering nuts.

▶ Decisions, Decisions, Decisions

The SUCCESS program is replete with decisions to be made. Teachers and students are constantly making choices. To recap, below are the types of choices teachers and students make in this module:

TEACHER DECISIONS

1. Do I use the Spelling Emphasis and/or Structural Emphasis suggested in the lessons or choose another?

2. How much do I discuss about each entry on the chart? What do I stress?

3. Do I write words, word clusters, or sentences on the chart?

4. What is "appropriate" in my classroom? Where do I draw the line about what is written on the charts?

5. Is what each student writes during the Writing time sufficient? Does it reflect their knowledge and ability?

6. How shall I assess each child's performance?

STUDENT DECISIONS

1. What shall I volunteer for the chart, if anything?

2. What shall I write during the Writing time? Only things from the chart? Only my original words? Or a combination?

▶ Summary Chart

Preplanning:	Teacher selects criteria.
Lesson:	
13–17 minutes	Chart development, group handwriting instruction.
13–17 minutes	Students writing, teacher-student conversations, dating and filing papers.

Chapter 6 Evaluation, Communication, and Materials

This chapter is about the general, everyday details that concern teachers who use *SUCCESS in Reading and Writing*, such as record-keeping and evaluation and grading, as well as communicating with parents and administrators about the progress of students. This chapter also discusses ways classroom teachers can work with resource teachers and ways resource teachers can adapt the program for use with their students. Another major topic is a summary list of the materials suggested in the Lessons, and, finally, suggestions about room arrangement.

▶ Evaluation and Assessment

All teachers have to gather documentation of students' progress. Beyond gathering information, teachers have to assess the strengths and weaknesses of each of their students and then be able to communicate each student's progress to parents, the principal, and the student. Most teachers have to translate their knowledge of the students into a letter grade or the equivalent. How can this be done credibly, since no formal tests are a part of the SUCCESS program? In actuality, teachers have far more documentation of students' true progress than they typically do with other approaches to teaching. Students (with the teacher's help) maintain longitudinal records of their work in every module. Teachers keep extensive notes of observations about each student. Plus they have more opportunities to know their students and how they think, as well as their academic strengths and weaknesses, because they spend two-thirds of the language arts teaching time working with individuals.

STUDENTS' FOLDERS: LONGITUDINAL RECORDS OF PROGRESS

In each module, the teacher keeps daily records of student work. Generally speaking, these are maintained by the student. In Research, Writing, and Word Study, students file their completed papers each day. For much of the year, students also keep a list of books they have read during Recreational Reading.

The daily records maintained by the students are: Recreational Reading, Writing, Research, and Word Study.

Recreational Reading   Students begin to record the books they have read as soon as doing so will not detract from their time for reading. Some teachers provide forms for the students. Others simply provide paper or notecards for students to list the books they have read.

Many teachers require students to take home a book each night to read or have read to them. These teachers can then refer to the list of books checked out by each student for additional records of the reading habits, interests, and, to some degree, the reading levels of their students.

Ashley Westmoreland

Writing   All compositions written during the Writing module are filed in the student's Writing folder. These folders contain more information about a student's progress in writing form, spelling, and composition techniques than dozens of artificial paper and pencil tasks such as workbook pages or formal tests.

Research   The papers completed by students in this module are also filed. Students should have a folder labeled Research for storing these papers. Sometimes two or more students will produce only one paper when working as a team. In that case, both students' names should go on the paper and it should be filed in one of the students' folders. Every student, therefore, will not have a paper for each day for Research. Individual papers produced during this module do not provide much obvious information about the student, but over time, the group of papers will provide detailed information about their reading, problem-solving, and other thinking skills.

Word Study   During the Word Study module, students copy parts of the chart or write things related to the chart. They are usually encouraged to practice their handwriting when writing in this module, so the papers are a source for teachers of examples of students' progress in handwriting, as well as the quantity and quality of their work related to the chart.

HOW TO MANAGE FILING

A SUCCESS teacher's goal is to have the students do most, if not all, of the filing. Teachers have developed clever systems and management techniques to make it possible for first-graders to file their own papers, without it taking half of the time scheduled for the module. By teaching one or two students a day how to find the right folder and place that day's paper either in the front or back of the other papers, many teachers reach this goal early in the year.

Some teachers color-code folders to make filing easier. They purchase colored folders, colored labels, or simply write the students' names in different colors. By color-coding the folders, teachers can then refer to Research folders as the red folders, Writing can be the green folders, and Word Study, the blue folders.

Many teachers place a sticker or a number next to the student's name on each of the folders. The stickers help students learn to find their own folders even before they can recognize the written form of their names. The number makes it possible for students to file other students' papers. Students learn to write their number next to their name on every paper that is filed. Then the designated student filer for the week can even file papers of students whose name he or she cannot read. If the numbers students write on their papers correspond to their alphabetical placement on the class list, and the folders are arranged in alphabetical order, filing by an adult is faster. The class set of papers can very quickly be put in numerical order and filed.

Another suggestion for simplifying filing and reducing the amount of time it takes is to have three or four stations around the room where folders are stored. All three of a student's folders would be stored at the same station. Lines for filing at the end of a module would be no longer than five to seven students.

DON'T PARENTS WANT TO SEE THE PAPERS?

Parents want to be informed of their child's progress. They want to be convinced that the teacher sees their child as a special individual, knows all about and has believable evidence of their child's strengths and weaknesses, and can tell them what they need to do to help him or her be even more successful in school. In some other programs, teachers send home countless graded dittos and worksheets. Parents look at the grade or number of teacher-written marks on the papers and form their own opinions. Their opinions are then supported or refuted by the grades on the periodic report card. If their opinion seems in line with the report card, often there is no further contact. If their opinion differs from that of the teacher, parents arrange meetings with the teacher. Traditionally the teacher's primary resource to support the opinion is the letters or grades in the grade book.

In SUCCESS the teacher has as many as three different papers from every school day that readily demonstrate the child's proficiency with written language. The teacher also has a list of books the child has read. The parents can look at the books on the list and compare them to others that average first-graders read with ease at that time of the year. The SUCCESS teacher's documentation is in a form parents can truly understand. It does not require any specialized knowledge of pedagogy; nor does it require that the teacher explain pedagogy or debate grading policies with the parents. The performance level of the child is obvious.

At the end of each grading period, teachers are encouraged to arrange the papers in date order and pull out every third or fourth paper from each folder. These smaller collections can be stapled together and sent home. There will be a sufficient number of papers to show clearly the student's growth. Sometimes a cover letter can delineate points parents should note when looking at the papers. For several reasons, a collection of papers communicates much more to parents even without a cover letter than if single papers went home each day. First of all, most of the papers do not look like traditional school work. Word Study and Research papers are rather uninteresting in isolation, but in a group they tell quite a story. Each daily Writing paper tells more about the student, but together with other papers, the picture of growth is far more evident. For this reason, teachers may choose to send home an occasional composition. The large majority of the papers should remain at school all year.

SUCCESS teachers have more than a collection of students' work and lists of books read. They have copious observation notes from most of the modules, as well as notes from studying the folders. SUCCESS teachers know their students and have no trouble convincing parents of that.

Below is a description of the records that SUCCESS teachers keep in addition to the collection of work in the students' folders.

RECORDS THAT TEACHERS KEEP

Teachers keep three main types of records on students: clipboard notes, conference notes, and periodic checklists for recording information gleaned from the folders. Below is a description of each of these.

Clipboard notes   These notes recorded during school include information about individuals or the whole class. Their name derives from forms teachers keep on a clipboard. Two types of clipboard note forms are included in the Recreational Reading module. On these forms teachers write general or specific observations they make during Recreational Reading. Making clipboard notes during the Writing and Research modules and other times of the day is also recommended. Whatever the teacher notices that attracts his or her attention should be written on the clipboard. The notes may reflect academic achievements or frustrations, social conflicts, examples of teamwork and mutual respect, and emotional highs and lows.

Each day the teacher begins with a new set of clipboard note forms, at least one for each module. Teachers use many styles of forms. The most common element in all of them, however, is that they have the students' names pre-printed next to or in a space large enough for the teacher's notes. Many forms have spaces for the teacher's objectives for that module. For example, the teacher may want to be particularly aware of who works with whom during Research and who the leaders of the teams seem to be. In Writing, the teacher may want to focus his or her attention and notes on students' use of capital letters. A focus for clipboard notes during Recreational Reading is suggested in the Lessons.

SUCCESS makes me feel more professional as a teacher since I can make flexible decisions about the sequence of the lessons, content, and choice of materials, within the structure of the modules. I know my children's needs much better since I am working with them all day and can catch problems, answer questions, and meet individual needs quickly. I feel I'm teaching children rather than materials.

Jean Weaver, teacher

Teachers do not make notes for each student during each module. Some days there are no notes at all on a student. Many teachers star the names of students they have made fewer notes about recently or that they want to be sure and notice for some other reason.

Teachers read over their clipboard notes regularly. Although some of the things they recorded seemed innocuous at the time, patterns usually emerge that are invaluable for teachers as they increase their knowledge of each student and modify their teaching to accommodate their new insights.

Conference notes   These are often more in-depth notes that result from In-Depth Recreational Reading conversations. Later in the year, teachers may also have more extensive editing conferences with accomplished first-grade writers during the Writing module. Since more information is recorded about each student, many teachers keep conference notes in a looseleaf binder, with a section for each student. The pages are simply notebook paper with the student's name at the top. Each entry is dated. At the end of an entry, the teacher draws a line. The next entry for that student is written below the line. Since the papers are in a looseleaf binder, more paper can be added as needed. (For teachers who prefer a form, there are suggestions in Chapter 3.)

Periodic checklists   SUCCESS teachers do more than store dozens of papers produced by each student. The papers form the basis for most of the curricular decisions teachers make each day. Teachers need to look through students' folders systematically and regularly, making notes about the students' progress and weaknesses. This could take hours of the teacher's time if the teacher does not have a predetermined objective as he or she looks through the papers. The teacher also needs a form on which he or she can record information quickly and meaningfully.

Each afternoon after school the teacher's time is spent looking through a fifth or a fourth (if Fridays are not included in the schedule) of his students' three folders. About five minutes is spent rereading and taking notes on each student's three sets of papers. Many teachers have found it useful to tell students what day they will be looking at their folders. That way the teacher can explain to a student that, even though he does not have time to read a student's composition right then, he will read it on Tuesday, since that one is in the Tuesday group.

The form on which the teacher records his or her notes is based on his or her objectives. Some teachers determine objectives for each week; other teachers have two- or three-week objectives. Below is a description of the process a first-grade teacher, David, went through to make his periodic checklist.

1. David decided to have two-week objectives for each area of language arts for which he had to assign a grade, except *reading*. He decided not to include *reading* on this form because he felt his conference and clipboard notes were sufficient. Some of his objectives were to check for mastery;

others were things he wanted to assess diagnostically, so he could adapt the specifics within some of the modules, if he found his students needed more instruction.

2. David's objectives for *language* were capitalization, final punctuation, and overuse of "and."

3. For *spelling* he chose to concentrate especially on the spelling of "was," "they," and "girl." His class frequently misspelled these three words. In addition, he decided to list two to four words each week that each student misspelled consistently. He would give these words to the student as their personal words to study, or at least be aware of when they write them. Likewise, he would note two to four words for each student that indicated growth in spelling. For some students, these words would not be the standard spelling yet, but they would show progress in developmental spelling.

4. For *handwriting* David chose to concentrate on reviewing three letters: *a, d,* and *g.* David had already introduced his students to the formation of every letter, but not everyone had mastered forming some letters; many students were having trouble with these in particular. He would note his students' progress on these three letters, as well as individuals' other strengths and weaknesses in handwriting. (In addition to recording his findings as he looked through the folders, he changed the spelling emphasis in Word Study on three different days to include one of the letters each time. After that, he noticed students' formation of these letters in particular whenever they wrote, and he helped those showing difficulty.)

5. David is also very interested in his students' growth as writers, even though he does not give a grade in composing. On his form he wanted to record his observations about his students' willingness to compose, who was hindered by overconcern about spelling, and who had awareness of sequence in their stories.

Once he determined his objectives, he developed a checklist and rating scale (Figure 6-1). He duplicated enough forms for each student. The bottom of the form and the entire back side could be used for additional anecdotal comments.

GRADING

Assigning grades in SUCCESS is actually very simple. That does not mean it is not scary for most teachers at first, because grading in SUCCESS is admittedly subjective. The fact that grading is subjective does not mean it is arbitrary. Nor does it mean that it is without documentation. Quite the contrary. SUCCESS teachers spend two-thirds of their language arts instructional time working with individuals, teaching and evaluating in the context of their work. While students are working, teachers are constantly observing *and* making notes about what they see happening, as well as what they discuss with students. After students go home, teachers spend their preparation time studying students' folders and, once again, making notes. At least once a week

Figure 6-1

Sample Periodic Checklist

STUDENT _____   DATES: Week 1 _____
                                            Week 2 _____

LANGUAGE	Week 1	Week 2		CODE	
1) Capitalization	_____	_____			
2) Final punctuation	_____	_____	1	Excellent	
3) Overuse of "and"	_____	_____	2	Good	
			3	OK	
			4-5	Below average	
SPELLING			N/A	Not applied	
1) Overall evaluation	_____	_____	0	Overconcern	
2) "was"	_____	_____	W	Willing to try	
3) "they"	_____	_____			
4) "girl"	_____	_____			

Strengths
Week 1 _____ _____ _____ _____
Week 2 _____ _____ _____ _____

Weaknesses
Week 1 _____ _____ _____ _____
Week 2 _____ _____ _____ _____

HANDWRITING	Week 1	Week 2
1) Overall evaluation	_____	_____
2) "a"	_____	_____
3) "d"	_____	_____
4) "g"	_____	_____

Strengths
Week 1 _____ _____ _____ _____
Week 2 _____ _____ _____ _____

Weaknesses
Week 1 _____ _____ _____ _____
Week 2 _____ _____ _____ _____

WRITING/COMPOSING		
1) Willingness to write	_____	_____
2) Overconcern re: spelling		
3) Sequence	_____	_____

COMMENTS:

teachers read (mostly they reread) papers students have written. They study them in the context of all the work students have produced since the beginning of the year. All of the teacher's evaluation is based on the student's applied knowledge, the thinking processes as they tackle problems and projects during school, and the written results of their work.

Sam Wyffles

WHEN DO I FIND THE TIME?

Teaching this way is not easier, it is just more rewarding. Teachers don't spend *more* time or effort, but they spend it differently. For most teachers, evaluation in SUCCESS represents a totally different focus. In the past, teachers spent hours before a school day preparing seatwork, making and duplicating worksheets, planning activities related to books or projects, and developing centers for independent work. During school they spent too much of their teaching time giving instructions again and again, so that students would stay meaningfully occupied while they worked with small groups. After school, teachers had to grade all of that work. Conscientious teachers responded to everything their students produced and usually made numerous comments. Then the cycle began all over.

In SUCCESS teachers work hard during the day teaching, observing, listening, and taking notes. They never sit down unless it is for one to three minutes beside a student who is writing, involved in a Research project, or reading. In the afternoon they spend thirty to forty minutes studying folders and making more notes. Then they go home and be an adult. They read books; they read the newspaper, watch TV, talk to adults and, generally, do adult things. They then return to school the next day ready to give their full attention to their students.

▶
Communicating with Parents and Others

Teachers need to be in constant communication with the parents of their students and the administrators to whom they report. This section outlines several strategies for keeping parents and others informed about what is happening in SUCCESS classrooms.

PARENTS

Teachers probably ought to worry more when parents do not ask questions about their philosophy and teaching practices than when they do. The more teachers and parents understand each other and work together, sharing their knowledge, the more the students will benefit. Teachers, therefore, should take the initiative to establish this type of relationship. Instead of waiting for parents to ask, teachers can inform parents of what is happening at school (and why) even before they ask. Following are several ways SUCCESS teachers communicate with parents. Often teachers who use SUCCESS are a minority within their school staff. If they are breaking away from the way others are teaching, they must know why and be able to explain it to anyone who asks. People will ask, "What is SUCCESS?" "How is it different?" "Why have you chosen to teach this way?" "What do you expect to accomplish?" "What can I do to help you and my child?" Teachers need to be confident and have plausible answers to these questions.

SUCCESS teachers can keep parents informed in several ways. First, they write letters at the beginning of the year explaining their goals and outlining the procedures they will be using. They plan Open House programs, invite parents to visit during school hours, and many send home regular newsletters. But mostly teachers send home each day students who are excited about learning, who have a book in their hands each afternoon that they are eager to read or have read to them, and who are growing in their awareness of the world around them and their important place in that world.

Letters to parents   At the beginning of the year teachers are encouraged to send a letter home to parents explaining their philosophy and how SUCCESS works. The following are some hints from veteran SUCCESS teachers that will make those first letters more effective:

1. Be brief. Parents don't want to hear your whole philosophy of education. Nor do they want to read a detailed description of what happens in your 2½-hour language arts block. Just include a summary of what your goals are and an outline of the program in a one- to two-page letter.

2. Be positive in your description of SUCCESS. Remember it has stood the test of time. Avoid such words as *new, innovative,* and especially *experimental.* Describe what your students will be doing, instead of what you will *not* be doing (reading groups, basals, workbooks).

3. Invite parents to come to school in a couple of weeks to see the program in action.

4. Inform them in a positive way that, except for the Storytime activity and an occasional composition, papers from SUCCESS will be in their child's folder at school and that they are welcome to look at the folders at any time.

5. Request that they read to or with their child nightly.

6. Ask them to donate magazines, catalogs, telephone books, and so on. Some parents may subscribe to a magazine as a gift to the class; others will send old magazines from home.

Open house The best way to understand SUCCESS is to experience it. For an Open House presentation, many teachers do abbreviated SUCCESS activities with the parents functioning as their students. One teacher wrote that he had his students bring their parents to the program. The parents sat in the students' desks and the children sat in chairs beside their parents. During the lessons, the children helped their parents when they had difficulty. Students' folders should be readily available to the parents. Also, papers should be displayed. Books, charts, and other key materials should be visible. Above all, concentrate on the students, not the program!

Keeping parents informed throughout the year There are many better ways to keep parents informed than by sending home papers. One way that many teachers have found effective is a weekly newsletter. The goal of these newsletters is to stimulate discussions between parent and child about what happened at school that week. A format that takes relatively little of the teacher's time is to scatter around the page blurbs about such things as the writing topics for that week, the letters studied in Word Study or sample words from some of the charts, book titles the teacher has read, findings or questions raised during Research, and so forth. Some teachers write these blurbs in what they call clouds that surround a student-drawn illustration. Others write them in different shapes, such as leaves in the fall or hearts around Valentine's Day. Teachers who have access to photocopiers that make reductions can simply assemble a collection of sample papers that different students produced during the week.

Having students write about the different parts of the program, assembling them into a book titled "Our Reading and Writing Program," and sending them home is something many teachers have also found effective. Others display papers throughout the school building that are produced in a SUCCESS module. It is most helpful if there is a brief explanation accompanying the display of what the project involved. More important than anything else is to send home excited, confident, aware children. When students are happy and they are learning, parents no longer ask, "*What* are you doing with my child?" They ask, "What *are* you doing with my child?"

VISITORS

Whenever parents, administrators, or other teachers visit a SUCCESS classroom, they are seldom permitted merely to sit in the back of the

As a ten-year veteran teacher of SUCCESS, I have seen a positive improvement in writing and thinking skills for first-graders.

Judith J. Barnes, teacher

room and watch. Instead they are encouraged to circulate around the room and talk with students. They may answer students' questions, listen to students read or discuss their book, comment on students' compositions, or simply ask the students to explain what they are doing. Visitors are usually impressed not only at the competence of the students, but they are amazed by the students' confidence in themselves.

In the spring of 1977, the year SUCCESS was begun in the inner city schools of Durham, North Carolina, a prominent politician visited a first-grade class. A first-grade boy walked up to the politician and said, "I know who you are. You are Lieutenant Governor Jimmy Green." That floored the governor and all of those around him. But the student continued, "I read something in the newspaper yesterday that you said, and I want to ask you about it." True story!

ADMINISTRATORS

Support from administrators is usually very important to the confidence teachers feel about trying new teaching strategies. SUCCESS is just as scary for some administrators as it is for some teachers. Many administrators not familiar with SUCCESS are wary of having some of their teachers organize their reading and writing instruction so differently from the others on the staff. In cases where administrators do not encourage teachers to try strategies like SUCCESS, teachers should make an appointment with their administrator(s) to discuss their request. Those SUCCESS teachers who have been in this situation recommend that teachers do three things:

1. Take the time and initiative to *write down* your reasons for using the program. Don't be negative about other programs; be positive about SUCCESS.

2. Agree to abandon the SUCCESS framework if, after a minimum trial of twelve weeks, it is not working for your students.

3. Invite the administrator to come into your classroom frequently to be an active visitor—after two to three weeks. Allow yourself time to get your program underway.

Administrators can show their support of teachers who use the SUCCESS program by providing the necessary materials and by visiting their classrooms often, talking with their students, and browsing through students' folders. Whenever an administrator visits a classroom, he or she should:

1. see the teacher circulating around the room talking with individual students,

2. see students reading alone (usually) or working in groups,

3. hear a buzz of purposeful activity,

4. see many current Word Study charts hanging around the room,

5. see boxes containing folders of students' papers from three modules,

6. talk to students about what they are doing, and

7. feel the excitement of learning in progress.

Most importantly, administrators can show their support for these risk-takers by patting them on the back regularly. These teachers have gone out on a limb to do something different because they are convinced it is for the good of their students.

▶ Using SUCCESS With Special Students

SUCCESS can be adapted easily to accommodate special students in resource or self-contained classes. It can also be adapted for use in special schedules, such as situations where teachers have less than 2½ hours with a student. A third consideration is how regular classroom and resource teachers work together.

SUCCESS has been used effectively in all classifications of special education and resource classes. The individualized nature of the teaching strategies and the real-life instructional materials are two reasons SUCCESS works with these students. School more readily relates to their life outside school and builds on their knowledge, however limited teachers think at first that the student's knowledge is. In SUCCESS learning to read and write is not abstract and meaningless. Many of these students have problems applying the isolated knowledge they have acquired through the type of instruction they have received. In SUCCESS all learning takes place through direct and immediate application.

Resource teachers rarely have 2½ hours with all of their students, so modifications have to be made in the lesson structure. Resource teachers who choose to use SUCCESS have several alternatives. Their choice of which alternative to use depends on whether the classroom teacher is using SUCCESS and whether theirs is a pull-out program or not.

1. Many resource teachers are currently choosing to work as a team teacher with the regular teacher, rather than pulling students out of class. This works very well, if both the classroom teacher and the

Abbie Chrisman

resource teacher are comfortable with using SUCCESS and with working together. Some school systems have to revise their federal program proposals or guidelines to allow for this restructuring, but it is possible. Resource teachers are rarely able to spend more than thirty to forty-five minutes in each teacher's class. Some are not able to schedule that much time every day. They elect to spend less time each day or more time two to four days a week. Once a schedule is worked out, the most effective system, teachers have found, is for the resource teacher to be in the regular classroom during Recreational Reading, Writing, or Research. Since most or all of the time in these modules teachers are working with individuals, having two professional educators in the room benefits everyone. Resource teachers emphasize working with students that classify for their programs, but they can still help other students. The more the teachers plan as a team, the more effectively this set-up works.

The next three options are for resource teachers who are restricted to pull-out programs or who prefer that plan.

2. If the regular classroom teacher is using SUCCESS, the resource teacher may concentrate on one or two modules. The resource students would have all of their instruction in that module from the resource teacher. Of the modules, Writing or Recreational Reading is probably the best choice for resource teachers. The only caution for resource teachers who work with small groups on either of these modules is to give students time to work independently. The resource teacher who has a group of five to eight students has time to assist each student and time for the student to read or write without constant interruption or dependence on the teacher.

3. Some resource teachers opt to expand on what the regular classroom teacher does. In this alternative the student would be in the regular class for all of the modules. Then the resource teacher expands on what the teacher does. Often resource students need more time than other students to complete their writing project. They can bring their composition to the resource class and continue writing. Another option is for the resource student to repeat an abbreviated form on two or more of the modules (especially Research or Word Study) that the regular teacher has done or will do that day. The resource teacher has the time to work more directly on the parts of the lesson the resource student is having difficulty with. The student rarely feels like he or she is repeating what he or she has already done, because every teacher approaches every lesson differently.

4. If the regular teacher is not using the SUCCESS program, the resource teacher has the option of teaching all of the modules. Obviously all four modules cannot be compressed into thirty to forty-five minutes each day. Therefore, resource teachers often do one module each day or two abbreviated modules each day. Rarely does a module that takes thirty minutes in a regular classroom take that amount of time with a small group of resource students. Regardless of the amount of time a resource teacher spends with his or her students each day, the teacher should reserve some time regularly to read to his or her students.

▶ Materials

With SUCCESS, teachers no longer need workbooks, basal readers, spelling books, language books, or even duplicated worksheets. The materials used in SUCCESS are, for the most part, common, everyday materials. Although they are far less expensive than the materials mentioned above, they are nonetheless important. In each of the preceding chapters there has been some mention of the materials used specifically for that module. Below is a comprehensive list. All of the materials specified in the Lessons are included.

1. *1 to 2 SUCCESS manuals.* If two are purchased, the second can be loaned to parents and others who are interested in learning more about the program.

2. *Children's books.* Thirty to fifty library books are rotated every two to three weeks. Teachers also supplement the library collection with books from their classroom collection, basal literature books, and any other source they can find.

3. *One to three newspaper subscriptions.* The newspaper should have both national and local news. If a local paper does not have national news, many schools get one subscription to the local paper and one or two to the national newspaper.

4. *Old magazines.* Most of the magazines used in the Research module are written for adults (*Life, People, Good Housekeeping, Ebony,* and so forth). Classroom subscriptions to children's magazines are recommended whenever funds allow.

5. *Collections of a variety of science, social studies, and math textbooks.* Ideally these should be several publishers' versions of textbooks for grades 1 to 4.

6. *Art prints, road maps, catalogs, telephone books, restaurant menus, and simple forms.* These are used during the second half of the year in the Research module.

7. *180 or more sheets of lined or unlined chart paper.* One sheet of chart paper (18″ × 24″ or larger) is used each day in Word Study. Some may occasionally be used in other modules for group displays and such. Paper the approximate weight of notebook paper is recommended. (Newsprint often tears when it is hung around the room, and tagboard is so heavy that it cannot be held securely to walls with masking tape.)

8. *Many dark-colored, wide-tipped felt markers.* Charts need to be visible from a distance. Teachers have noticed that some colors are hard to read and some markers fade easily.

9. *Masking tape* or other devices for hanging Word Study charts. Many teachers string wire from corner to corner around the room and tape over the wire. PTAs in some schools have purchased cork strips or soft wood strips that teachers can use to staple or tack charts onto.

10. *Assorted dictionaries.* In a SUCCESS classroom a wide assortment of dictionaries is preferable to having a class set of elementary dictionaries. The teacher needs a good, current dictionary. Students need every-

Jason Workman

thing from rather simple dictionaries appropriate to their age level that they can use effectively for looking up definitions, but they also need dictionaries that they will use to spell words they have in their spoken vocabularies. Having only elementary dictionaries will teach students that dictionaries are not very useful, because they do not have the words in them that students need.

11. *Large world, United States, and state or regional map.* If these are displayed in the classroom, students will learn all about geography and map-reading skills as they look up places they read about in newspapers and magazines.

12. *Three file folders per student.* These sturdy folders are stored in sets of boxes or plastic crates in three to four stations around the room. When they are filled, some of the papers are removed and stored in the teacher's file drawer or a cabinet. The entire collection goes home with the students at the end of the year.

Having several stations around the room for storing each of the materials is recommended. Teachers who have four to five students pass out paper and four to five students who distribute each of the other materials find that less time is spent getting ready for a module, leaving more time for the actual project. When materials are not all in the same location, bottlenecks are avoided.

▶
Classroom Arrangement

The most important factor in arranging a SUCCESS classroom is that all students need to feel a part of the group. Can everyone see the chart as the teacher writes on it? Can they comfortably see to copy parts of the chart? Can everyone hear the teacher read during Storytime? Can they see the pictures? Is it easy for students to interact with each other during the modules?

In SUCCESS, talking to others is essential. That does not mean that there is chaos, but it does mean that few modules, if any, are absolutely quiet. The way the room is arranged helps to encourage interaction without the need for extensive movement. Many teachers organize desks into groups of four. Others have students sit at tables of four to six. If the desks are arranged in rows, they will need to be moved at the beginning of Research (at least) and returned to their rows at the end.

Conversation during the other modules is also important, as is sitting in close proximity to other students. During Writing, students often need to confer with someone other than the teacher about how the composition is progressing. Many teachers place tubs of books in strategic areas around the room for students to select books during Recreational Reading. If books are within reach, in the middle of a table of four to six students, movement is decreased.

Another consideration in room arrangement is that space is available on the floor for large- or small-group gatherings. Most teachers gather their students around them for Storytime. A carpeted area is a wonderful thing to have! Students often move to the floor when working with newspapers. Some students prefer to read on the floor, in windowsills, or under desks during Recreational Reading. Student-to-student writing conferences work best if the students have a place away from other writers to confer.

SUCCESS classrooms should appear to be as student-centered as the instructional practices are. Students' words and ideas fill the room. The most recent charts from Word Study are everywhere. Students, busy and involved in their own pursuits, are often scattered around the room. The teacher is usually not immediately evident to the visitor, because he or she is somewhere mingling among the students, conferring about something of immediate concern only to that student. Learning is happening!

▶
A Community of Teachers

Just as students work and plan together, SUCCESS teachers are encouraged to work together. In many areas groups of teachers have formed regional networks. They meet regularly to share ideas, solve problems, and inspire each other. On a smaller scale, when like-minded teachers in the same building or in the same district get together frequently to plan and confer, the SUCCESS teacher feels like a member of a community. The framework of SUCCESS not only allows, but depends on teachers making decisions that focus their program on their students. The reinforcement of a group is important in building and maintaining confidence. Whether the gathering is an informal meeting in the teachers' lounge or a follow-up workshop, teachers learn that there is always more to learn about teaching and learning the SUCCESS way.

Lessons

Walls, roof, and floor alone do not make a house a home, but the people inside certainly count on the building's firm framework. Similarly, these lessons do not constitute a rich language arts program in themselves, but the SUCCESS framework gives students and teachers freedom to form literary communities in schools.

The lesson plans are centered around themes that are highlighted in two or three of the modules. Blank lines indicate many opportunities for teachers to substitute different themes, either relating the activities in a day's lesson more closely, or making them more diverse in their themes.

Books are suggested in every lesson for the teacher to read aloud to the class. There is no prescribed list of books for SUCCESS. Teachers should read their own favorite books and investigate new books that become available to them. They should read some books over and over throughout the year, and they should consider scheduling books for reading aloud that enhance the class's study of a particular theme. Most important of all, the teacher should read aloud to the class every day.

Lesson 1

Research

LEAD-IN
Teacher introduces the Project Idea.
Letters: *b* B or _____
Material: Newspapers or _____
Reading Focus: Letter recognition or _____

SEARCH & RECORD
Project Idea: Individually, students cut or tear the lesson's letters or words containing the letters from newspapers. They paste or tape the letters or words on their papers. Encourage discussion of findings with neighbors.
   Teacher checks for letter recognition.

SHARING
Compare letters and words found with another student or _____.
   Papers are dated and filed.

Recreational Reading

For approximately 10 minutes all students read or look at books.

CONVERSATIONS
Getting Started: The teacher reads silently with the class. During the last 2 to 3 minutes the teacher may choose to talk with some individuals about what they have read.

CLIPBOARD NOTES
Teacher notes who reads or attempts to read or _____.

BOOK SHARING
Each person tells another person something he or she has read about that day.

and Storytime

READ ALOUD
Brown Bear, Brown Bear by Bill Martin, Jr., or _____
   Read the book. Discuss the pattern. Reread the book, encouraging the students to join in.

ACTIVITY (Optional)
Draw a picture of "what you see looking at you." Make a class book.

Writing

MINI-LESSON
Teacher leads a 5- to 7-minute discussion about possible interpretations of the Writing Topic: Me: What I Like or _____.

COMPOSING
Each student writes (by drawing or developmental spelling) on
■ the lesson's topic
■ a personally chosen topic

SHARING
Papers are read to a classmate or the teacher, dated, and filed.

Word Study

CHART DEVELOPMENT
Spelling Emphasis: *b* and/or _____

   On the chart, the teacher writes any words containing the day's letter or _____.

WRITING
On their papers, students write
■ their favorite words from the chart
■ other words/clusters/sentences that would be appropriate for the chart
Papers are dated and filed.

Lesson 2

Research

LEAD-IN
Teacher introduces the Project Idea.
Letters: *c C* or _____
Material: Newspapers or _____
Reading Focus: Letter recognition or
_____

SEARCH & RECORD
Project Idea: Individually, students cut or tear the lesson's letters or words containing the letters from newspapers. They paste or tape the letters or words on their papers. Encourage discussion of findings with neighbors.
   Teacher checks for letter recognition.

SHARING
Compare letters and words found with another student or _____.
   Papers are dated and filed.

Recreational Reading and Storytime

For approximately 10 minutes all students read or look at books.

CONVERSATIONS
Getting Started: The teacher reads silently with the class. During the last 2 to 3 minutes the teacher may choose to talk with some individuals about their reading.

CLIPBOARD NOTES
Teacher notes who reads or attempts to read or_____.

READ ALOUD
Are You My Mother? by P. D. Eastman or
_____
   Discuss the humor in the book.

ACTIVITY (Optional)
Make a bird similar to the one in the illustration. Attach the bird's wings with a brad.

BOOK SHARING
Each person tells another person something he or she has read about that day.

Writing

MINI-LESSON
Teacher leads a 5- to 7-minute discussion about possible interpretations of the Writing Topic: Me: What I Like to Do or
_____

COMPOSING
Each student writes on
■ the lesson's topic
■ a personally chosen topic
■ a topic begun previously

SHARING
Papers are read to a classmate or the teacher, dated, and filed.

Word Study

CHART DEVELOPMENT
Spelling Emphasis: *c* and/or
_____
   On the chart, the teacher writes any words containing the day's letter or
_____.

WRITING
On their papers, students write
■ their favorite words from the chart
■ other words/clusters/sentences that would be appropriate for the chart
Papers are dated and filed.

Lesson 3

Research

LEAD-IN
Teacher introduces the Project Idea.
Letters: *b* or *c* or _____
Material: math textbooks or nonfiction books or
Reading Focus: words or pictures with certain letters or _____

SEARCH & RECORD
Project Idea: Students explore math textbooks identifying words or pictures with the letters *b* or *c* or _____.

Students should report their ideas to the class or teacher before recording with drawing and/or developmental spelling.
    Teacher checks students for ideas associated with the text's content.

SHARING
Students compare the items found that contain the letters *b* or *c* or _____.
    Papers are dated and filed.

Recreational Reading

For approximately 10 minutes all students read or look at books.

CONVERSATIONS
Getting Started: The teacher reads silently with the class. During the last 2 to 3 minutes the teacher may choose to talk to some individuals about their reading.

CLIPBOARD NOTES
Teacher notes who reads or attempts to read or _____.

BOOK SHARING
Each person tells another person something he or she has read about that day.

and Storytime

READ ALOUD
Sleepy Book by Charlotte Zolotow or _____
    Discuss *where* and *when* things happened in the story.

ACTIVITY (Optional)
Make a face whose eyelids close. Paste flap eyelids over the eyes. Use a paper

plate or large circle of construction paper for the face.

Writing

MINI-LESSON
Teacher leads a 5- to 7-minute discussion about possible interpretations of the Writing Topic: Me: What I Do Before School or _____.

COMPOSING
Each student writes on
■ the lesson's topic
■ a personally chosen topic
■ a topic begun previously

SHARING
Papers are read to a classmate or the teacher, dated, and filed.

Word Study

CHART DEVELOPMENT
Spelling Emphasis: *d* and/or
_____.
    On the chart, the teacher writes any words containing the day's letter or _____.

WRITING
On their papers, students write
■ their favorite words from the chart
■ other words/clusters/sentences that would be appropriate for the chart
    Papers are dated and filed.

Lesson 4

Research

LEAD-IN
Teacher introduces the Project Idea.
Theme: Food or _____
Material: Math textbooks or
_____

Reading Focus: Classification or
_____

SEARCH & RECORD
Project Idea: Students explore math textbooks identifying words or pictures that they associate with food or
_____ .

Students should report their ideas to the class or the teacher before recording with drawing and/or developmental spelling.
Teachers check students for association of pictures/words with theme.

SHARING
Students discuss the items found that relate to the day's theme or _____ .
Papers are dated and filed.

Recreational Reading

For approximately 10 minutes all students read or look at books.

CONVERSATIONS
Getting Started: The teacher reads silently with the class. During the last 2 to 3 minutes the teacher may choose to talk to some individuals about their reading.

CLIPBOARD NOTES
Teacher notes titles or types of books chosen or _____ .

BOOK SHARING
Each person tells another person something he or she has read about that day.

and Storytime

READ ALOUD
In the Forest by Marie Hall Ets or
_____

Discuss what is real and make-believe in the story.

ACTIVITY (Optional)
Make paper hats from newspaper. Fold a single sheet of newspaper in half. Bring

the two corners of the folded edge toward the center of the paper, making a point at the midpoint of the folded edge. Fold the lower edges twice each to make the brim.
After making paper hats, class parades around the room with pretend bugles looking for imaginary friends to join them. Encourage students to discuss who they invite along.

Writing

MINI-LESSON
Teacher leads a 5- to 7-minute discussion about possible interpretations of the Writing Topic: Me: What I Do After School or _____ .

COMPOSING
Each student writes on
■ the lesson's topic
■ a personally chosen topic
■ a topic begun previously

SHARING
Papers are read to a classmate or the teacher, dated, and filed.

Word Study

CHART DEVELOPMENT
Spelling Emphasis: *f* and/or
_____

On the chart, the teacher writes any words containing the day's letter or _____ .

WRITING
On their papers, students write
■ their favorite words from the chart
■ other words/clusters/sentences that would be appropriate for the chart
Papers are dated and filed.

Lesson 5

Research

LEAD-IN
Teacher introduces the Project Idea.
Theme: Food or _____
Material: Magazines or _____
Reading Focus: Classification or
_____

SEARCH & RECORD
Project Idea: Individually, students cut or tear from magazines pictures or words related to the lesson's theme. They paste or tape the pictures or words on their papers. Encourage discussion of findings with neighbors.
  Teachers check students or association of pictures/words with theme.

SHARING
Students discuss the items found that relate to the day's theme or _____.
  Papers are dated and filed.

Recreational Reading and Storytime

For approximately 10 minutes all students read or look at books.

CONVERSATIONS
Getting Started: The teacher reads silently with the class. During the last 2 to 3 minutes the teacher may choose to talk to some individuals about their reading.

CLIPBOARD NOTES
Teacher notes titles or types of books chosen or _____.

BOOK SHARING
Each person tells another person something he or she has read about that day.

READ ALOUD
Gregory the Terrible Eater by Mitchell Sharmat or _____
  Discuss the title.

ACTIVITY (Optional)
Make a paper-bag puppet of a goat. Cut pictures of food that a goat eats (a typical goat or Gregory) from magazines. Put the food in the paper bag.

Writing

MINI-LESSON
Teacher leads a 5- to 7-minute discussion about possible interpretations of the Writing Topic: Me: What I Do at School or _____.

COMPOSING
Each student writes (by drawing or developmental spelling) on
■ the lesson's topic
■ a personally chosen topic
■ a topic begun previously

SHARING
Papers are read to a classmate or the teacher, dated, and filed.

Word Study

CHART DEVELOPMENT
Spelling Review: *b c* and/or
_____
  Students locate words on the room's charts which contain either review letter. On today's chart the teacher writes additional word clusters that contain either letter or _____.

WRITING
On their papers, students write
■ their favorite words from the chart
■ other words/clusters/sentences that would be appropriate for the chart
Papers are dated and filed.

Lesson **6**

Research

LEAD-IN
Teacher introduces the Project Idea.
Theme: Events, what's happening? or
_____

Material: Magazines or _____
Reading Focus: Interpretation or
_____

SEARCH & RECORD
Project Idea: Students locate pictures in magazines and discuss events or what

is happening in the pictures. They cut or tear the pictures out and paste them on their paper. Using developmental spelling, some children record what is happening in their pictures.

SHARING
Students compare the pictures found and what they think is happening in each or
_____.

Papers are dated and filed.

Recreational Reading

and Storytime

For approximately 15 minutes all students read or look at books.

CONVERSATIONS
Getting Started: The teacher reads silently with the class. During the last 3 to 5 minutes the teacher may choose to talk to some individuals about their reading.

CLIPBOARD NOTES
Teacher notes titles or types of books chosen or _____.

READ ALOUD
It's Mine, It's Mine by Leo Lionni or
_____

Discuss the times things happened in the book.

ACTIVITY (Optional)
Make a frog whose legs move. Use brads.

BOOK SHARING
Each person tells another person something he or she has read about that day.

Writing

MINI-LESSON
Teacher leads a 5- to 7-minute discussion about possible interpretations of the Writing Topic: Me: What I Do on Weekends or _____.

COMPOSING
Each student writes on
■ the lesson's topic
■ a personally chosen topic
■ a topic begun previously

SHARING
Papers are read to a classmate or the teacher, dated, and filed.

Word Study

CHART DEVELOPMENT
Spelling Emphasis: *g* and/or
_____

On the chart, the teacher writes any words containing the day's letter or
_____.

WRITING
On their papers, students write
■ their favorite words from the chart
■ other words/clusters/sentences that would be appropriate for the chart
Papers are dated and filed.

Lesson 7

Research

LEAD-IN
Teacher introduces the Project Idea.
Theme: Events—what's happening? or
_____

Material: Library books or _____
Reading Focus: Interpretation or
_____

SEARCH & RECORD
Project Idea: Students locate pictures in library books and discuss events or what is happening in the pictures.

Students should discuss ideas with the class or teacher before recording what is happening in the book with drawing and/ or developmental spelling.

SHARING
Students compare the pictures found and what they think is happening in each or
_____.

Papers are dated and filed.

Recreational Reading and Storytime

For approximately 15 minutes all students read or look at books.

CONVERSATIONS
Getting Started: The teacher reads silently with the class. During the last 3 to 5 minutes the teacher may choose to talk to some individuals about their reading.

CLIPBOARD NOTES
Teacher notes who seems excited about books and reading or _____.

READ ALOUD
Parade by Donald Crews or _____
Discuss the sequence of events in the book.

ACTIVITY (Optional)
Make a picture similar to the illustrations in the book. Use shapes of colored construction paper.

BOOK SHARING
Each person tells another person something he or she has read about that day.

Writing

MINI-LESSON
Teacher leads a 5- to 7-minute discussion about possible interpretations of the Writing Topic: Me: I Can or _____.

COMPOSING
Each student writes on
■ the lesson's topic
■ a personally chosen topic
■ a topic begun previously

SHARING
Papers are read to a classmate or the teacher, dated, and filed.

Word Study

CHART DEVELOPMENT
Spelling Emphasis: *h* and/or
_____
On the chart, the teacher writes any words containing the day's letter or
_____.

WRITING
On their papers, students write
■ their favorite words from the chart
■ other words/clusters/sentences that would be appropriate for the chart
Papers are dated and filed.

Lesson 8

Research

LEAD-IN
Teacher introduces the Project Idea.
Theme: Events—what's happening? or
_____

Material: Library books or _____
Reading Focus: Interpretation or
_____

SEARCH & RECORD
Project Idea: Students locate pictures in library books and discuss events or what is happening in the pictures.

Students should discuss ideas with the class or teacher before recording what is happening in the book with drawing and/or developmental spelling.

SHARING
Students compare the pictures found and what they think is happening in each or
_____.

Papers are dated and filed.

Recreational Reading

and Storytime

For approximately 15 minutes all students read or look at books.

CONVERSATIONS
Getting Started: The teacher reads silently with the class. During the last 3 to 5 minutes the teacher may choose to talk to some individuals about their reading.

CLIPBOARD NOTES
Teacher notes who seems excited about books and reading or _____.

BOOK SHARING
Each person tells another person something he or she has read about that day.

READ ALOUD
The Biggest Bear by Lynd Ward or
_____

  Discuss problems in the story and how they were solved.

ACTIVITY (Optional)
Make a bearskin from construction paper or fake-fur cloth.

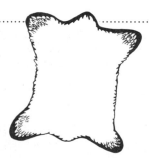

Writing

MINI-LESSON
Teacher leads a 5- to 7-minute discussion about possible interpretations of the Writing Topic: Me: I'm Good At or
_____.

COMPOSING
Each student writes on
■ the lesson's topic
■ a personally chosen topic
■ a topic begun previously

SHARING
Papers are read to a classmate or the teacher, dated, and filed.

Word Study

CHART DEVELOPMENT
Spelling Emphasis: *j* and/or
_____

  On the chart, the teacher writes any words containing the day's letter or
_____.

WRITING
On their papers, students write
■ their favorite words from the chart
■ other words/clusters/sentences that would be appropriate for the chart
Papers are dated and filed.

Lesson 9

Research

LEAD-IN
Teacher introduces the Project Idea.
Letters: *d D* or _____
Material: Newspapers or _____
Reading Focus: Letter Recognition or _____

SEARCH & RECORD
Project Idea: Individually, students cut or tear the lesson's letters or words containing the letters from newspapers. They paste or tape them on their papers. Encourage discussion of findings with neighbors.
   Teacher checks for letter recognition.

SHARING
Students compare letters and words found with another student or _____.
   Papers are dated and filed.

Recreational Reading

For approximately 15 minutes all students read or look at books.

CONVERSATIONS
Getting Started: The teacher reads silently with the class. During the last 3 to 5 minutes the teacher may choose to talk to some individuals about their reading.

CLIPBOARD NOTES
Teacher notes who seems excited about books and reading or _____.

BOOK SHARING
Each person tells another person something he or she has read about that day.

and Storytime

READ ALOUD
Alexander and the Terrible, Horrible, Very Bad, No-Good Day, by Judith Viorst or
_____
   Relate the story to the students' experiences.

ACTIVITY (Optional)
Students draw a picture of themselves having a very bad day.

Writing

MINI-LESSON
Teacher leads a 5- to 7-minute discussion about possible interpretations of the Writing Topic: Me: What I Have Trouble Doing or _____.

COMPOSING
Each student writes (by drawing or developmental spelling) on
■ the lesson's topic
■ a personally chosen topic
■ a topic begun previously

SHARING
Papers are read to a classmate or the teacher, dated, and filed.

Word Study

CHART DEVELOPMENT
Spelling Emphasis: *k* and/or
_____
   On the chart, the teacher writes any words containing the day's letter or _____.

WRITING
On their papers, students write
■ their favorite words from the chart
■ other words/clusters/sentences that would be appropriate for the chart.
Papers are dated and filed.

Lesson 10

Research

LEAD-IN
Teacher introduces the Project Idea.
Letters: *f F* or _____
Material: Newspapers or _____
Reading Focus: Letter recognition or _____

SEARCH & RECORD
Project Idea: Individually, students cut or tear the lesson's letters or words containing the letters from newspapers. They paste or tape the letters or words on their papers. Encourage discussion of findings with neighbors.
  Teacher checks for letter recognition.

SHARING
Students compare letters and words found with another student or _____.
  Papers are dated and filed.

Recreational Reading

For approximately 15 minutes all students read or look at books.

CONVERSATIONS
Getting Started: The teacher reads silently with the class. During the last 3 to 5 minutes the teacher may choose to talk to some individuals about their reading.

CLIPBOARD NOTES
Teacher notes who stays seated and who walks around or _____.

BOOK SHARING
Each person tells another person something he or she has read about that day.

and Storytime

READ ALOUD
Runaway Bunny by Margaret Wise Brown or _____
  Discuss the beginning, middle, and end of the story.

ACTIVITY (Optional)
Students make wings out of construction paper. Teacher pins them on. Class acts out the story.

Writing

MINI-LESSON
Teacher leads a 5- to 7-minute discussion about possible interpretations of the Writing Topic: If I Wasn't Me I'd Like to Be or _____.

COMPOSING
Each student writes on
- the lesson's topic
- a personally chosen topic
- a topic begun previously

SHARING
Papers are read to a classmate or the teacher, dated, and filed.

Word Study

CHART DEVELOPMENT
Spelling Review: *d f* and/or _____
  Students locate words on the room's charts that contain either review letter. On today's chart, the teacher writes additional word clusters that contain either letter or _____.

WRITING
On their papers, students write
- their favorite words from the chart
- other words/clusters/sentences that would be appropriate for the chart
Papers are dated and filed.

Lesson **11**

Research

LEAD-IN
Teacher introduces the Project Idea.
Letters: *d* or *f* or _____
Material: Science textbooks or nonfiction books or _____
Reading Focus: Words or pictures with certain letters or _____.

SEARCH & RECORD
Project Idea: Students explore science textbooks identifying words or pictures with the day's letters or _____.
Students should discuss their ideas with the class or teacher before recording with developmental spelling and/or drawing.
   Teacher checks groups for ideas associated with the text's content.

SHARING
Students compare the items found that contain the letters *d* or *f* or _____.
   Papers are dated and filed.

Recreational Reading

For approximately 20 minutes all students read or look at books.

CONVERSATIONS
Getting Started: The teacher reads silently with the class. During the last 5 to 7 minutes the teacher may choose to talk to some individuals about their reading.

CLIPBOARD NOTES
Teacher notes who stays seated and who walks around or _____.

BOOK SHARING
Each person tells another person something he or she has read about that day.

and Storytime

READ ALOUD
Any book about fall, such as *Apples and Pumpkins* by Anne Rockwell or *Frog and Toad All Year* by Arnold Lobel or *Seasons* by Brian Wildsmith or *January Brings the Snow* by Sara Coleridge or

_____

   Discuss colors seen in the book that are seen in the fall.

ACTIVITY (Optional)
Students make a crayon-resist picture about fall. Paint over with light mixture of grey paint so it looks foggy.

Writing

MINI-LESSON
Teacher leads a 5- to 7-minute discussion about possible interpretations of the Writing Topic: Early Signs of Fall or

_____

COMPOSING
Each student writes on
■ the lesson's topic
■ a personally chosen topic
■ a topic begun previously

SHARING
Papers are read to a classmate or the teacher, dated, and filed.

Word Study

CHART DEVELOPMENT
Spelling Emphasis: *l* and/or

_____

   On the chart, the teacher writes any words containing the day's letter or _____.

WRITING
On their papers, students write
■ their favorite words from the chart
■ other words/clusters/sentences that would be appropriate for the chart
Papers are dated and filed.

Lesson 12

Research

LEAD-IN
Teacher introduces the Project Idea.
Theme: Seasons or _____
Material: Science textbooks or
_____
Reading Focus: Classification or
_____

SEARCH & RECORD
Project Idea: Students explore science textbooks identifying words or pictures which they can associate with seasons or
_____.

Students should discuss their ideas with the class or teacher before recording with developmental spelling and/or drawing.
Teachers check students for association of pictures/words with theme.

SHARING
Students meet in groups of 4 or 5 and discuss the items found that relate to the day's theme or _____.
Papers are dated and filed.

Recreational Reading

For approximately 20 minutes all students read or look at books.

CONVERSATIONS
Getting Started: The teacher reads silently with the class. During the last 5 to 7 minutes the teacher may choose to talk to some individuals about their reading.

CLIPBOARD NOTES
Teacher notes who stays seated and who walks around or _____.

BOOK SHARING
Each person tells another person something he or she has read about that day.

and Storytime

READ ALOUD
Any book of riddles such as *Riddles about the Seasons* by Jacqueline Ball or *What Am I? Very First Riddles* by Stephanie Calmenson or _____
Discuss humor. What makes the riddles funny?

ACTIVITY (Optional)
Class goes for a walk outside and gathers fall objects that they will write about in the Writing module. Each student takes one item home.

Writing

MINI-LESSON
Teacher leads a 5- to 7-minute discussion about possible interpretations of the Writing Topic: Jokes or Riddles About Fall or _____.

COMPOSING
Each student writes on
■ the lesson's topic
■ a personally chosen topic
■ a topic begun previously

SHARING
Papers are read to a classmate or the teacher, dated, and filed.

Word Study

CHART DEVELOPMENT
Spelling Emphasis: *m* and/or
_____
On the chart, the teacher writes any words containing the day's letter or _____.

WRITING
On their papers, students write
■ their favorite words from the chart
■ other words/clusters/sentences that would be appropriate for the chart
Papers are dated and filed.

115

Lesson 13

Research

LEAD-IN
Teacher introduces the Project Idea.
Theme: Seasons or _____
Material: Magazines or _____
Reading Focus: Classification or
_____

SEARCH & RECORD
Project Idea: Individually, students cut or tear from magazines pictures or words related to the lesson's theme. They paste or tape them on their papers. Encourage discussion of findings with neighbors.
    Teachers check students for association of pictures/words with theme.

SHARING
Students discuss the items found that relate to the day's theme or _____.
    Papers are dated and filed.

Recreational Reading

For approximately 20 minutes all students read or look at books.

CONVERSATIONS
Getting Started: The teacher reads silently with the class. During the last 5 to 7 minutes the teacher may choose to talk to some individuals about their reading.

CLIPBOARD NOTES
Teacher notes where students choose to read or _____.

BOOK SHARING
Each person tells another person something he or she has read about that day.

and Storytime

READ ALOUD (Optional)
The Tale of Squirrel Nutkin by Beatrix Potter or *The Meanest Squirrel I Ever Met* by Gene Zion or _____
    Teacher rereads part of the story. Discuss pronouns and their referents.

ACTIVITY (Optional)
Sort and classify remaining objects from day before yesterday's walk. Teacher adds a variety of nuts to the collection. Work in teams or small groups. Make a group display. Glue on objects.

Writing

MINI-LESSON
Teacher leads a 5- to 7-minute discussion about possible interpretations of the Writing Topic: Nuts or _____.

COMPOSING
Each student writes (by drawing or developmental spelling) on
 ▪ the lesson's topic
 ▪ a personally chosen topic
 ▪ a topic begun previously

SHARING
Papers are read to a classmate or the teacher, dated, and filed.

Word Study

CHART DEVELOPMENT
Spelling Emphasis: *n* and/or
_____
    On the chart, the teacher writes any words containing the day's letter or
_____.

WRITING
On their papers, students write
 ▪ their favorite words from the chart
 ▪ other words/clusters/sentences that would be appropriate for the chart
Papers are dated and filed.

Lesson 14

Research

LEAD-IN
Teacher introduces the Project Idea.
Theme: Colors or _____
Material: Magazines or _____
Reading Focus: Color discrimination or _____

SEARCH & RECORD
Project Idea: Students locate pictures in magazines and discuss colors of items in the pictures. They cut or tear the pictures out and paste the pictures on their papers. Using developmental spelling, some children record what is happening in their pictures.

SHARING
Students compare the pictures found and what they think is happening in each or _____.

   Papers are dated and filed.

Recreational Reading and Storytime

For approximately 20 minutes all students read or look at books.

CONVERSATIONS
Getting Started: The teacher reads silently with the class. During the last 5 to 7 minutes the teacher may choose to talk to some individuals about their reading.

CLIPBOARD NOTES
Teacher notes where students choose to read or _____.

BOOK SHARING
Each person tells another person something he or she has read about that day.

READ ALOUD
Any book about shapes or textures such as *Color Zoo* by Lois Ehlert or *Color Farm* by Lois Ehlert or *Is It Rough? Is It Smooth? Is it Shiny?* by Tana Hoban or _____

   Discuss classifications related to textures or shapes.

ACTIVITY (Optional)
Teacher makes many varied sized shapes from painted tagboard or colored paper. Students construct animals or other objects using the pre-cut shapes as the basis.

Writing

MINI-LESSON
Teacher leads a 5- to 7-minute discussion about possible interpretations of the Writing Topic: Textures of Fall or _____.

COMPOSING
Each student writes on
■ the lesson's topic
■ a personally chosen topic
■ a topic begun previously

SHARING
Papers are read to a classmate or the teacher, dated, and filed.

Word Study

CHART DEVELOPMENT
Spelling Emphasis: *p* and/or _____

   On the chart, the teacher writes any words containing the day's letter or _____.

WRITING
On their papers, students write
■ their favorite words from the chart
■ other words/clusters/sentences that would be appropriate for the chart
Papers are dated and filed.

Lesson 15

Research

LEAD-IN
Teacher introduces the Project Idea.
Theme: Colors or _____
Material: Library books or _____
Reading Focus: Color discrimination
or _____

SEARCH & RECORD
Project Idea: Students locate pictures in library books and discuss colors of items in the pictures.

Students should discuss ideas with the class or teacher before recording the colors with drawing and/or developmental spelling.

SHARING
Students compare the pictures found and the colors of things in the pictures or
_____.

Papers are dated and filed.

Recreational Reading

and

Storytime

For approximately 20 minutes all students read or look at books.

CONVERSATIONS
Getting Started: The teacher reads silently with the class. During the last 5 to 7 minutes the teacher may choose to talk to some individuals about their reading.

CLIPBOARD NOTES
Teacher notes where students choose to read or _____.

READ ALOUD
Any "color" book or *Planting a Rainbow* by Lois Ehlert or *A Rainbow of My Own* by Don Freeman or _____
Discuss colors and shapes and how the author/illustrator used them in the book.

ACTIVITY (Optional)
Plant a seed in a paper cup. Or, make a colorful flower out of paper.

BOOK SHARING
Each person tells another person something he or she has read about that day.

Writing

MINI-LESSON
Teacher leads a 5- to 7-minute discussion about possible interpretations of the Writing Topic: Colors of Fall or
_____.

COMPOSING
Each student writes on
■ the lesson's topic
■ a personally chosen topic
■ a topic begun previously

SHARING
Papers are read to a classmate or the teacher, dated, and filed.

Word Study

CHART DEVELOPMENT
Spelling Review: *g h* and/or

_____
Students locate words on the room's charts that contain either review letter. On today's chart the teacher writes additional word clusters that contain either letter or _____.

WRITING
On their papers, students write
■ their favorite words from the chart
■ other words/clusters/sentences that would be appropriate for the chart
Papers are dated and filed.

Lesson 16

Research

LEAD-IN
Teacher introduces the Project Idea.
Theme: Colors or _____
Material: Library books or _____
Reading Focus: Color discrimination
or _____

SEARCH & RECORD
Project Idea: Students locate pictures
in library books and discuss colors of
items in the pictures.

Students should discuss ideas with the
class or teacher before recording the
colors with drawing and/or developmental
spelling.

SHARING
Students compare the pictures found and
what color each is or _____.
Papers are dated and filed.

Recreational Reading

For approximately 25 minutes all
students read or look at books.

CONVERSATIONS
Getting Started: The teacher reads
silently with the class. During the last 7
to 10 minutes the teacher may choose to
talk to some individuals about their
reading.

CLIPBOARD NOTES
Teacher notes who studies or learns from
pictures or _____.

BOOK SHARING
Each person tells another person
something he or she has read about that
day.

yellow

and Storytime

READ ALOUD
Any "color" book such as *Samuel Todd's
Book of Colors* by E. L. Konigsburg or
The Mixed-Up Chameleon by Eric Carle
or *Rainbow Crow* by N. Van Laan or
_____

Discuss words that describe colors.

ACTIVITY (Optional)
Use magazine pictures (cut or torn out) to
make individual color collages. Each
student also contributes one item to the
class collage.

Writing

MINI-LESSON
Teacher leads a 5- to 7-minute discussion
about possible interpretations of the
Writing Topic: My Favorite Color or
_____.

COMPOSING
Each student writes on
■ the lesson's topic
■ a personally chosen topic
■ a topic begun previously

SHARING
Papers are read to a classmate or the
teacher, dated, and filed.

Word Study

CHART DEVELOPMENT
Spelling Emphasis: q and/or _____

On the chart, the teacher writes any
words containing the day's letter or
_____

WRITING
On their papers, students write
■ their favorite words from the chart
■ other words/clusters/sentences that
would be appropriate for the chart
Papers are dated and filed.

Lesson 17

Research

LEAD-IN
Teacher introduces the Project Idea.
Letters: *g G* or _____
Material: Newspapers or _____
Reading Focus: Letter Recognition or _____

SEARCH & RECORD
Project Idea: Individually, students cut or tear the lesson's letters or words

containing the letters from newspapers. They paste or tape the letters or words on their papers. Encourage discussion of findings with neighbors.
Teacher checks for letter recognition.

SHARING
Compare letters and words found with another student or _____.
Papers are dated and filed.

Recreational Reading

For approximately 25 minutes all students read or look at books.

CONVERSATIONS
Getting Started: The teacher reads silently with the class. During the last 7 to 10 minutes the teacher may choose to talk to some individuals about their reading.

CLIPBOARD NOTES
Teacher notes who studies or learns from pictures or _____.

BOOK SHARING
Each person tells another person something he or she has read about that day.

and Storytime

READ ALOUD
Someday by Charlotte Zolotow or
_____
Discuss times in the book.

ACTIVITY (Optional)
Draw a picture of what you'd like to do someday. Make a class book.

Writing

MINI-LESSON
Teacher leads a 5- to 7-minute discussion about possible interpretations of the Writing Topic: Colors of Food or _____.

COMPOSING
Each student writes (by drawing or developmental spelling) on
- the lesson's topic
- a personally chosen topic
- a topic begun previously

SHARING
Papers are read to a classmate or the teacher, dated, and filed.

Word Study

CHART DEVELOPMENT
Spelling Emphasis: *r* and/or _____
On the chart, the teacher writes any words containing the day's letter or _____.

WRITING
On their papers, students write
- their favorite words from the chart
- other words/clusters/sentences that would be appropriate for the chart
Papers are dated and filed.

Lesson 18

Research

LEAD-IN
Teacher introduces the Project Idea.
Letters: *h H* or _____
Material: Newspapers or _____
Reading Focus: Letter recognition or
_____

SEARCH & RECORD
Project Idea: Individually, students cut or tear the lesson's letters or words containing the letters from newspapers. They paste or tape the letters or words on their papers. Encourage discussion of findings with neighbors.
   Teacher checks for letter recognition.

SHARING
Compare letters and words found with another student or _____.
   Papers are dated and filed.

Recreational Reading

For approximately 25 minutes all students read or look at books.

CONVERSATIONS
Getting Started: The teacher reads silently with the class. During the last 7 to 10 minutes the teacher may choose to talk to some individuals about their reading.

CLIPBOARD NOTES
Teacher notes who studies or learns from pictures or _____.

BOOK SHARING
Each person tells another person something he or she has read about that day.

and Storytime

READ ALOUD
Any book involving camouflage such as *How to Hide a Gray Treefrog* by Ruth Heller or *How to Hide a Polar Bear* by Ruth Heller or _____
   Discuss camouflage. Show pictures, camouflaged items, hunting clothes, etc. Develop a chart of some unusual examples of camouflage. For example:

camouflage to make you look like a chair when your mother is looking for someone to take out the garbage.

ACTIVITY (Optional)
Find a picture of an animal or object. Glue it on a piece of paper. Draw around the picture to camouflage the magazine picture.

Writing

MINI-LESSON
Teacher leads a 5- to 7-minute discussion about possible interpretations of the Writing Topic: Animal Coloring or
_____

COMPOSING
Each student writes on
■ the lesson's topic
■ a personally chosen topic
■ a topic begun previously

SHARING
Papers are read to a classmate or the teacher, dated, and filed.

Word Study

CHART DEVELOPMENT
Spelling Emphasis: *s* and/or
_____

   On the chart, the teacher writes any words containing the day's letter or
_____

WRITING
On their papers, students write
■ their favorite words from the chart
■ other words/clusters/sentences that would be appropriate for the chart
Papers are dated and filed.

Lesson 19

Research

LEAD-IN
Teacher introduces the Project Idea.
Letters: *g* or *h* or _____
Material: Social studies textbooks or nonfiction books or _____
Reading Focus: Words or pictures with certain letters or _____

SEARCH & RECORD
Project Idea: Students explore social studies textbooks identifying words or pictures with the letters *g* or *h* or _____.

Students should report their ideas to the class or teacher before recording with drawing and/or developmental spelling.
Teacher checks students for ideas associated with the text's content.

SHARING
Students compare the items found that contain the letters *g* or *h* or _____.
Papers are dated and filed.

Recreational Reading

For approximately 25 minutes all students read or look at books.

CONVERSATIONS
Getting Started: The teacher reads silently with the class. During the last 7 to 10 minutes the teacher may choose to talk to some individuals about their reading.

CLIPBOARD NOTES
Teacher notes who seeks meaning from books or _____.

BOOK SHARING
Each person tells another person something he or she has read about that day.

and Storytime

READ ALOUD
Petunia by Roger Duvoisin or _____
Discuss the places in the book.

ACTIVITY (Optional)
Make a duck whose wing is a pocket and can hold things, like a little book.

Writing

MINI-LESSON
Teacher leads a 5- to 7-minute discussion about possible interpretations of the Writing Topic: Colors in the Classroom or _____.

COMPOSING
Each student writes on
■ the lesson's topic
■ a personally chosen topic
■ a topic begun previously

SHARING
Papers are read to a classmate or the teacher, dated, and filed.

Word Study

CHART DEVELOPMENT
Spelling Emphasis: *t* and/or _____
On the chart, the teacher writes any words containing the day's letter or _____

WRITING
On their papers, students write
■ their favorite words from the chart
■ other words/clusters/sentences that would be appropriate for the chart
Papers are dated and filed.

Research

LEAD-IN
Teacher introduces the Project Idea.
Theme: Jobs or _____
Material: Social studies textbooks or _____

Reading Focus: Classification or _____

SEARCH & RECORD
Project Idea: Students explore social studies textbooks identifying words or pictures which they associate with jobs or _____.

Students should report their ideas to the class or the teacher before recording with drawing and/or developmental spelling.
Teachers check students for association of pictures/words with theme.

SHARING
Students discuss the items found that relate to the day's theme or _____.
Papers are dated and filed.

Recreational Reading

For approximately 25 minutes all students read or look at books.

CONVERSATIONS
Getting Started: The teacher reads silently with the class. During the last 7 to 10 minutes the teacher may choose to talk to some individuals about their reading.

CLIPBOARD NOTES
Teacher notes who seeks meaning from books or _____.

BOOK SHARING
Each person tells another person something he or she has read about that day.

and Storytime

READ ALOUD
My Teacher Sleeps in School by Leatie Weiss or *John Patrick Norman McHennessy, The Boy Who Was Always Late* by John Burningham or _____
Discuss *where* and *when* things happened in the story.

ACTIVITY (Optional)
Make a class book about the teacher. Children contribute writings and illustrations showing places the teacher might sleep in their classroom.

Writing

MINI-LESSON
Teacher leads a 5- to 7-minute discussion about possible interpretations of the Writing Topic: Jobs in School or _____.

COMPOSING
Each student writes on
■ the lesson's topic
■ a personally chosen topic
■ a topic begun previously

SHARING
Papers are read to a classmate or the teacher, dated, and filed.

Word Study

CHART DEVELOPMENT
Spelling Review: *j k* and/or _____

Students locate words on the room's charts which contain either review letter. On today's chart the teacher writes additional word clusters that contain either letter or _____.

WRITING
On their papers, students write
■ their favorite words from the chart
■ other words/clusters/sentences that would be appropriate for the chart
Papers are dated and filed.

Lesson 21

Research

LEAD-IN
Teacher introduces the Project Idea.
Theme: Jobs or _____
Material: Magazines or _____
Reading Focus: Classification or _____

SEARCH & RECORD
Project Idea: Individually, students cut or tear from magazines pictures or words related to the lesson's theme. They paste or tape them on their papers. Encourage discussion of findings with neighbors.
    Teachers check students for association of pictures/words with theme.

SHARING
Students discuss the items found that relate to the day's theme or _____.
    Papers are dated and filed.

Recreational Reading and Storytime

For approximately 30 minutes all students read or look at books.

CONVERSATIONS
Check-In: Teacher moves among students, having 2- to 3-minute conversations with as many individuals as possible. If appropriate, discuss main idea(s) and/or _____.

CLIPBOARD NOTES
Teacher notes who seeks meaning from books or _____.

BOOK SHARING
Each person tells another person something he or she has read about that day.

READ ALOUD
Owliver by Robert Kraus or _____
    Discuss *who* is in the story and *what* happened.

ACTIVITY (Optional)
Make an Owliver paper doll. Design a work costume for the job you would choose for Owliver.

Writing

MINI-LESSON
Teacher leads a 5- to 7-minute discussion about possible interpretations of the Writing Topic: Other Jobs in School or _____.

COMPOSING
Each student writes (by drawing or developmental spelling) on
■ the lesson's topic
■ a personally chosen topic
■ a topic begun previously

SHARING
Papers are read to a classmate or the teacher, dated, and filed.

Word Study

CHART DEVELOPMENT
Spelling Emphasis: *v* and/or _____

    On the chart, the teacher writes any word clusters that contain the day's letter or _____.

WRITING
On their papers, students write
■ their favorite words from the chart
■ other words/clusters/sentences that would be appropriate for the chart
Papers are dated and filed.

Lesson 22

Research

LEAD-IN
Teacher introduces the Project Idea.
Theme: Eyes or _____
Material: Magazines or _____
Reading Focus: Description and analysis or _____

SEARCH & RECORD
Project Idea: Individually, students cut or tear from magazines pictures or words related to the lesson's theme. They paste or tape the pictures or words on their papers. Encourage discussion of findings with neighbors.
Teachers check students for association of pictures/words with theme.

SHARING
Students discuss the items found that relate to the day's theme or _____.
Papers are dated and filed.

Recreational Reading

For approximately 30 minutes all students read or look at books.

CONVERSATIONS
Check-In: Teacher moves among students, having 2- to 3-minute conversations with as many individuals as possible. If appropriate, discuss main idea(s) and/or _____.

CLIPBOARD NOTES
Teacher notes who gets up often or _____.

BOOK SHARING
Each person tells another person something he or she has read about that day.

and Storytime

READ ALOUD
Any book about eyes, such as *Eyes* by Jill Bailey or *The Eye Book* by Theodore LeSieg or *Look at Your Eyes* by Paul Showers or _____
Discuss similarities and differences.

ACTIVITY (Optional)
Make a class book about "Things We Like to See."

Writing

MINI-LESSON
Teacher leads a 5- to 7-minute discussion about possible interpretations of the Writing Topic: A Place in the Classroom or _____.

COMPOSING
Each student writes on
■ the lesson's topic
■ a personally chosen topic
■ a topic begun previously

SHARING
Papers are read to a classmate or the teacher, dated, and filed.

Word Study

CHART DEVELOPMENT
Spelling Emphasis: *w* and/or
_____
On the chart, the teacher writes any word clusters that contain the day's letter or _____.

WRITING
On their papers, students write
■ their favorite words from the chart
■ other words/clusters/sentences that would be appropriate for the chart
Papers are dated and filed.

Lesson 23

Research

LEAD-IN
Teacher introduces the Project Idea.
Theme: Character traits or _____
Material: Library books or _____
Reading Focus: Description &
analysis or _____

SEARCH & RECORD
Project Idea: Students locate pictures
in library books and discuss the
characters in the pictures.

Students should discuss ideas with the
class or teacher before recording the
book's character traits with drawing and/
or developmental spelling.

SHARING
Students compare the pictures found and
what the characters are like or
_____.

Papers are dated and filed.

Recreational Reading

For approximately 30 minutes all
students read or look at books.

CONVERSATIONS
Check-In: Teacher moves among
students, having 2- to 3-minute
conversations with as many individuals
as possible. If appropriate, discuss main
idea(s) and/or _____.

CLIPBOARD NOTES
Teacher notes who gets up often or
_____.

BOOK SHARING
Each person tells another person
something he or she has read about that
day.

and Storytime

READ ALOUD
Leo the Late Bloomer by Robert Kraus or
_____
Discuss the title.

ACTIVITY (Optional)
Make a large flower with a large center.
In the center draw a picture of something
you have just learned how to do.

Writing

MINI-LESSON
Teacher leads a 5- to 7-minute discussion
about possible interpretations of the
Writing Topic: Something I Do Inside the
Classroom or _____.

COMPOSING
Each student writes on
■ the lesson's topic
■ a personally chosen topic
■ a topic begun previously

SHARING
Papers are read to a classmate or the
teacher, dated, and filed.

Word Study

CHART DEVELOPMENT
Spelling Emphasis: *x* and/or
_____
On the chart, the teacher writes any
word clusters that contain the day's letter
or _____.

WRITING
On their papers, students write
■ their favorite words from the chart
■ other words/clusters/sentences that
would be appropriate for the chart
Papers are dated and filed.

Lesson 24

Research

LEAD-IN
Teacher introduces the Project Idea.
Theme: Character traits or _____
Material: Library books or _____
Reading Focus: Description & analysis or _____

SEARCH & RECORD
Project Idea: Students locate pictures in library books and discuss the characters in the pictures.

Students should discuss ideas with the class or teacher before recording the book's character traits with drawing and/or developmental spelling.

SHARING
Students compare the pictures found and what the characters are like or

_____.

Papers are dated and filed.

Recreational Reading

For approximately 30 minutes all students read or look at books.

CONVERSATIONS
Check-In: Teacher moves among students, having 2- to 3-minute conversations with as many individuals as possible. If appropriate, discuss details and/or _____.

CLIPBOARD NOTES
Teacher notes who gets up often or

_____.

BOOK SHARING
Each person tells another person something he or she has read about that day.

and

Storytime

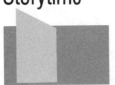

READ ALOUD
Mike Mulligan and His Steam Shovel by Virginia Lee Burton or _____
   Discuss the sequence of events.

ACTIVITY (Optional)
Enlarge a picture of a steam shovel. Cut out and assemble with brads.

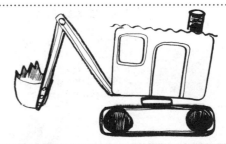

Writing

MINI-LESSON
Teacher leads a 5- to 7-minute discussion about possible interpretations of the Writing Topic: Compare Two Classmates or _____.

COMPOSING
Each student writes on
■ the lesson's topic
■ a personally chosen topic
■ a topic begun previously

SHARING
Papers are read to a classmate or the teacher, dated, and filed.

Word Study

CHART DEVELOPMENT
Spelling Emphasis: *y* and/or

_____

   On the chart, the teacher writes any word clusters that contain the day's letter or _____.

WRITING
On their papers, students write
■ their favorite words from the chart
■ other words/clusters/sentences that would be appropriate for the chart
Papers are dated and filed.

Lesson 25

Research

LEAD-IN
Teacher introduces the Project Idea.
Letters: *j J* or _____
Material: Newspapers or _____
Reading Focus: Letter recognition or
_____

SEARCH & RECORD
Project Idea: Individually, students
cut or tear the lesson's letters or words

containing the letters from newspapers.
They paste or tape the letters or words on
their papers. Encourage discussion of
findings with neighbors.
   Teacher checks for letter recognition.

SHARING
Compare letters and words found with
another student or _____.
   Papers are dated and filed.

Recreational Reading

For approximately 30 minutes all
students read or look at books.

CONVERSATIONS
Teacher Reads: For approximately
20 minutes the teacher reads silently
with the class. During the last 10
minutes the teacher may chose to talk
with some individuals about what they
have read.

CLIPBOARD NOTES
Teacher notes who re-reads the same book
or _____.

BOOK SHARING
Each person tells another person
something he or she has read about that
day.

and Storytime

READ ALOUD
Any book featuring a parent such as
Gorilla by Anthony Browne or *The
Wednesday Surprise* by Eve Bunting or
The Wall by Eve Bunting or _____
   Describe the characters. Compare them
with your parents.

ACTIVITY (Optional)
Make a colored paper portrait of one of
your parents.

Writing

MINI-LESSON
Teacher leads a 5- to 7-minute discussion
about possible interpretations of the
Writing Topic: Describe Mother or Father
or _____.

COMPOSING
Each student writes (by drawing or
developmental spelling) on
■ the lesson's topic
■ a personally chosen topic
■ a topic begun previously

SHARING
Papers are read to a classmate or the
teacher, dated, and filed.

Word Study

CHART DEVELOPMENT
Spelling Review: *l m* and/or

   Students locate words on the room's
charts which contain either review letter.
On today's chart the teacher writes
additional word clusters that contain
either review letter or _____.

WRITING
On their papers, students write
■ their favorite words from the chart
■ other words/clusters/sentences that
   would be appropriate for the chart
   Papers are dated and filed.

Lesson 26

Research

LEAD-IN
Teacher introduces the Project Idea.
Letters: *k K* or _____
Material: Newspapers or _____
Reading Focus: Letter recognition or _____

SEARCH & RECORD
Project Idea: Individually, students cut or tear the lesson's letters or words containing the letters from newspapers. They paste or tape the letters or words on their papers. Encourage discussion of findings with neighbors.
   Teacher checks for letter recognition.

SHARING
Compare letters and words found with another student or _____.
   Papers are dated and filed.

Recreational Reading

For approximately 30 minutes all students read or look at books.

CONVERSATIONS
Check-In: Teacher moves among students, having 2- to 3-minute conversations with as many individuals as possible. If appropriate, discuss details and/or _____.

CLIPBOARD NOTES
Teacher notes who re-reads the same book or _____.

BOOK SHARING
Each person tells another person something he or she has read about that day.

and Storytime

READ ALOUD
Any book featuring parents such as *Weird Parents* by Audrey Wood or *Blueberries for Sal* by Robert McCloskey or *Follow Me* by Nancy Tafuri or *River Dream* by Allan Say or _____
   Compare the parents in today's book to the parents in yesterday's book.

ACTIVITY (Optional)
Make a colored paper portrait of your other parent.

Writing

MINI-LESSON
Teacher leads a 5- to 7-minute discussion about possible interpretations of the Writing Topic: A Memory with Mother or Father (a special time you were with one of them, perhaps just the two of you) or _____.

COMPOSING
Each student writes on
- the lesson's topic
- a personally chosen topic
- a topic begun previously

SHARING
Papers are read to a classmate or the teacher, dated, and filed.

Word Study

CHART DEVELOPMENT
Spelling Emphasis: *z* and/or
_____
   On the chart, the teacher writes any word clusters that contain the day's letter or _____.

WRITING
On their papers, students write
- their favorite words from the chart
- other words/clusters/sentences that would be appropriate for the chart
Papers are dated and filed.

Lesson 27

Research

LEAD-IN
Teacher introduces the Project Idea.
Letters: *j* or *k* or _____
Material: Math textbooks or nonfiction books or _____
Reading Focus: Words or pictures with certain letters

SEARCH & RECORD
Project Idea: Students explore math textbooks identifying words or pictures with the letters *j* or *k* or _____.

Students should report their ideas to the class or teacher before recording with drawing and/or developmental spelling.
Teacher checks students for ideas associated with the text's content.

SHARING
Students compare the items found that contain the letters *j* or *k* or _____.
Papers are dated and filed.

Recreational Reading

For approximately 30 minutes all students read or look at books.

CONVERSATIONS
Check-In: Teacher moves among students, having 2- to 3-minute conversations with as many individuals as possible. If appropriate, discuss details and/or _____.

CLIPBOARD NOTES
Teacher notes who re-reads the same book or _____.

BOOK SHARING
Each person tells another person something he or she has read about that day.

---

and Storytime

READ ALOUD
Any book about babies such as *The Baby* by John Burningham or *Earthlets* by Tony Ross or *The Baby's Catalogue* by Janet & Allan Ahlberg or *She Come Bringing Me That Little Baby Girl* by Eloise Greenfield or _____
Help students relate the events in the book to their own experience.

ACTIVITY (Optional)
Draw a picture of yourself or a sibling as a baby. Make a class book.

Writing

MINI-LESSON
Teacher leads a 5- to 7-minute discussion about possible interpretations of the Writing Topic: Describe Brother or Sister (one you have or would like to have) or
_____.

COMPOSING
Each student writes on
■ the lesson's topic
■ a personally chosen topic
■ a topic begun previously

SHARING
Papers are read to a classmate or the teacher, dated, and filed.

Word Study

CHART DEVELOPMENT
Spelling Emphasis: *a* and/or
_____.
On the chart, the teacher writes any word clusters that contain the day's letter or _____.

WRITING
On their papers, students write
■ their favorite words from the chart
■ other words/clusters/sentences that would be appropriate for the chart
Papers are dated and filed.

Lesson 28

Research

LEAD-IN
Teacher introduces the Project Idea.
Theme: Math words or _____
Material: Math textbooks or _____

Reading Focus: Specialized vocabulary or _____

SEARCH & RECORD
Project Idea: Students explore math textbooks identifying words or pictures which they associate with mathematics or _____.

Students should report their ideas to the class or the teacher before recording with drawing and/or developmental spelling.
Teachers check students for association of pictures/words with theme.

SHARING
Students discuss the items found that relate to the day's theme or _____.
Papers are dated and filed.

Recreational Reading

For approximately 30 minutes all students read or look at books.

CONVERSATIONS
Check-In: Teacher moves among students, having 2- to 3-minute conversations with as many individuals as possible. If appropriate, discuss prediction or inference and/or _____.

CLIPBOARD NOTES
Teacher notes who daydreams or watches the teacher or _____.

BOOK SHARING
Each person tells another person something he or she has read about that day.

and Storytime

READ ALOUD
Abby by Jeanette Caines or *Stevie* by John Steptoe or _____
Discuss the sequence of events.

ACTIVITY (Optional)
Make a collage of things cut out of magazines that a baby needs.

Writing

MINI-LESSON
Teacher leads a 5- to 7-minute discussion about possible interpretations of the Writing Topic: A Memory With a Brother or Sister (or what you would do with a brother or sister) or _____.

COMPOSING
Each student writes on
■ the lesson's topic
■ a personally chosen topic
■ a topic begun previously

SHARING
Papers are read to a classmate or the teacher, dated, and filed.

Word Study

CHART DEVELOPMENT
Spelling Emphasis: *e* and/or _____

On the chart, the teacher writes any word clusters that contain the day's letter or _____.

WRITING
On their papers, students write
■ their favorite words from the chart
■ other words/clusters/sentences that would be appropriate for the chart
Papers are dated and filed.

Lesson 29

Research

LEAD-IN
Teacher introduces the Project Idea.
Theme: Math words or _____
Material: Magazines or _____
Reading Focus: Specialized
vocabulary or _____

SEARCH & RECORD
Project Idea: Individually, students
cut or tear from magazines pictures or
words related to the lesson's theme. They
paste or tape them on their papers.
Encourage discussion of findings with
neighbors.
   Teachers check students for association
of pictures/words with theme.

SHARING
Students discuss the items found that
relate to the day's theme or _____.
   Papers are dated and filed.

Recreational Reading

For approximately 30 minutes all
students read or look at books.

CONVERSATIONS
Check-In: Teacher moves among
students, having 2- to 3-minute
conversations with as many individuals
as possible. If appropriate, discuss
prediction or inference and/or _____.

CLIPBOARD NOTES
Teacher notes who daydreams or watches
the teacher or _____.

BOOK SHARING
Each person tells another person
something he or she has read about that
day.

and Storytime

READ ALOUD
Any book featuring neighbors such as
Wilfrid Gordon McDonald Partridge by
Mem Fox or *Miss Rumphius* by Barbara
Cooney or *Harry and the Lady Next Door*
by Gene Zion or _____
   Discuss students' neighbors.

ACTIVITY (Optional)
Class makes presents to give to
neighbors.

Writing

MINI-LESSON
Teacher leads a 5- to 7-minute discussion
about possible interpretations of the
Writing Topic: Write About a Neighbor or

_____.

COMPOSING
Each student writes (by drawing or
developmental spelling) on
■ the lesson's topic
■ a personally chosen topic
■ a topic begun previously

SHARING
Papers are read to a classmate or the
teacher, dated, and filed.

Word Study

CHART DEVELOPMENT
Spelling Emphasis: *i* and/or

_____

   On the chart, the teacher writes any
word clusters that contain the day's letter
or _____.

WRITING
On their papers, students write
■ their favorite words from the chart
■ other words/clusters/sentences that
   would be appropriate for the chart
   Papers are dated and filed.

Lesson 30

Research

LEAD-IN
Teacher introduces the Project Idea.
Theme: Feet or _____
Material: Magazines or _____
Reading Focus: Classification and inference or _____

SEARCH & RECORD
Project Idea: Individually, students cut or tear from magazines pictures or words related to the lesson's theme. They paste or tape the pictures or words on their papers. Encourage discussion of findings with neighbors.
　Teachers check students or association of pictures/words with theme.

SHARING
Students discuss the feet found and what the feet are doing or _____.
　Papers are dated and filed.

Recreational Reading

and

Storytime

For approximately 30 minutes all students read or look at books.

CONVERSATIONS
Teacher Reads: For approximately 20 minutes the teacher reads silently with the class. During the last 10 minutes the teacher may choose to talk with some individuals about what they have read.

CLIPBOARD NOTES
Teacher notes who daydreams or watches the teacher or _____.

BOOK SHARING
Each person tells another person something he or she has read about that day.

READ ALOUD
Any book about feet such as *Feet!* by Peter Parnell or *The Foot Book* by Dr. Seuss or _____
　Discuss words that describe feet.

ACTIVITY (Optional)
Make tempera paint footprints. Roll tempera paint on a cookie sheet with a brayer. Students make footprints with bare feet. Use more than one color of paint for the footprints.
　Cut out footprints. Make footprint patterns based on the color. Decorate the room with footprints.

Writing

MINI-LESSON
Teacher leads a 5- to 7-minute discussion about possible interpretations of the Writing Topic: Write About Some Feet Found in *Research* or _____.

COMPOSING
Each student writes on
■ the lesson's topic
■ a personally chosen topic
■ a topic begun previously

SHARING
Papers are read to a classmate or the teacher, dated, and filed.
　Each student chooses a composition from their folder for the teacher to display in the classroom. Students may modify their writing and/or illustration as they see fit.

Word Study

CHART DEVELOPMENT
Spelling Review: *n p* and/or _____
　Students locate words on the room's charts which contain either review letter. On today's chart the teacher writes additional word clusters that contain either letter or _____.

WRITING
On their papers, students write
■ their favorite words from the chart
■ other words/clusters/sentences that would be appropriate for the chart
Papers are dated and filed.

Lesson 31

Research

LEAD-IN
Teacher introduces the Project Idea.
Theme: Feet—what they are doing now/next or _____
Material: Library books or _____
Reading Focus: Sequence or _____

SEARCH & RECORD
Project Idea: In teams of 2 or 3, students locate pictures of feet in library books and discuss what the feet are doing now and what they will be doing next.

Team members should discuss ideas until all agree before recording what the feet are doing and will be doing. Recording will be with drawing and/or developmental spelling.

SHARING
Two or three teams compare the pictures found and what the feet are doing or _____.

Papers are dated and filed.

Recreational Reading and Storytime

For approximately 30 minutes all students read or look at books.

CONVERSATIONS
Check-In: Teacher moves among students, having 2- to 3-minute conversations with as many individuals as possible. If appropriate, discuss prediction or inference and/or _____.

CLIPBOARD NOTES
Teacher notes who reads or attempts to read or _____.

BOOK SHARING
Each person tells another person something he or she has read about that day.

READ ALOUD
A book about shoes and/or feet such as *Making Shoes* by Nancy Tafuri or *Shoes* by Elizabeth Winthrop or *Big Shoe, Little Shoe* by Denys Cazet or _____
    Compare and classify shoe types found in the classroom.

ACTIVITY (Optional)
Students make a contour drawing of their shoe. ("Without looking at your paper, try to draw the outline of your shoe.")

Writing

MINI-LESSON
Teacher leads a 5- to 7-minute discussion about possible interpretations of the Writing Topic: Shoes or _____.

COMPOSING
Each student writes on
- the lesson's topic
- a personally chosen topic
- a topic begun previously

SHARING
Papers are read to a classmate or the teacher, dated, and filed.

Word Study

CHART DEVELOPMENT
Spelling Emphasis: *o* and/or _____

    On the chart, the teacher writes any word clusters that contain the day's letter or _____.

WRITING
On their papers, students write
- their favorite words from the chart
- other words/clusters/sentences that would be appropriate for the chart
Papers are dated and filed.

Research

LEAD-IN
Teacher introduces the Project Idea.
Theme: Events—now/next or

_____
Material: Library books or _____
Reading Focus: Sequence or
_____

SEARCH & RECORD
Project Idea: In teams of 2 or 3, students locate pictures of events in library books and discuss what is happening now and will happen next.

Team members should discuss ideas until all agree before recording what is happening now and will happen next in the book. Recording will be with drawing and/or developmental spelling.

SHARING
Two or three teams compare the pictures found and the sequence of events or
_____
Papers are dated and filed.

Recreational Reading

For approximately 30 minutes all students read or look at books.

CONVERSATIONS
Check-In: Teacher moves among students, having 2- to 3-minute conversations with as many individuals as possible. If appropriate, discuss comparison and/or _____.

CLIPBOARD NOTES
Teacher notes who reads or attempts to read or _____.

BOOK SHARING
Each person tells another person something he or she has read about that day.

and Storytime

READ ALOUD
Ramona the Pest by Beverly Cleary (chapter about school) or _____
Help the students relate the events in the book to their experiences.

ACTIVITY (Optional)
Draw or paint a picture of yourself in kindergarten.

Writing

MINI-LESSON
Teacher leads a 5- to 7-minute discussion about possible interpretations of the Writing Topic: Write a daily school schedule. Work with a partner or
_____.

COMPOSING
Each student writes on
■ the lesson's topic
■ a personally chosen topic
■ a topic begun previously

SHARING
Papers are read to a classmate or the teacher, dated, and filed.

Word Study

CHART DEVELOPMENT
Spelling Emphasis: *u* and/or

_____
On the chart, the teacher writes any word clusters that contain the day's letter or _____.

WRITING
On their papers, students write
■ their favorite words from the chart
■ other words/clusters/sentences that would be appropriate for the chart
Papers are dated and filed.

Lesson **33**

Research

LEAD-IN
Teacher introduces the Project Idea.
Letters: *l L* or _____
Material: Newspapers or _____
Reading Focus: Letter recognition or
_____

SEARCH & RECORD
Project Idea: Individually, students cut or tear the lesson's letters or words containing the letters from newspapers. They paste or tape the letters or words on their papers. Encourage discussion of findings with neighbors.
Teacher checks for letter recognition.

SHARING
Compare letters and words found with another student or _____.
Papers are dated and filed.

Recreational Reading

For approximately 30 minutes all students read or look at books.

CONVERSATIONS
Check-In: Teacher moves among students, having 2- to 3-minute conversations with as many individuals as possible. If appropriate, discuss comparison and/or _____.

CLIPBOARD NOTES
Teacher notes who reads or attempts to read or _____.

BOOK SHARING
Each person tells another person something he or she has read about that day.

and Storytime

READ ALOUD
A Tree Is Nice by Janice May Udry or
_____
Describe the places in the book.

ACTIVITY (Optional)
Make a class book about trees. Each student contributes a page about trees.

Writing

MINI-LESSON
Teacher leads a 5- to 7-minute discussion about possible interpretations of the Writing Topic: Write a plan for making a sandwich. Work with a partner or
_____.

COMPOSING
Each student writes (by drawing or developmental spelling) on
■ the lesson's topic
■ a personally chosen topic
■ a topic begun previously

SHARING
Papers are read to a classmate or the teacher, dated, and filed.

Word Study

CHART DEVELOPMENT
Spelling Emphasis: *A** and/or
_____
On the chart, the teacher writes any word clusters that contain the day's letter or _____.

WRITING
On their papers, students write
■ their favorite words from the chart
■ other words/clusters/sentences that would be appropriate for the chart
Papers are dated and filed.

Lesson 34

Research

LEAD-IN
Teacher introduces the Project Idea.
Letters: *m M* or _____
Material: Newspapers or _____
Reading Focus: Letter recognition or _____

SEARCH & RECORD
Project Idea: Individually, students cut or tear the lesson's letters or words containing the letters from newspapers. They paste or tape the letters or words on their papers. Encourage discussion of findings with neighbors.
Teacher checks for letter recognition.

SHARING
Compare letters and words found with another student or _____.
Papers are dated and filed.

Recreational Reading

For approximately 30 minutes all students read or look at books.

CONVERSATIONS
Check-In: Teacher moves among students, having 2- to 3-minute conversations with as many individuals as possible. If appropriate, discuss comparison and/or _____.

CLIPBOARD NOTES
Teacher notes titles or types of books chosen or _____.

BOOK SHARING
Each person tells another person something he or she has read about that day.

and Storytime

READ ALOUD
Spot's Birthday Party by Eric Hill and *Clifford's Birthday Party* by Norman Bridwell or _____
Compare the two books.

ACTIVITY (Optional)
Make a birthday cake out of construction paper. Add the number of candles that represent your age. Decorate your cake as you like.

Writing

MINI-LESSON
Teacher leads a 5- to 7-minute discussion about possible interpretations of the Writing Topic: Write about anything that happened first, second, third or _____.

COMPOSING
Each student writes on
■ the lesson's topic
■ a personally chosen topic
■ a topic begun previously

SHARING
Papers are read to a classmate or the teacher, dated, and filed.

Word Study

CHART DEVELOPMENT
Spelling Emphasis: *B* and/or _____
On the chart, the teacher writes any word clusters that contain the day's letter or _____.

WRITING
On their papers, students write
■ their favorite words from the chart
■ other words/clusters/sentences that would be appropriate for the chart
Papers are dated and filed.

Lesson **35**

Research

LEAD-IN
Teacher introduces the Project Idea.
Letters: *l* or *m* or _____
Material: Science textbooks or nonfiction books or _____
Reading Focus: Words or pictures with certain letters

SEARCH & RECORD
Project Idea: In teams of 2 or 3, students explore science textbooks identifying words or pictures with the letters *l* or *m* or _____.

Team members should discuss their ideas until all agree before recording with drawing and/or developmental spelling.
Teacher checks students for ideas associated with the text's content.

SHARING
Two or three teams compare the items found that contain the letters *l* or *m* or _____.

Papers are dated and filed.

Recreational Reading

For approximately 30 minutes all students read or look at books.

CONVERSATIONS
Teacher Reads: For approximately 20 minutes the teacher reads silently with the class. During the last 10 minutes the teacher may choose to talk with some individuals about what they have read.

CLIPBOARD NOTES
Teacher notes titles or types of books chosen or _____.

BOOK SHARING
Each person tells another person something he or she has read about that day.

and Storytime

READ ALOUD
Any book about birthdays such as *Birthday Presents* by Cynthia Rylant or *The Birthday Moon* by Lois Duncan or *June 7!* by Aliki or _____
Discuss the number of times that things happened in each book.

ACTIVITY (Optional)
Make a special birthday book for yourself. Your book should have one page for every year of your age. Take the book home and finish drawing in special events that occurred in your life.

Writing

MINI-LESSON
Teacher leads a 5- to 7-minute discussion about possible interpretations of the Writing Topic: Birthdays or _____.

COMPOSING
Each student writes on
■ the lesson's topic
■ a personally chosen topic
■ a topic begun previously

SHARING
Papers are read to a classmate or the teacher, dated, and filed.

Word Study

CHART DEVELOPMENT
Spelling Review: *q r* and/or
_____
Students locate words on the room's charts which contain either review letter. On today's chart the teacher writes word clusters that contain either letter or
_____.

WRITING
On their papers, students write
■ their favorite words from the chart
■ other words/clusters/sentences that would be appropriate for the chart
Papers are dated and filed.

Lesson 36

Research

LEAD-IN
Teacher introduces the Project Idea.
Theme: Science words or _____
Material: Science textbooks or

_____

Reading Focus: Specialized
vocabulary or _____

SEARCH & RECORD
Project Idea: In teams of 2 or 3,
students explore science textbooks
identifying words or pictures which they
associate with science or _____ .

Team members should discuss their
ideas until all agree before recording with
drawing and/or developmental spelling.
Teachers check students for association
of pictures/words with theme.

SHARING
Students meet in groups of 4 or 5 and
discuss the items found that relate to the
day's theme or _____ .
Papers are dated and filed.

Recreational Reading

For approximately 30 minutes all
students read or look at books.

CONVERSATIONS
In-Depth: Teacher holds 7- to 10-
minute conversations with 3 or 4 students
(individually) discussing main idea(s),
details, and/or _____ .

CLIPBOARD NOTES
Teacher notes titles or types of books
chosen or _____ .

BOOK SHARING
Each person tells another person
something he or she has read about that
day.

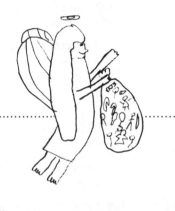

and Storytime

READ ALOUD
Poems by Myra Cohn Livingston such as
"Celebrations" or "Birthday Poems" or

_____

Paraphrase the poems.

ACTIVITY (Optional)
Make a class book of family celebrations
or school celebrations.

Writing

MINI-LESSON
Teacher leads a 5- to 7-minute discussion
about possible interpretations of the
Writing Topic: Family Celebrations or

_____ .

COMPOSING
Each student writes
- the lesson's topic
- a personally chosen topic
- a topic begun previously

SHARING
Papers are read to a classmate or the
teacher, dated, and filed.

Word Study

CHART DEVELOPMENT
Spelling Emphasis: *c* and/or

_____

On the chart, the teacher writes any
word clusters that contain the day's letter
or _____ .

WRITING
On their papers, students write
- their favorite words from the chart
- other words/clusters/sentences that
would be appropriate for the chart
Papers are dated and filed.

Lesson 37

Research

LEAD-IN
Teacher introduces the Project Idea.
Theme: Science or _____
Material: Magazines or _____
Reading Focus: Association or _____

SEARCH & RECORD
Project Idea: Individually, students cut or tear from magazines pictures or words related to the lesson's theme. They paste or tape the pictures or words on their papers. Encourage discussion of findings with neighbors.

Teachers check students for association of pictures/words with theme.

SHARING
Students discuss the items found that relate to the day's theme or _____.

Papers are dated and filed.

Recreational Reading

For approximately 30 minutes all students read or look at books.

CONVERSATIONS
In-Depth: Teacher holds 7- to 10-minute conversations with 3 or 4 students (individually) discussing main idea(s), details, and/or _____.

CLIPBOARD NOTES
Teacher notes who seems excited about books and reading or _____.

BOOK SHARING
Each person tells another person something he or she has read about that day.

and Storytime

READ ALOUD
Polar Express by Chris Van Allsburg or _____

Discuss *when* and *where* events in the story took place.

ACTIVITY (Optional)
Wrap a small box with wrapping paper. Put a ribbon on it. Enclose an imaginary present. Decide what it is and who it is for.

Writing

MINI-LESSON
Teacher leads a 5- to 7-minute discussion about possible interpretations of the Writing Topic: Holidays or _____.

COMPOSING
Each student writes (by drawing or developmental spelling) on
- the lesson's topic
- a personally chosen topic
- a topic begun previously

SHARING
Papers are read to a classmate or the teacher, dated, and filed.

Word Study

CHART DEVELOPMENT
Spelling Emphasis: *D* and/or _____

On the chart, the teacher writes any word clusters that contain the day's letter or _____.

WRITING
On their papers, students write
- their favorite words from the chart
- other words/clusters/sentences that would be appropriate for the chart

Papers are dated and filed.

Lesson 38

Research

LEAD-IN
Teacher introduces the Project Idea.
Theme: Hands—what they are doing now/before or _____
Material: Magazines or _____
Reading Focus: Sequence or _____

SEARCH & RECORD
Project Idea: Individually, students cut or tear from magazines pictures or words related to the lesson's theme. They paste or tape them on their papers. Encourage discussion with neighbors of what the hands are doing now and were doing before.
Teachers check students for association of pictures/words with theme.

SHARING
Students discuss the hands found, what they are doing now and were doing before or _____.
Papers are dated and filed.

Recreational Reading and Storytime

For approximately 30 minutes all students read or look at books.

CONVERSATIONS
In-Depth: Teacher holds 7- to 10-minute conversations with 3 or 4 students (individually) discussing main idea(s), details, and/or _____.

CLIPBOARD NOTES
Teacher notes who seems excited about books and reading or _____.

READ ALOUD
Crictor by Tomi Ungerer or _____
Discuss *why* things happened.

ACTIVITY (Optional)
Make a Crictor paper doll. Make clothes for him.

BOOK SHARING
Each person tells another person something he or she has read about that day.

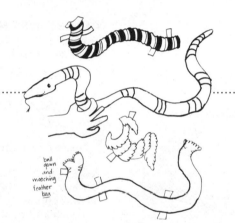

ball gown and matching feather boa

Writing

MINI-LESSON
Teacher leads a 5- to 7-minute discussion about possible interpretations of the Writing Topic: Draw and Label a Pet or _____.

COMPOSING
Each student writes on
- the lesson's topic
- a personally chosen topic
- a topic begun previously

SHARING
Papers are read to a classmate or the teacher, dated, and filed.

Word Study

CHART DEVELOPMENT
Spelling Emphasis: *E* and/or _____
On the chart, the teacher writes any word clusters that contain the day's letter or _____.

WRITING
On their papers, students write
- their favorite words from the chart
- other words/clusters/sentences that would be appropriate for the chart
Papers are dated and filed.

Lesson **39**

Research

LEAD-IN
Teacher introduces the Project Idea.
Theme: Events—now/before or
_____

Material: Library books or _____
Reading Focus: Sequence or
_____

SEARCH & RECORD
Project Idea: In teams of 2 or 3, students locate pictures in library books and discuss what is happening now and what happened before.

Team members should discuss ideas until all agree before recording what is happening now and happened before. Recording will be with drawing and/or developmental spelling.

SHARING
Two or three teams compare the pictures found and the sequence of events recorded or _____.
Papers are dated and filed.

Recreational Reading

For approximately 30 minutes all students read or look at books.

CONVERSATIONS
In-Depth: Teacher holds 7- to 10-minute conversations with 3 or 4 students (individually) discussing main idea(s), details, and/or _____.

CLIPBOARD NOTES
Teacher notes who seems excited about books and reading or _____.

BOOK SHARING
Each person tells another person something he or she has read about that day.

and Storytime

READ ALOUD
Can I Keep Him? by Steven Kellogg or
_____

Discuss *who* and *what*.

ACTIVITY (Optional)
Draw a picture of a pet you would like to have. Tell your neighbors why it would or would not work for you to have this pet.

Writing

MINI-LESSON
Teacher leads a 5- to 7-minute discussion about possible interpretations of the Writing Topic: Describe a Pet or
_____.

COMPOSING
Each student writes on
■ the lesson's topic
■ a personally chosen topic
■ a topic begun previously

SHARING
Papers are read to a classmate or the teacher, dated, and filed.

Word Study

CHART DEVELOPMENT
Spelling Emphasis: *F* and/or
_____

On the chart, the teacher writes any word clusters that contain the day's letter or _____.

WRITING
On their papers, students write
■ their favorite words from the chart
■ other words/clusters/sentences that would be appropriate for the chart
Papers are dated and filed.

Research

LEAD-IN
Teacher introduces the Project Idea.
Theme: Events—now/before or _____

Material: Library books or _____
Reading Focus: Sequence or _____

SEARCH & RECORD
Project Idea: In teams of 2 or 3, students locate pictures in library books and discuss what is happening now and what happened before.

Team members should discuss ideas until all agree before recording the book's sequence of events with drawing and/or developmental spelling.

SHARING
Two or three teams compare the pictures found and the sequence of events recorded or _____.
   Papers are dated and filed.

Recreational Reading

For approximately 30 minutes all students read or look at books.

CONVERSATIONS
In-Depth: Teacher holds 7- to 10-minute conversations with 3 or 4 students (individually) discussing main idea(s), details, and/or _____.

CLIPBOARD NOTES
Teacher notes who stays seated and who walks around or _____.

BOOK SHARING
Each person tells another person something he or she has read about that day.

and Storytime

READ ALOUD
Lyle, Lyle, Crocodile by Bernard Waber or _____
   Describe the characters.

ACTIVITY (Optional)
Make a crocodile. Use a brad to make his jaw move.

Writing

MINI-LESSON
Teacher leads a 5- to 7-minute discussion about possible interpretations of the Writing Topic: Write a Story about a Pet or _____

COMPOSING
Each student writes on
■ the lesson's topic
■ a personally chosen topic
■ a topic begun previously

SHARING
Papers are read to a classmate or the teacher, dated, and filed.

Word Study

CHART DEVELOPMENT
Spelling Review: *s t* and/or _____
   Students locate words on the room's charts that contain either review letter. On today's chart the teacher writes word clusters that contain either letter or _____.

WRITING
On their papers, students write
■ their favorite words from the chart
■ other words/clusters/sentences that would be appropriate for the chart
Papers are dated and filed.

Lesson **41**

Research

LEAD-IN
Teacher introduces the Project Idea.
Letters: *n N* or _____
Material: Newspapers or _____
Reading Focus: Letter recognition or _____

SEARCH & RECORD
Project Idea: Individually, students cut or tear the lesson's letters or words containing the letters from newspapers. They paste or tape the letters or words on their papers. Encourage discussion of findings with neighbors.
   Teacher checks for letter recognition.

SHARING
Compare letters and words found with another student or _____.
   Papers are dated and filed.

Recreational Reading

For approximately 30 minutes all students read or look at books.

CONVERSATIONS
In-Depth: Teacher holds 7- to 10-minute conversations with 3 or 4 students (individually) discussing main idea(s), details, and/or _____.

CLIPBOARD NOTES
Teacher notes who stays seated and who walks around or _____.

BOOK SHARING
Each person tells another person something he or she has read about that day.

and Storytime

READ ALOUD
The Paper Crane by Molly Bang or _____
   Discuss the sequence of events.

ACTIVITY (Optional)
Using large sheets of paper, make an origami crane or other item from folded paper.

Writing

MINI-LESSON
Teacher leads a 5- to 7-minute discussion about possible interpretations of the Writing Topic: A Favorite Meal or a Least Favorite Meal or _____.

COMPOSING
Each student writes (by drawing or developmental spelling) on
■ the lesson's topic
■ a personally chosen topic
■ a topic begun previously

SHARING
Papers are read to a classmate or the teacher, dated, and filed.

Word Study

CHART DEVELOPMENT
Spelling Emphasis: *G* and/or _____
   On the chart, the teacher writes any word clusters that contain the day's letter or _____.

WRITING
On their papers, students write
■ their favorite words from the chart
■ other words/clusters/sentences that would be appropriate for the chart
Papers are dated and filed.

Research

LEAD-IN
Teacher introduces the Project Idea.
Letters: *p P* or _____
Material: Newspapers or _____
Reading Focus: Letter recognition or _____

SEARCH & RECORD
Project Idea: Individually, students cut or tear the lesson's letters or words containing the letters from newspapers. They paste or tape the letters or words on their papers. Encourage discussion of findings with neighbors.
   Teacher checks for letter recognition.

SHARING
Compare letters and words found with another student or _____.
   Papers are dated and filed.

Recreational Reading

For approximately 30 minutes all students read or look at books.

CONVERSATIONS
In-Depth: Teacher holds 7- to 10-minute conversations with 3 or 4 students (individually) discussing main idea(s), details, and/or _____.

CLIPBOARD NOTES
Teacher notes who stays seated and who walks around or _____.

BOOK SHARING
Each person tells another person something@he or she has read about that day.

and Storytime

READ ALOUD
Eating the Alphabet by Lois Ehlert or
Growing Vegetable Soup by Lois Ehlert or
Feathers for Lunch by Lois Ehlert or
_____
   Discuss classifications.

ACTIVITY (Optional)
Make a bowl of alphabet soup. Cut letters from magazines.

Writing

MINI-LESSON
Teacher leads a 5- to 7-minute discussion about possible interpretations of the Writing Topic: Breakfast or _____.

COMPOSING
Each student writes on
■ the lesson's topic
■ a personally chosen topic
■ a topic begun previously

SHARING
Papers are read to a classmate or the teacher, dated, and filed.

Word Study

CHART DEVELOPMENT
Spelling Emphasis: *H* and/or

   On the chart, the teacher writes any word clusters that contain the day's letter or _____.

WRITING
On their papers, students write
■ their favorite words from the chart
■ other words/clusters/sentences that would be appropriate for the chart
Papers are dated and filed.

Lesson 43

Research

LEAD-IN
Teacher introduces the Project Idea.
Letters: *n* or *p* or _____
Material: Social studies textbooks or nonfiction books or _____
Reading Focus: Words or pictures with certain letters

SEARCH & RECORD
Project Idea: In teams of 2 or 3, students explore social studies textbooks identifying words or pictures with the letters *n* or *p* or _____.

Team members should discuss their ideas until all agree before recording with drawing and/or developmental spelling.

Teacher checks students for ideas associated with the text's content.

SHARING
Two or three teams compare the items found that contain the letters *n* or *p* or _____.

Papers are dated and filed.

Recreational Reading

For approximately 30 minutes all students read or look at books.

CONVERSATIONS
Check-In: Teacher moves among students, having 2- to 3-minute conversations with as many individuals as possible. If appropriate, discuss cause and effect and/or _____.

CLIPBOARD NOTES
Teacher notes where students choose to read or _____.

BOOK SHARING
Each person tells another person something he or she has read about that day.

and Storytime

READ ALOUD
Heckety Peg by Don and Audrey Wood or _____
Discuss problem-solving.

ACTIVITY (Optional)
Make a class book. Each student draws two pictures. One is of what he or she would ask their mother to bring them from town. The other is what food the witch would turn them into.

Writing

MINI-LESSON
Teacher leads a 5- to 7-minute discussion about possible interpretations of the Writing Topic: Lunch or _____.

COMPOSING
Each student writes on
- the lesson's topic
- a personally chosen topic
- a topic begun previously

SHARING
Papers are read to a classmate or the teacher, dated, and filed.

Word Study

CHART DEVELOPMENT
Spelling Emphasis: *I* and/or

_____

On the chart, the teacher writes any word clusters that contain the day's letter or _____.

WRITING
On their papers, students write
- their favorite words from the chart
- other words/clusters/sentences that would be appropriate for the chart
Papers are dated and filed.

Lesson 44

Research

LEAD-IN
Teacher introduces the Project Idea.
Theme: Objects that could be purchased or _____
Material: Social studies textbooks or _____

Reading Focus: Classification or _____

SEARCH & RECORD
Project Idea: In teams of 2 or 3, students explore social studies textbooks identifying words or pictures of objects which can be purchased or _____.

Team members should discuss their ideas until all agree before recording with drawing and/or developmental spelling.

Teachers check students for association of pictures/words with theme.

SHARING
Students meet in groups of 4 or 5 and discuss the items found that relate to the day's theme or _____.

Papers are dated and filed.

Recreational Reading

For approximately 30 minutes all students read or look at books.

CONVERSATIONS
Check-In: Teacher moves among students, having 2- to 3-minute conversations with as many individuals as possible. If appropriate, discuss cause and effect and/or _____.

CLIPBOARD NOTES
Teacher notes where students choose to read or _____.

BOOK SHARING
Each person tells another person something he or she has read about that day.

and Storytime

READ ALOUD
Stone Soup (any version) or _____
  Discuss cause and effect.

ACTIVITY (Optional)
Go outside. Find a stone that you think will make good soup.

Writing

MINI-LESSON
Teacher leads a 5- to 7-minute discussion about possible interpretations of the Writing Topic: Dinner or _____.

COMPOSING
Each student writes on
- the lesson's topic
- a personally chosen topic
- a topic begun previously

SHARING
Papers are read to a classmate or the teacher, dated, and filed.

Word Study

CHART DEVELOPMENT
Spelling Emphasis: *J K* and/or _____

  On the chart, the teacher writes any word clusters that contain either letter or _____.

WRITING
On their papers, students write
- their favorite words from the chart
- other words/clusters/sentences that would be appropriate for the chart
Papers are dated and filed.

Lesson 45

Research

LEAD-IN
Teacher introduces the Project Idea.
Theme: Money or _____
Material: Magazines or _____
Reading Focus: Association or
_____

SEARCH & RECORD
Project Idea: Individually, students cut or tear from magazines pictures or words related to the lesson's theme. They paste or tape the pictures or words on their papers. Encourage discussion of findings with neighbors.
   Teachers check students for association of pictures/words with theme.

SHARING
Students discuss the items found that relate to the day's theme or _____.
   Papers are dated and filed.

Recreational Reading and Storytime

For approximately 30 minutes all students read or look at books.

CONVERSATIONS
Teacher Reads: For approximately 20 minutes the teacher reads silently with the class. During the last 10 minutes the teacher may choose to talk with some individuals about what they have read.

CLIPBOARD NOTES
Teacher notes where students choose to read or _____.

READ ALOUD
Umbrella by Taro Yashima or _____
   Reread parts of the book. Discuss the pronouns and what they refer to.

ACTIVITY (Optional)
Decorate a drawing of an umbrella.

BOOK SHARING
Each person tells another person something he or she has read about that day.

Writing

MINI-LESSON
Teacher leads a 5- to 7-minute discussion about possible interpretations of the Writing Topic: Dessert or _____.

COMPOSING
Each student writes (by drawing or developmental spelling) on
■ the lesson's topic
■ a personally chosen topic
■ a topic begun previously

SHARING
Papers are read to a classmate or the teacher, dated, and filed.
   Each student chooses a composition from his or her folder for the teacher to display in the classroom. Students may modify their writing and/or illustration as they choose.

Word Study

CHART DEVELOPMENT
Spelling Review: *v w* and/or
_____
   Students locate words on the room's charts which contain either review letter. On today's chart the teacher writes additional word clusters that contain either letter or _____.

WRITING
On their papers, students write
■ their favorite words from the chart
■ other words/clusters/sentences that would be appropriate for the chart
Papers are dated and filed.

Research

LEAD-IN
Teacher introduces the Project Idea.
Theme: Relative cost of items or _____

Material: Magazines or _____
Reading Focus: Comparison or _____

SEARCH & RECORD
Project Idea: Individually, students cut or tear from magazines pictures or words related to the lesson's theme. They paste or tape the pictures or words on their papers. Encourage discussion of findings with neighbors.
    Teachers check students for association of pictures/words with theme.

SHARING
Students discuss the items found that relate to the day's theme or _____.
    Papers are dated and filed.

Recreational Reading

and

Storytime

For approximately 30 minutes all students read or look at books.

CONVERSATIONS
Check-In: Teacher moves among students, having 2- to 3-minute conversations with as many individuals as possible. If appropriate, discuss cause and effect and/or _____.

CLIPBOARD NOTES
Teacher notes who studies or learns from pictures or _____.

READ ALOUD
Marge's Diner by Gail Gibbons or _____
    Describe the places in the book.

ACTIVITY (Optional)
Make props and act out being in a diner.

BOOK SHARING
Each person tells another person something he or she has read about that day.

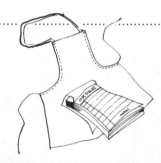

Writing

MINI-LESSON
Teacher leads a 5- to 7-minute discussion about possible interpretations of the Writing Topic: Eating Out or _____.

COMPOSING
Each student writes on
■ the lesson's topic
■ a personally chosen topic
■ a topic begun previously

SHARING
Papers are read to a classmate or the teacher, dated, and filed.

Word Study

CHART DEVELOPMENT
Spelling Emphasis: *L* and/or _____
    On the chart, the teacher writes any word clusters that contain the day's letter or _____.

WRITING
On their papers, students write
■ their favorite words from the chart
■ other words/clusters/sentences that would be appropriate for the chart
Papers are dated and filed.

Lesson 47

Research

LEAD-IN
Teacher introduces the Project Idea.
Theme: Places or _____
Material: Library books or _____
Reading Focus: Description or
_____

SEARCH & RECORD
Project Idea: In teams of 2 or 3, students locate pictures in library books and discuss places in the pictures.

Team members should discuss ideas until all agree before recording what each place is and what it is like. Recording will be with drawing and/or developmental spelling.

SHARING
Two or three teams compare the pictures found and the places represented or
_____.
Papers are dated and filed.

Recreational Reading

For approximately 30 minutes all students read or look at books.

CONVERSATIONS
Check-In: Teacher moves among students, having 2- to 3-minute conversations with as many individuals as possible. If appropriate, discuss sequence and/or _____.

CLIPBOARD NOTES
Teacher notes who studies or learns from pictures or _____.

BOOK SHARING
Each person tells another person something he or she has read about that day.

and Storytime

READ ALOUD
The Mitten by Jan Brett and *The Mitten* by Alvin Tresselt or _____
Compare the two books.

ACTIVITY (Optional)
Make mittens with construction paper and yarn.

Writing

MINI-LESSON
Teacher leads a 5- to 7-minute discussion about possible interpretations of the Writing Topic: A Meal Prepared by the Student or _____.

COMPOSING
Each student writes on
- the lesson's topic
- a personally chosen topic
- a topic begun previously

SHARING
Papers are read to a classmate or the teacher, dated, and filed.

Word Study

CHART DEVELOPMENT
Spelling Emphasis: *M* and/or
_____
On the chart, the teacher writes any word clusters that contain the day's letter or _____.

WRITING
On their papers, students write
- their favorite words from the chart
- other words/clusters/sentences that would be appropriate for the chart
Papers are dated and filed.

Lesson 48

Research

LEAD-IN
Teacher introduces the Project Idea.
Theme: Places or _____
Material: Library books or _____
Reading Focus: Description or _____

SEARCH & RECORD
Project Idea: In teams of 2 or 3, students locate pictures in library books and discuss places in the pictures.

Team members should discuss ideas until all agree before recording what each place is and what it is like. Recording will be with drawing and/or developmental spelling.

SHARING
Two or three teams compare the pictures found and the places represented or _____.

Papers are dated and filed.

Recreational Reading

For approximately 30 minutes all students read or look at books.

CONVERSATIONS
Check-In: Teacher moves among students having 2- to 3-minute conversations with as many individuals as possible. If appropriate, discuss sequence and/or _____.

CLIPBOARD NOTES
Teacher notes who studies or learns from pictures or _____.

BOOK SHARING
Each person tells another person something he or she has read about that day.

and Storytime

READ ALOUD
Poems about food in poetry books such as *The New Kid on the Block* by Jack Prelutsky or _____
Discuss rhyming words in the poetry.

ACTIVITY (Optional)
Make a food collage using pictures and words from magazines.

Writing

MINI-LESSON
Teacher leads a 5- to 7-minute discussion about possible interpretations of the Writing Topic: A Shopping List or _____.

COMPOSING
Each student writes on
■ the lesson's topic
■ a personally chosen topic
■ a topic begun previously

SHARING
Papers are read to a classmate or the teacher, dated, and filed.

Word Study

CHART DEVELOPMENT
Spelling Emphasis: *M* and/or _____

On the chart, the teacher writes any word clusters that contain the day's letter or _____.

WRITING
On their papers, students write
■ their favorite words from the chart
■ other words/clusters/sentences that would be appropriate for the chart
Papers are dated and filed.

Lesson 49

Research

?

LEAD-IN
Teacher introduces the Project Idea.
Letters: *q Q* or _____
Material: Newspapers or _____
Reading Focus: Letter recognition or
_____

SEARCH & RECORD
Project Idea: Individually, students
cut or tear the lesson's letters or words

containing the letters from newspapers.
They paste or tape the letters or words on
their papers. Encourage discussion of
findings with neighbors.
  Teacher checks for letter recognition.

SHARING
Compare letters and words found with
another student or _____.
  Papers are dated and filed.

Recreational Reading

and

Storytime

For approximately 30 minutes all
students read or look at books.

CONVERSATIONS
Check-In: Teacher moves among
students, having 2- to 3-minute
conversations with as many individuals
as possible. If appropriate, discuss
sequence and/or _____.

CLIPBOARD NOTES
Teacher notes who seeks meaning from
books or _____.

BOOK SHARING
Each person tells another person
something he or she has read about that
day.

READ ALOUD
Peanut Butter and Jelly by Nadine B.
Westcott or *Bread and Jam for Frances*
by Russell Hoban or *Bread, Bread, Bread*
by Ann Morris or _____
  Students discuss how the story relates
to their own experiences.

ACTIVITY (Optional)
Make a sandwich out of construction
paper. Glue the sandwich pieces together
only in the center of the sandwich, so you
can show others what is in your
sandwich.

Writing

MINI-LESSON
Teacher leads a 5- to 7-minute discussion
about possible interpretations of the
Writing Topic: A Snack or _____.

COMPOSING
Each student writes on
■ the lesson's topic
■ a personally chosen topic
■ a topic begun previously

SHARING
Papers are read to a classmate or the
teacher, dated, and filed.

Word Study

CHART DEVELOPMENT
Spelling Emphasis: *o* and/or
_____
  On the chart, the teacher writes any
word clusters that contain the day's letter
or _____.

WRITING
On their papers, students write
■ their favorite words from the chart
■ other words/clusters/sentences that
  would be appropriate for the chart
  Papers are dated and filed.

Lesson 50

Research

LEAD-IN
Teacher introduces the Project Idea.
Letters: *r R* or _____
Material: Newspapers or _____
Reading Focus: Letter recognition or _____

SEARCH & RECORD
Project Idea: Individually, students cut or tear the lesson's letters or words containing the letters from newspapers. They paste or tape the letters or words on their papers. Encourage discussion of findings with neighbors.

Teacher checks for letter recognition.

SHARING
Compare letters and words found with another student or _____.

Papers are dated and filed.

Recreational Reading

For approximately 30 minutes all students read or look at books.

CONVERSATIONS
Teacher Reads: For approximately 20 minutes the teacher reads silently with the class. During the last 10 minutes the teacher may choose to talk with some individuals about what they have read.

CLIPBOARD NOTES
Teacher notes who seeks meaning from books or _____.

BOOK SHARING
Each person tells another person something he or she has read about that day.

and Storytime

READ ALOUD
This is the first "Get to Know an Author" Series: Arnold Lobel *Frog and Toad Are Friends* by Arnold Lobel "Lost Buttons" or _____

Discuss opposites. What opposites do you remember in "Lost Buttons"?

ACTIVITY (Optional)
Make a paper shirt or other article of clothing. Glue buttons on the clothes.

Writing

MINI-LESSON
Teacher leads a 5- to 7-minute discussion about possible interpretations of the Writing Topic: A Cartoon or _____.

COMPOSING
Each student writes (by drawing or developmental spelling) on
■ the lesson's topic
■ a personally chosen topic
■ a topic begun previously

SHARING
Papers are read to a classmate or the teacher, dated, and filed.

Word Study

CHART DEVELOPMENT
Spelling Review: *x y* and/or

_____

Students locate words on the room's charts which contain either review letter. On today's chart the teacher writes additional word clusters that contain either letter or _____.

WRITING
On their papers, students write
■ their favorite words from the chart
■ other words/clusters/sentences that would be appropriate for the chart
Papers are dated and filed.

Lesson **51**

Research

LEAD-IN
Teacher introduces the Project Idea.
Letters: *q* or *r* or _____
Material: Math textbooks or nonfiction books or _____
Reading Focus: Words or pictures with certain letters

SEARCH & RECORD
Project Idea: In teams of 2 or 3, students explore math textbooks identifying words or pictures with the letters *q* or *r* or _____.

Team members should discuss their ideas until all agree before recording with drawing and/or developmental spelling.
   Teacher checks students for ideas associated with the text's content.

SHARING
Two or three teams compare the items found that contain the letters *q* or *r* or _____.
   Papers are dated and filed.

Recreational Reading

For approximately 30 minutes all students read or look at books.

CONVERSATIONS
Check-In: Teacher moves among students, having 2- to 3-minute conversations with as many individuals as possible. If appropriate, discuss parts of books and/or _____.

CLIPBOARD NOTES
Teacher notes who seeks meaning from books or _____.

BOOK SHARING
Each person tells another person something he or she has read about that day.

and Storytime

READ ALOUD
Prince Bertram the Bad by Arnold Lobel or _____
   Discuss times you misbehaved and what happened.

ACTIVITY (Optional)
Make a crown out of construction paper.

Writing

MINI-LESSON
Teacher leads a 5- to 7-minute discussion about possible interpretations of the Writing Topic: A Favorite TV Program or _____.

COMPOSING
Each student writes on
■ the lesson's topic
■ a personally chosen topic
■ a topic begun previously

SHARING
Papers are read to a classmate or the teacher, dated, and filed.

Word Study

CHART DEVELOPMENT
Spelling Emphasis: *P* and/or

_____
   On the chart, the teacher writes any word clusters that contain the day's letter or _____.

WRITING
On their papers, students write
■ their favorite words from the chart
■ other words/clusters/sentences that would be appropriate for the chart
Papers are dated and filed.

Lesson 52

Research

LEAD-IN
Teacher introduces the Project Idea.
Theme: Television or _____
Material: Math textbooks or
_____

Reading Focus: Association or
_____

SEARCH & RECORD
Project Idea: In teams of 2 or 3, students explore math textbooks identifying words or pictures they associate with television or _____.

Team members should discuss their ideas until all agree before recording with drawing and/or developmental spelling.
Teacher checks students for association of pictures/words with theme.

SHARING
Students meet in groups of 4 or 5 and discuss the items found that relate to the day's theme or _____.
Papers are dated and filed.

Recreational Reading

For approximately 30 minutes all students read or look at books.

CONVERSATIONS
Check-In: Teacher moves among students, having 2- to 3-minute conversations with as many individuals as possible. If appropriate, discuss parts of books and/or _____.

CLIPBOARD NOTES
Teacher notes who gets up often or
_____.

BOOK SHARING
Each person tells another person something he or she has read about that day.

and Storytime

READ ALOUD
Mouse Tales by Arnold Lobel or
_____

Retell a favorite part of one of the stories.

ACTIVITY (Optional)
With white crayons or white chalk, draw cloud pictures on black or dark blue paper.

Writing

MINI-LESSON
Teacher leads a 5- to 7-minute discussion about possible interpretations of the Writing Topic: A Least Favorite Program or _____.

COMPOSING
Each student writes on
- the lesson's topic
- a personally chosen topic
- a topic begun previously

SHARING
Papers are read to a classmate or the teacher, dated, and filed.

Word Study

CHART DEVELOPMENT
Spelling Emphasis: Q R and/or
_____

On the chart, the teacher writes any word clusters that contain either letter or
_____.

WRITING
On their papers, students write
- their favorite words from the chart
- other words/clusters/sentences that would be appropriate for the chart
Papers are dated and filed.

155

Lesson 53

Research

LEAD-IN
Teacher introduces the Project Idea.
Theme: Television or _____
Material: Magazines or _____
Reading Focus: Association or
_____

SEARCH & RECORD
Project Idea: Individually, students cut or tear from magazines pictures or words related to the lesson's theme. They paste or tape the pictures or words on their papers. Encourage discussion of findings with neighbors.

Teachers check students for association of pictures/words with theme.

SHARING
Students discuss the items found that relate to the day's theme or _____.

Papers are dated and filed.

Recreational Reading

For approximately 30 minutes all students read or look at books.

CONVERSATIONS
Check-In: Teacher moves among students, having 2- to 3-minute conversations with as many individuals as possible. If appropriate, discuss parts of books and/or _____.

CLIPBOARD NOTES
Teacher notes who gets up often or
_____.

BOOK SHARING
Each person tells another person something he or she has read about that day.

and Storytime

READ ALOUD
Uncle Elephant by Arnold Lobel or
_____

Discuss *where* and *when* things happened in the stories.

ACTIVITY (Optional)
Make ring hats. Decorate them with pictures of flowers.

Writing

MINI-LESSON
Teacher leads a 5- to 7-minute discussion about possible interpretations of the Writing Topic: A TV Character or
_____.

COMPOSING
Each student writes on
- the lesson's topic
- a personally chosen topic
- a topic begun previously

SHARING
Papers are read to a classmate or the teacher, dated, and filed.

Word Study

CHART DEVELOPMENT
Spelling Emphasis: *S* and/or _____

On the chart, the teacher writes any word clusters that contain the day's letter or _____.

WRITING
On their papers, students write
- their favorite words from the chart
- other words/clusters/sentences that would be appropriate for the chart
Papers are dated and filed.

Research

LEAD-IN
Teacher introduces the Project Idea.
Theme: Describing words or _____

Material: Magazines or _____
Reading Focus: Description or _____

SEARCH & RECORD
Project Idea: Individually, students cut or tear from magazines pictures or words related to the lesson's theme. They paste or tape them on their papers. Encourage discussion of findings with neighbors.
   Teachers check students for association of pictures/words with theme.

SHARING
Students discuss the items found that relate to the day's theme or _____.
   Papers are dated and filed.

Recreational Reading

For approximately 30 minutes all students read or look at books.

CONVERSATIONS
Check-In: Teacher moves among students, having 2- to 3-minute conversations with as many individuals as possible. If appropriate, discuss description and/or _____.

CLIPBOARD NOTES
Teacher notes who gets up often or _____.

BOOK SHARING
Each person tells another person something he or she has read about that day.

and Storytime

READ ALOUD
Oh! Were They Ever Happy by Peter Spier or _____
   Discuss things you have done to try to please your parents. Talk about the good things the children in the story did.

ACTIVITY (Optional)
Color a picture of a house the way you would like it painted.

Writing

MINI-LESSON
Teacher leads a 5- to 7-minute discussion about possible interpretations of the Writing Topic: News on TV or _____.

COMPOSING
Each student writes (by drawing or developmental spelling) on
■ the lesson's topic
■ a personally chosen topic
■ a topic begun previously

SHARING
Papers are read to a classmate or the teacher, dated, and filed.

Word Study

CHART DEVELOPMENT
Spelling Emphasis: *T* and/or _____
   On the chart, the teacher writes any word clusters that contain the day's letter or _____.

WRITING
On their papers, students write
■ their favorite words from the chart
■ other words/clusters/sentences that would be appropriate for the chart
Papers are dated and filed.

Lesson 55

Research

LEAD-IN
Teacher introduces the Project Idea.
Theme: People or _____
Material: Library books or _____
Reading Focus: Description or
_____

SEARCH & RECORD
Project Idea: In teams of 2 or 3, students locate people in library books and discuss ways the people could be described.

Team members should discuss ideas until all agree before recording the book's descriptions of people with drawing and/or developmental spelling.

SHARING
Two or three teams compare the pictures found and descriptions recorded or
_____

Papers are dated and filed.

Recreational Reading

For approximately 30 minutes all students read or look at books.

CONVERSATIONS
Teacher Reads: For approximately 20 minutes the teacher reads silently with the class. During the last 10 minutes the teacher may choose to talk with some individuals about what they have read.

CLIPBOARD NOTES
Teacher notes who rereads the same book or _____.

BOOK SHARING
Each person tells another person something he or she has read about that day.

and Storytime

READ ALOUD
Any book about weather such as *Flash, Crash, Rumble, and Roll* by Franklyn Branley or *Hurricane Watch* by Franklyn Branley or *Rain & Hail* by Franklyn Branley or *The Storm Book* by Charlotte Zolotow or _____
Discuss ways to describe weather.

ACTIVITY (Optional)
Make a weather vane. Attach it to a stick or hang it with a string from the ceiling of the classroom.

Writing

MINI-LESSON
Teacher leads a 5- to 7-minute discussion about possible interpretations of the Writing Topic: Weather on TV or
_____ .

COMPOSING
Each student writes on
- the lesson's topic
- a personally chosen topic
- a topic begun previously

SHARING
Papers are read to a classmate or the teacher, dated, and filed.

Word Study

CHART DEVELOPMENT
Spelling Review: *z a* and/or _____

Students locate words on the room's charts which contain either review letter. On today's chart the teacher writes additional word clusters that contain either letter or _____ .

WRITING
On their papers, students write
- their favorite words from the chart
- other words/clusters/sentences that would be appropriate for the chart
Papers are dated and filed.

Research

LEAD-IN
Teacher introduces the Project Idea.
Theme: Places or _____
Material: Library books or _____
Reading Focus: Description or
_____

SEARCH & RECORD
Project Idea: In teams of 2 or 3,
students locate places in library books
and discuss how they could be described.

Team members should discuss ideas
until all agree before recording the book's
descriptions of places with drawing and/or
developmental spelling.

SHARING
Two or three teams compare the pictures
found and their descriptions or
_____.

Papers are dated and filed.

Recreational Reading

and

Storytime

For approximately 30 minutes all
students read or look at books.

CONVERSATIONS
Check-In: Teacher moves among
students, having 2- to 3-minute
conversations with as many individuals
as possible. If appropriate, discuss
description and/or _____.

CLIPBOARD NOTES
Teacher notes who rereads the same book
or _____.

BOOK SHARING
Each person tells another person
something he or she has read about that
day.

READ ALOUD
The Little House by Virginia Lee Burton
or _____
  Discuss changes you have seen in
places and people.

ACTIVITY (Optional)
Make construction-paper houses.

Writing

MINI-LESSON
Teacher leads a 5- to 7-minute discussion
about possible interpretations of the
Writing Topic: Sports on TV or
_____.

COMPOSING
Each student writes on
■ the lesson's topic
■ a personally chosen topic
■ a topic begun previously

SHARING
Papers are read to a classmate or the
teacher, dated, and filed.

Word Study

CHART DEVELOPMENT
Spelling Emphasis: *U V* and/or
_____

  On the chart, the teacher writes any
word clusters that contain either letter or
_____.

WRITING
On their papers, students write
■ their favorite words from the chart
■ other words/clusters/sentences that
  would be appropriate for the chart
Papers are dated and filed.

Lesson 57

Research

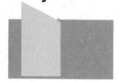

LEAD-IN
Teacher introduces the Project Idea.
Letters: *s S* or _____
Material: Newspapers or _____
Reading Focus: Letter recognition or _____

SEARCH & RECORD
Project Idea: Individually, students cut or tear the lesson's letters or words containing the letters from newspapers. They paste or tape the letters or words on their papers. Encourage discussion of findings with neighbors.
  Teacher checks for letter recognition.

SHARING
Compare letters and words found with another student or _____.
  Papers are dated and filed.

Recreational Reading and Storytime

For approximately 30 minutes all students read or look at books.

CONVERSATIONS
Check-In: Teacher moves among students, having 2- to 3-minute conversations with as many individuals as possible. If appropriate, discuss description and/or _____.

CLIPBOARD NOTES
Teacher notes who re-reads the same book or _____.

READ ALOUD
Owl Moon by Jane Yolen or _____
  Discuss the times things happened in the book.

ACTIVITY (Optional)
Using brads, make an owl whose wings spread.

BOOK SHARING
Each person tells another person something he or she has read about that day.

Writing

MINI-LESSON
Teacher leads a 5- to 7-minute discussion about possible interpretations of the Writing Topic: A Place to Walk To or _____.

COMPOSING
Each student writes on
- the lesson's topic
- a personally chosen topic
- a topic begun previously

SHARING
Papers are read to a classmate or the teacher, dated, and filed.

Word Study

CHART DEVELOPMENT
Spelling Emphasis: *W X* and/or

_____
  On the chart, the teacher writes any word clusters that contain either letter or _____.

WRITING
On their papers, students write
- their favorite words from the chart
- other words/clusters/sentences that would be appropriate for the chart
Papers are dated and filed.

Lesson 58

Research

LEAD-IN
Teacher introduces the Project Idea.
Letters: *t T* or _____
Material: Newspapers or _____
Reading Focus: Letter recognition or
_____

SEARCH & RECORD
Project Idea: Individually, students cut or tear the lesson's letters or words

containing the letters from newspapers. They paste or tape the letters or words on their papers. Encourage discussion of findings with neighbors.
   Teacher checks for letter recognition.

SHARING
Compare letters and words found with another student or _____.
   Papers are dated and filed.

Recreational Reading

For approximately 30 minutes all students read or look at books.

CONVERSATIONS
Check-In: Teacher moves among students, having 2- to 3-minute conversations with as many individuals as possible. If appropriate, discuss real and make-believe and/or _____.

CLIPBOARD NOTES
Teacher notes who daydreams or watches the teacher or _____.

BOOK SHARING
Each person tells another person something he or she has read about that day.

and Storytime

READ ALOUD
Airport by Byron Barton and *Flying* by Donald Crews or _____
   Compare the two books.

ACTIVITY (Optional)
Make a paper airplane. Fly it outside.

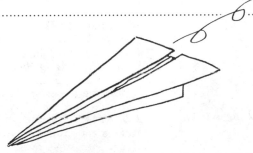

Writing

MINI-LESSON
Teacher leads a 5- to 7-minute discussion about possible interpretations of the Writing Topic: A Place to Go in a Car or _____.

COMPOSING
Each student writes (by drawing or developmental spelling) on
- the lesson's topic
- a personally chosen topic
- a topic begun previously

SHARING
Papers are read to a classmate or the teacher, dated, and filed.

Word Study

CHART DEVELOPMENT
Spelling Emphasis: *Y Z* and/or
_____
   On the chart, the teacher writes any word clusters that contain either letter or _____.

WRITING
On their papers, students write
- their favorite words from the chart
- other words/clusters/sentences that would be appropriate for the chart
Papers are dated and filed.

Lesson 59

Research

LEAD-IN
Teacher introduces the Project Idea.
Letters: *s* or *t* or _____
Material: Science textbooks or nonfiction books or _____
Reading Focus: Words or pictures with certain letters

SEARCH & RECORD
Project Idea: In teams of 2 or 3, students explore science textbooks identifying words or pictures with the letters *s* or *t* or _____.

Team members should discuss their ideas until all agree before recording with drawing and/or developmental spelling.
Teacher checks students for ideas associated with the text's content.

SHARING
Two or three teams compare the items found that contain the letters *s* or *t* or _____.
Papers are dated and filed.

Recreational Reading

For approximately 30 minutes all students read or look at books.

CONVERSATIONS
Check-In: Teacher moves among students, having 2- to 3-minute conversations with as many individuals as possible. If appropriate, discuss real and make-believe and/or _____.

CLIPBOARD NOTES
Teacher notes who daydreams or watches the teacher or _____.

BOOK SHARING
Each person tells another person something he or she has read about that day.

and Storytime

READ ALOUD
The Magic Schoolbus Visits the Waterworks by Joanna Cole or *The Great White Man-Eating Shark* by Margaret Mahy or _____.
Describe places in the story.

ACTIVITY (Optional)
Make a construction paper or tagboard diver's face mask or shark fins.

Writing

MINI-LESSON
Teacher leads a 5- to 7-minute discussion about possible interpretations of the Writing Topic: A Ride in a Bus, Plane, or Train or _____.

COMPOSING
Each student writes on
■ the lesson's topic
■ a personally chosen topic
■ a topic begun previously

SHARING
Papers are read to a classmate or the teacher, dated, and filed.

Word Study

CHART DEVELOPMENT
Spelling Emphasis: *br* and/or _____

On the chart, the teacher writes any word clusters that contain the day's letters or _____.

WRITING
On their papers, students write
■ their favorite words from the chart
■ other words/clusters/sentences that would be appropriate for the chart
Papers are dated and filed.

162

Lesson 60

Research

LEAD-IN
Teacher introduces the Project Idea.
Theme: Water or _____
Material: Science textbooks or
_____
Reading Focus: Association or
_____

SEARCH & RECORD
Project Idea: In teams of 2 or 3,
students explore science textbooks
identifying words or pictures which they
can associate with water or _____.

Team members should discuss their
ideas until all agree before recording with
drawing and/or developmental spelling.
Teachers check students for association
of pictures/words with theme.

SHARING
Students meet in groups of 4 or 5 and
discuss the items found that relate to the
day's theme or _____.
Papers are dated and filed.

Recreational Reading

For approximately 30 minutes all
students read or look at books.

CONVERSATIONS
In-Depth: Teacher holds 7- to 10-
minute conversations with 3 or 4 students
(individually) discussing prediction,
inference, comparison, and/or _____.

CLIPBOARD NOTES
Teacher notes who daydreams or watches
the teacher or _____.

BOOK SHARING
Each person tells another person
something he or she has read about that
day.

and Storytime

READ ALOUD
Swimmy by Leo Lionni or _____
Discuss problem solving. What was the
problem? How did Swimmy solve it?

ACTIVITY (Optional)
Make a tissue-paper picture.

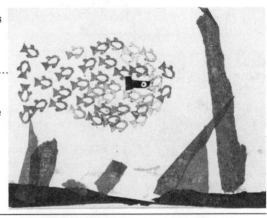

Writing

MINI-LESSON
Teacher leads a 5- to 7-minute discussion
about possible interpretations of the
Writing Topic: Something You Do in
Water or _____.

COMPOSING
Each student writes on
- the lesson's topic
- a personally chosen topic
- a topic begun previously

SHARING
Papers are read to a classmate or the
teacher, dated, and filed.
Each student chooses a composition
from his or her folder for the teacher to
display in the classroom. Students may
modify their writing and/or illustration as
they choose.

Word Study

CHART DEVELOPMENT
Spelling Review: *e i* and/or

_____
Students locate words on the room's
charts that contain either review letter.
On today's chart the teacher writes
additional word clusters that contain
either letter or _____.

WRITING
On their papers, students write
- their favorite words from the chart
- other words/clusters/sentences that
would be appropriate for the chart
Papers are dated and filed.

Lesson 61

Research

LEAD-IN
Teacher introduces the Project Idea.
Theme: Water or _____
Material: Magazines or _____
Reading Focus: Association or

_____

SEARCH & RECORD
Project Idea: Individually, students cut or tear from magazines pictures or words related to the lesson's theme. They paste or tape the pictures or words on their papers. Encourage discussion of findings with neighbors.
   Teacher checks students for association of pictures/words with theme.

SHARING
Students discuss the items found that relate to the day's theme or _____.
   Papers are dated and filed.

Recreational Reading

For approximately 30 minutes all students read or look at books.

CONVERSATIONS
In-Depth: Teacher holds 7- to 10-minute conversations with 3 or 4 students (individually) discussing prediction, inference, comparison, and/or _____.

CLIPBOARD NOTES
Teacher notes who reads with whom or

_____.

BOOK SHARING
Each person tells another person something he or she has read about that day.

and Storytime

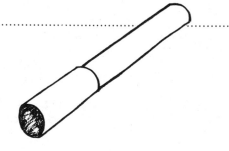

READ ALOUD
Little Tim and the Brave Sea Captain by Edward Ardizonne or _____
   Discuss the sequence of events.

ACTIVITY (Optional)
Make a telescope using paper-towel rolls.

Writing

MINI-LESSON
Teacher leads a 5- to 7-minute discussion about possible interpretations of the Writing Topic: Swimming or _____.

COMPOSING
Each student writes on
- the lesson's topic
- a personally chosen topic
- a topic begun previously

SHARING
Papers are read to a classmate or the teacher, dated, and filed.

Word Study

CHART DEVELOPMENT
Spelling Emphasis: *bl* and/or

   On the chart, the teacher writes any word clusters that contain the day's letters or _____.

WRITING
On their papers, students write
- their favorite words from the chart
- other words/clusters/sentences that would be appropriate for the chart
Papers are dated and filed.

Lesson 62

Research

LEAD-IN
Teacher introduces the Project Idea.
Theme: Words for actions or
_____

Material: Magazines or _____
Reading Focus: Verbs or _____

SEARCH & RECORD
Project Idea: Individually, students cut or tear from magazines pictures or words related to the lesson's theme. They paste or tape the pictures or words on their papers. Encourage discussion of findings with neighbors.
     Teacher checks students for association of pictures/words with theme.

SHARING
Students discuss the items found that relate to the day's theme or _____.
     Papers are dated and filed.

Recreational Reading and Storytime

For approximately 30 minutes all students read or look at books.

CONVERSATIONS
In-Depth: Teacher holds 7- to 10-minute conversations with 3 or 4 students (individually) discussing prediction, inference, comparison, and/or _____.

CLIPBOARD NOTES
Teacher notes who reads with whom or _____

BOOK SHARING
Each person tells another person something he or she has read about that day.

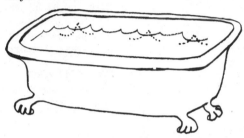

READ ALOUD
King Bidgood's in the Bathtub by Don and Audrey Wood or _____
     On a second reading encourage students to join in the refrain, "Oh, what shall we do?"
     Discuss how the story relates to students' experiences (playing in the tub, toys for the tub, effects of staying in the tub too long, etc.)

ACTIVITY (Optional)
Enlarge and reproduce the bathtub illustration. Students work with partners to think of new situations for King Bidgood. Each pair decorates the tub for the occasion.

Writing

MINI-LESSON
Teacher leads a 5- to 7-minute discussion about possible interpretations of the Writing Topic: Tub of Shower Baths or _____.

COMPOSING
Each student writes (by drawing or developmental spelling) on
■ the lesson's topic
■ a personally chosen topic
■ a topic begun previously

SHARING
Papers are read to a classmate or the teacher, dated, and filed.

Word Study

CHART DEVELOPMENT
Spelling Emphasis: *cr* and/or _____
     On the chart, the teacher writes any word clusters that contain the day's letters or _____.

WRITING
On their papers, students write
■ their favorite words from the chart
■ other words/clusters/sentences that would be appropriate for the chart
     Papers are dated and filed.

Lesson 63

Research

LEAD-IN
Teacher introduces the Project Idea.
Theme: Words ending in -ing or
_____

Material: Library books or _____
Reading Focus: Word endings or
_____

SEARCH & RECORD
Project Idea: In teams of 2 or 3, students locate words and pictures in library books and discuss words ending in -ing.

Team members should discuss and record words ending in *ing* found in library books. Recording will be with drawing and/or developmental spelling.

SHARING
Two or three teams compare the words and pictures that end in -ing or
_____.
   Papers are dated and filed.

Recreational Reading

For approximately 30 minutes all students read or look at books.

CONVERSATIONS
In-Depth: Teacher holds 7- to 10-minute conversations with 3 or 4 students (individually) discussing prediction, inference, comparison, and/or _____.

CLIPBOARD NOTES
Teacher notes who reads with whom or
_____.

BOOK SHARING
Each person tells another person something he or she has read about that day.

and Storytime

READ ALOUD
The Tub People by Pam Conrad or *Time to Get Out of the Bath, Shirley* by John Burningham or _____
   Discuss real and make-believe.

ACTIVITY (Optional)
Make a class book about real or imagined adventures in the tub.

Writing

MINI-LESSON
Teacher leads a 5- to 7-minute discussion about possible interpretations of the Writing Topic: Toys in the Tub or Pool or
_____.

COMPOSING
Each student writes on
■ the lesson's topic
■ a personally chosen topic
■ a topic begun previously

SHARING
Papers are read to a classmate or the teacher, dated, and filed.

Word Study

CHART DEVELOPMENT
Spelling Emphasis: *dr* and/or
_____

   On the chart, the teacher writes any word clusters that contain the day's letters or _____.

WRITING
On their papers, students write
■ their favorite words from the chart
■ other words/clusters/sentences that would be appropriate for the chart
   Papers are dated and filed.

Lesson 64

Research

LEAD-IN
Teacher introduces the Project Idea.
Theme: Words ending in -ed or
_____

Material: Library books or _____
Reading Focus: Word endings or
_____

SEARCH & RECORD
Project Idea: In teams of 2 or 3, students locate words and pictures in library books and discuss words ending in -ed.

Team members should discuss and record words ending in ed found in library books. Recording will be with drawing and/or developmental spelling.

SHARING
Two or three teams compare the words and pictures that end in -ed or
_____.

Papers are dated and filed.

Recreational Reading

For approximately 30 minutes all students read or look at books.

CONVERSATIONS
In-Depth: Teacher holds 7- to 10-minute conversations with 3 or 4 students (individually) discussing prediction, inference, comparison, and/or _____.

CLIPBOARD NOTES
Teacher notes which students read audibly or _____.

BOOK SHARING
Each person tells another person something he or she has read about that day.

and Storytime

READ ALOUD
Fire! Fire! by Gail Gibbons or *The Fire Cat* by Esther Averill or _____
Discuss *where* and *when* things happened in the story.

ACTIVITY (Optional)
Make fire hats from red construction paper. Cut a large oval of red paper. Cut out a smaller oval in the big oval that is

just big enough to fit your head. Attach a firefighter's badge to the front with tabs.

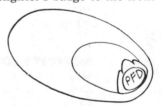

Writing

MINI-LESSON
Teacher leads a 5- to 7-minute discussion about possible interpretations of the Writing Topic: Firefighters or _____.

COMPOSING
Each student writes on
■ the lesson's topic
■ a personally chosen topic
■ a topic begun previously

SHARING
Papers are read to a classmate or the teacher, dated, and filed.

Word Study

CHART DEVELOPMENT
Spelling Emphasis: *fl* and/or
_____

On the chart, the teacher writes any word clusters that contain the day's letters or _____.

WRITING
On their papers, students write
■ their favorite words from the chart
■ other words/clusters/sentences that would be appropriate for the chart
Papers are dated and filed.

Lesson 65

Research

LEAD-IN
Teacher introduces the Project Idea.
Letters: *v V* or _____
Material: Newspapers or _____
Reading Focus: Letter recognition or _____

SEARCH & RECORD
Project Idea: Individually, students cut or tear the lesson's letters or words containing the letters from newspapers. They paste or tape the letters or words on their papers. Encourage discussion of findings with neighbors.
    Teacher checks for letter recognition.

SHARING
Compare letters and words found with another student or _____.
    Papers are dated and filed.

Recreational Reading

For approximately 30 minutes all students read or look at books.

CONVERSATIONS
In-Depth: Teacher holds 7- to 10-minute conversations with 3 or 4 students (individually) discussing prediction, inference, comparison, and/or _____.

CLIPBOARD NOTES
Teacher notes which students read audibly or _____.

BOOK SHARING
Each person tells another person something he or she has read about that day.

and Storytime

READ ALOUD
Make Way for Ducklings by Robert McCloskey or _____
    Discuss the beginning, middle, and end of the story.

ACTIVITY (Optional)
Make a duck out of modeling clay or crumpled aluminum foil.

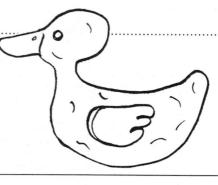

Writing

MINI-LESSON
Teacher leads a 5- to 7-minute discussion about possible interpretations of the Writing Topic: Police or _____.

COMPOSING
Each student writes on
■ the lesson's topic
■ a personally chosen topic
■ a topic begun previously

SHARING
Papers are read to a classmate or the teacher, dated, and filed.

Word Study

CHART DEVELOPMENT
Spelling Review: *o u* and/or

_____
    Students locate words on the room's charts which contain either review letter. On today's chart the teacher writes additional word clusters that contain either letter or _____.

WRITING
On their papers, students write
■ their favorite words from the chart
■ other words/clusters/sentences that would be appropriate for the chart
Papers are dated and filed.

Lesson **66**

Research

LEAD-IN
Teacher introduces the Project Idea.
Letters: *w W* or _____
Material: Newspapers or _____
Reading Focus: Letter recognition or
_____

SEARCH & RECORD
Project Idea: Individually, students cut or tear the lesson's letters or words containing the letters from newspapers. They paste or tape the letters or words on their papers. Encourage discussion of findings with neighbors.
  Teacher checks for letter recognition.

SHARING
Compare letters and words found with another student or _____.
  Papers are dated and filed.

Recreational Reading

For approximately 30 minutes all students read or look at books.

CONVERSATIONS
In-Depth: Teacher holds 7- to 10-minute conversations with 3 or 4 students (individually) discussing prediction, inference, comparison, and/or _____.

CLIPBOARD NOTES
Teacher notes which students read audibly or _____.

BOOK SHARING
Each person tells another person something he or she has read about that day.

and Storytime

READ ALOUD
Imogene's Antlers by David Small or *Mother, Mother, I Feel Sick . . .* by Remy Charlip or _____
  Discuss *who* was in the story and *what* happened.

ACTIVITY (Optional)
Make some doctor's equipment, such as a headband reflector or a stethoscope. Act out the story.

Writing

MINI-LESSON
Teacher leads a 5- to 7-minute discussion about possible interpretations of the Writing Topic: Doctors and Nurses or
_____

COMPOSING
Each student writes on
■ the lesson's topic
■ a personally chosen topic
■ a topic begun previously

SHARING
Papers are read to a classmate or the teacher, dated, and filed.

Word Study

CHART DEVELOPMENT
Spelling Emphasis: *fr* and/or
_____
  On the chart, the teacher writes any word clusters that contain the day's letters or _____.

WRITING
On their papers, students write
■ their favorite words from the chart
■ other words/clusters/sentences that would be appropriate for the chart
Papers are dated and filed.

Lesson 67

Research

LEAD-IN
Teacher introduces the Project Idea.
Letters: *v* or *w* or _____
Material: Social studies textbooks or nonfiction books or _____
Reading Focus: Words or pictures with certain letters

SEARCH & RECORD
Project Idea: In teams of 2 or 3, students explore social studies textbooks identifying words or pictures with the letters *v* or *w* or _____.

Team members should discuss their ideas until all agree before recording with drawing and/or developmental spelling.
Teacher checks students for ideas associated with the text's content.

SHARING
Two or three teams compare the items found that contain the letters *v* or *w* or _____.
Papers are dated and filed.

Recreational Reading and Storytime

For approximately 30 minutes all students read or look at books.

CONVERSATIONS
Check-In: Teacher moves among students, having 2- to 3-minute conversations with as many individuals as possible. If appropriate, discuss real and make-believe and/or _____.

CLIPBOARD NOTES
Teacher notes who talks spontaneously about books or _____.

READ ALOUD
Arthur's Loose Tooth by Lillian Hoban or *Dr. DeSoto* by William Stieg or
_____
Reread parts of the story. Discuss the pronouns and whom they refer to.

ACTIVITY (Optional)
Make a large mouth out of tag or heavy paper. Draw in all but one tooth. Draw a

BOOK SHARING
Each person tells another person something he or she has read about that day.

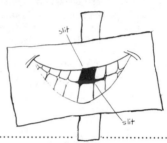

tooth on a strip of paper. Cut slits above and below where the tooth belongs. Make a tachistoscope using the strip. Pull the strip and the tooth comes out, leaving a big space.

Writing

MINI-LESSON
Teacher leads a 5- to 7-minute discussion about possible interpretations of the Writing Topic: Dentists or _____.

COMPOSING
Each student writes (by drawing or developmental spelling) on
- the lesson's topic
- a personally chosen topic
- a topic begun previously

SHARING
Papers are read to a classmate or the teacher, dated, and filed.

Word Study

CHART DEVELOPMENT
Spelling Emphasis: *gr* and/or
_____
On the chart, the teacher writes any word clusters that contain the day's letters or _____.

WRITING
On their papers, students write
- their favorite words from the chart
- other words/clusters/sentences that would be appropriate for the chart
Papers are dated and filed.

Research

LEAD-IN
Teacher introduces the Project Idea.
Theme: What people are doing or _____

Material: Social studies textbooks or _____

Reading Focus: Interpretation or _____

SEARCH & RECORD
Project Idea: In teams of 2 or 3, students explore social studies textbooks identifying words or pictures they

associate with what people are doing or _____.

Team members should discuss their ideas until all agree before recording with drawing and/or developmental spelling.

Teachers check students for association of pictures/words with theme.

SHARING
Students meet in groups of 4 or 5 and discuss the items found that relate to the day's theme or _____.

Papers are dated and filed.

Recreational Reading

and

Storytime

For approximately 30 minutes all students read or look at books.

CONVERSATIONS
Check-In: Teacher moves among students, having 2- to 3-minute conversations with as many individuals as possible. If appropriate, discuss how events in the book relate to the student's experience and/or _____.

CLIPBOARD NOTES
Teacher notes who talks spontaneously about books or _____.

BOOK SHARING
Each person tells another person something he or she has read about that day.

READ ALOUD
Machines at Work by Byron Barton or *Machines* by Anne and Harlow Rockwell or *Building a House* by Byron Barton or _____

Discuss classifications or types of machines.

ACTIVITY (Optional)
Make a class book about real or imaginary machines.

Writing

MINI-LESSON
Teacher leads a 5- to 7-minute discussion about possible interpretations of the Writing Topic: Builders of Houses, Roads, Furniture, etc. or _____.

COMPOSING
Each student writes on
- the lesson's topic
- a personally chosen topic
- a topic begun previously

SHARING
Papers are read to a classmate or the teacher, dated, and filed.

Word Study

CHART DEVELOPMENT
Spelling Emphasis: *pr* and/or _____

On the chart, the teacher writes any word clusters that contain the day's letters or _____.

WRITING
On their papers, students write
- their favorite words from the chart
- other words/clusters/sentences that would be appropriate for the chart

Papers are dated and filed.

Lesson 69

Research

LEAD-IN
Teacher introduces the Project Idea.
Theme: What people are doing or _____

Material: Magazines or _____
Reading Focus: Interpretation or _____

SEARCH & RECORD
Project Idea: Individually, students cut or tear from magazines pictures or words related to the lesson's theme. They paste or tape the pictures or words on their papers. Encourage discussion of findings with neighbors.
   Teachers check students for association of pictures/words with theme.

SHARING
Students discuss the items found that relate to the day's theme or _____.
   Papers are dated and filed.

Recreational Reading

For approximately 30 minutes all students read or look at books.

CONVERSATIONS
Check-In: Teacher moves among students, having 2- to 3-minute conversations with as many individuals as possible. If appropriate, discuss how events in the book relate to student's experience and/or _____.

CLIPBOARD NOTES
Teacher notes who talks spontaneously about books or _____.

BOOK SHARING
Each person tells another person something he or she has read about that day.

and

Storytime

READ ALOUD
Katy and the Big Snow by Virginia Lee Burton or _____
   Discuss *why* things happened in the story.

ACTIVITY (Optional)
Draw a picture of a snow scene. Coat the snow with glue and attach cotton.

Writing

MINI-LESSON
Teacher leads a 5- to 7-minute discussion about possible interpretations of the Writing Topic: Other Jobs or _____.

COMPOSING
Each student writes on
- the lesson's topic
- a personally chosen topic
- a topic begun previously

SHARING
Papers are read to a classmate or the teacher, dated, and filed.

Word Study

CHART DEVELOPMENT
Spelling Emphasis: *sl* and/or _____

   On the chart, the teacher writes any word clusters that contain the day's letters or _____.

WRITING
On their papers, students write
- their favorite words from the chart
- other words/clusters/sentences that would be appropriate for the chart
Papers are dated and filed.

Research

LEAD-IN
Teacher introduces the Project Idea.
Theme: Transportation or _____
Material: Magazines or _____
Reading Focus: Classification or
_____

SEARCH & RECORD
Project Idea: Individually, students cut or tear from magazines pictures or words related to the lesson's theme. They paste or tape the pictures or words on their papers. Encourage discussion of findings with neighbors.
    Teachers check students for association of pictures/words with theme.

SHARING
Students discuss the items found that relate to the day's theme or _____.
    Papers are dated and filed.

Recreational Reading

For approximately 30 minutes all students read or look at books.

CONVERSATIONS
Teacher Reads: For approximately 20 minutes the teacher reads silently with the class. During the last 10 minutes the teacher may choose to talk with some individuals about what they have read.

CLIPBOARD NOTES
Teacher notes who recommends books to others or _____.

BOOK SHARING
Each person tells another person something he or she has read about that day.

and Storytime

READ ALOUD
Any of the transportation books by Byron Barton *Airplanes* or *Boats* or *Trains* or *Trucks* or *Wheels* or _____
    Discuss similarities and differences in different transportation vehicles.

ACTIVITY (Optional)
Turn blocks of wood into transportation vehicles by adding other pieces of wood, attaching paper adornments, or painting features on the block.

Writing

MINI-LESSON
Teacher leads a 5- to 7-minute discussion about possible interpretations of the Writing Topic: A Story About a Worker or _____.

COMPOSING
Each student writes on
■ the lesson's topic
■ a personally chosen topic
■ a topic begun previously

SHARING
Papers are read to a classmate or the teacher, dated, and filed.

Word Study

CHART DEVELOPMENT
Spelling Emphasis: *sk* and/or
_____
    On the chart, the teacher writes any word clusters that contain the day's letters or _____.

WRITING
On their papers, students write
■ their favorite words from the chart
■ other words/clusters/sentences that would be appropriate for the chart
Papers are dated and filed.

173

Lesson 71

Research

LEAD-IN
Teacher introduces the Project Idea.
Theme: Transportation or _____
Material: Library books or _____
Reading Focus: Classification or
_____

SEARCH & RECORD
Project Idea: In teams of 2 or 3, students locate pictures in library books and discuss modes of transportation in the pictures.

Team members should discuss ideas until all agree before recording modes of transportation found in the book. Recording will be with drawing and/or developmental spelling.

SHARING
Two or three teams compare the pictures found about transportation or _____.
   Papers are dated and filed.

Recreational Reading

For approximately 30 minutes all students read or look at books.

CONVERSATIONS
Check-In: Teacher moves among students, having 2- to 3-minute conversations with as many individuals as possible. If appropriate, discuss how events in the book relate to student's experience and/or _____.

CLIPBOARD NOTES
Teacher notes who recommends books to others or _____.

BOOK SHARING
Each person tells another person something he or she has read about that day.

and Storytime

READ ALOUD
Round Trip by Ann Jonas or _____
   Discuss the places they saw on their trip.

ACTIVITY (Optional)
Make a picture in black and white only. Start with either black or white paper. Draw with a crayon of the opposite color or cut out pieces of the other color paper

and assemble the pieces to make your picture.

Writing

MINI-LESSON
Teacher leads a 5- to 7-minute discussion about possible interpretations of the Writing Topic: What You Want to Be or
_____.

COMPOSING
Each student writes on
■ the lesson's topic
■ a personally chosen topic
■ a topic begun previously

SHARING
Papers are read to a classmate or the teacher, dated, and filed.

Word Study

CHART DEVELOPMENT
Spelling Emphasis: *sc* and/or

_____
   On the chart, the teacher writes any word clusters that contain the day's letters or _____.

WRITING
On their papers, students write
■ their favorite words from the chart
■ other words/clusters/sentences that would be appropriate for the chart
   Papers are dated and filed.

Research

LEAD-IN
Teacher introduces the Project Idea.
Theme: Transportation or _____
Material: Library books or _____
Reading Focus: Classification or
_____

SEARCH & RECORD
Project Idea: In teams of 2 or 3, students locate pictures in library books and discuss modes of transportation found in the pictures.

Team members should discuss ideas until all agree before recording modes of transportation found in the book. Recording will be with drawing and/or developmental spelling.

SHARING
Two or three teams compare the pictures found and the methods of transportation or _____.
Papers are dated and filed.

Recreational Reading

and Storytime

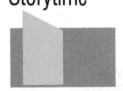

For approximately 30 minutes all students read or look at books.

CONVERSATIONS
Check-In: Teacher moves among students, having 2- to 3-minute conversations with as many individuals as possible. If appropriate, discuss humor and what makes something funny and/or _____.

CLIPBOARD NOTES
Teacher notes who recommends books to others or _____.

BOOK SHARING
Each person tells another person something he or she has read about that day.

READ ALOUD
I Want to Be an Astronaut by Byron Barton or _____
Discuss space travel and what the students want to be.

ACTIVITY (Optional)
Make a space helmet with white construction paper. Cut a hole for the face

mask from a cylinder that is large enough to fit over student's head.

Writing

MINI-LESSON
Teacher leads a 5- to 7-minute discussion about possible interpretations of the Writing Topic: Space Travel or _____.

COMPOSING
Each student writes on
■ the lesson's topic
■ a personally chosen topic
■ a topic begun previously

SHARING
Papers are read to a classmate or the teacher, dated, and filed.

Word Study

CHART DEVELOPMENT
Spelling Emphasis: *sp* and/or
_____
On the chart, the teacher writes any word clusters that contain the day's letters or _____.

WRITING
On their papers, students write
■ their favorite words from the chart
■ other words/clusters/sentences that would be appropriate for the chart
Papers are dated and filed.

Lesson 73

Research

LEAD-IN
Teacher introduces the Project Idea.
Letters: *x X z Z* or _____
Material: Newspapers or _____
Reading Focus: Letter recognition or
_____

SEARCH & RECORD
Project Idea: Individually, students cut or tear the lesson's letters or words containing the letters from newspapers. They paste or tape the letters or words on their papers. Encourage discussion of findings with neighbors.
   Teacher checks for letter recognition.

SHARING
Compare letters and words found with another student or _____.
   Papers are dated and filed.

Recreational Reading

For approximately 30 minutes all students read or look at books.

CONVERSATIONS
Check-In: Teacher moves among students, having 2- to 3-minute conversations with as many individuals as possible. If appropriate, discuss humor and what makes something funny and/or _____.

CLIPBOARD NOTES
Teacher notes who seeks recommendations from others or _____.

BOOK SHARING
Each person tells another person something he or she has read about that day.

and Storytime

READ ALOUD
Shooting Stars by Franklyn Branley or
_____
   Discuss *who* is in the story and *what* happened.

ACTIVITY (Optional)
Draw a picture on dark blue or black paper. Add foil stars.

Writing

MINI-LESSON
Teacher leads a 5- to 7-minute discussion about possible interpretations of the Writing Topic: Planets and/or Stars or
_____.

COMPOSING
Each student writes on
■ the lesson's topic
■ a personally chosen topic
■ a topic begun previously

SHARING
Papers are read to a classmate or the teacher, dated, and filed.

Word Study

CHART DEVELOPMENT
Spelling Emphasis: *st* and/or
_____
   On the chart, the teacher writes any word clusters that contain the day's letters or _____.

WRITING
On their papers, students write
■ their favorite words from the chart
■ other words/clusters/sentences that would be appropriate for the chart
Papers are dated and filed.

Lesson **74**

Research

LEAD-IN
Teacher introduces the Project Idea.
Letters: *y Y* or _____
Material: Newspapers or _____
Reading Focus: Letter recognition or
_____

SEARCH & RECORD
Project Idea: Individually, students
cut or tear the lesson's letters or words
containing the letters from newspapers.
They paste or tape the letters or words on
their papers. Encourage discussion of
findings with neighbors.
   Teacher checks for letter recognition.

SHARING
Compare letters and words found with
another student or _____.
   Papers are dated and filed.

Recreational Reading

For approximately 30 minutes all
students read or look at books.

CONVERSATIONS
Check-In: Teacher moves among
students, having 2- to 3-minute
conversations with as many individuals
as possible. If appropriate, discuss humor
and what makes something funny and/or
_____.

CLIPBOARD NOTES
Teacher notes who seeks
recommendations from others or
_____.

BOOK SHARING
Each person tells another person
something he or she has read about that
day.

and Storytime

READ ALOUD
Happy Birthday Moon by Frank Asch or
Moongame by Frank Asch or _____
   Discuss *why* things happened.

ACTIVITY (Optional)
Make a birthday card for the moon.

Writing

MINI-LESSON
Teacher leads a 5- to 7-minute discussion
about possible interpretations of the
Writing Topic: Moon or _____.

COMPOSING
Each student writes on
■ the lesson's topic
■ a personally chosen topic
■ a topic begun previously

SHARING
Papers are read to a classmate or the
teacher, dated, and filed.

Word Study

CHART DEVELOPMENT
Spelling Emphasis: *sh* and/or
_____
   On the chart, the teacher writes any
word clusters that contain the day's
letters or _____.

WRITING
On their papers, students write
■ their favorite words from the chart
■ other words/clusters/sentences that
   would be appropriate for the chart
Papers are dated and filed.

Lesson **75**

Research

LEAD-IN
Teacher introduces the Project Idea.
Letters: *x y* or *z* or _____
Material: Math textbooks or nonfiction books or _____
Reading Focus: Words or pictures with certain letters

SEARCH & RECORD
Project Idea: In teams of 2 or 3, students explore math textbooks identifying words or pictures with the letters *x, y,* or *z* or _____.

Team members should discuss their ideas until all agree before recording with drawing and/or developmental spelling.
Teacher checks students for ideas associated with the text's content.

SHARING
Two or three teams compare the items found that contain the letters *x, y,* or *z* or _____.
Papers are dated and filed.

Recreational Reading

For approximately 30 minutes all students read or look at books.

CONVERSATIONS
Teacher Reads: For approximately 20 minutes the teacher reads silently with the class. During the last 10 minutes the teacher may choose to talk with some individuals about what they have read.

CLIPBOARD NOTES
Teacher notes who seeks recommendations from others or _____.

BOOK SHARING
Each person tells another person something he or she has read about that day.

and Storytime

READ ALOUD
Moon Man by Tomi Ungerer or _____
Discuss the beginning, middle, and end of the story.

ACTIVITY (Optional)
Make a Moon Man mask.

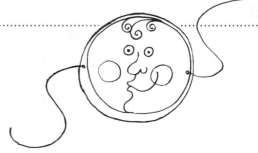

Writing

MINI-LESSON
Teacher leads a 5- to 7-minute discussion about possible interpretations of the Writing Topic: An Adventure in Space or _____.

COMPOSING
Each student writes (by drawing or developmental spelling) on
■ the lesson's topic
■ a personally chosen topic
■ a topic begun previously

SHARING
Papers are read to a classmate or the teacher, dated, and filed.
Each student chooses a composition from his or her folder for the teacher to display in the classroom. Students may modify their writing and/or illustration as they choose.

Word Study

CHART DEVELOPMENT
Spelling Emphasis: *ch* and/or _____
On the chart, the teacher writes any word clusters that contain the day's letters or _____.

WRITING
On their papers, students write
■ their favorite words from the chart
■ other words/clusters/sentences that would be appropriate for the chart
Papers are dated and filed.

Lesson 76

Research

LEAD-IN
Teacher introduces the Project Idea.
Theme: Opposites or _____
Material: Math textbooks or
_____

Reading Focus: Opposites or
_____

SEARCH & RECORD
Project Idea: In teams of 2 or 3, students explore math textbooks identifying words or pictures which they think are opposites or _____.

Team members should discuss their ideas until all agree before recording with drawing and/or developmental spelling.
Teachers check students for association of pictures/words with theme.

SHARING
Students meet in groups of 4 or 5 and discuss the items found that relate to the day's theme or _____.
Papers are dated and filed.

Recreational Reading

For approximately 30 minutes all students read or look at books.

CONVERSATIONS
Check-In: Teacher moves among students, having 2- to 3-minute conversations with as many individuals as possible. If appropriate, discuss words that tell *when* and/or _____.

CLIPBOARD NOTES
Teacher notes titles or types of books chosen or _____.

BOOK SHARING
Each person tells another person something he or she has read about that day.

and Storytime

READ ALOUD
Fortunately by Remy Charlip or
_____
Discuss opposites and the pattern of the book.

ACTIVITY (Optional)
Make a class book in the pattern of the read-aloud book.

Writing

MINI-LESSON
Teacher leads a 5- to 7-minute discussion about possible interpretations of the Writing Topic: Things That Are Opposites or _____.

COMPOSING
Each student writes on
- the lesson's topic
- a personally chosen topic
- a topic begun previously

SHARING
Papers are read to a classmate or the teacher, dated, and filed.

Word Study

CHART DEVELOPMENT
Spelling Emphasis: *ai* and/or
_____
On the chart, the teacher writes any word clusters that contain the day's letters or _____.

WRITING
On their papers, students write
- their favorite words from the chart
- other words/clusters/sentences that would be appropriate for the chart
Papers are dated and filed.

179

Lesson 77

Research

LEAD-IN
Teacher introduces the Project Idea.
Theme: Opposites or _____
Material: Magazines or _____
Reading Focus: Opposites or _____

SEARCH & RECORD
Project Idea: Individually, students cut or tear from magazines pictures or words related to the lesson's theme. They paste or tape the pictures or words on their papers. Encourage discussion of findings with neighbors.
 Teachers check students for association of pictures/words with theme.

SHARING
Students discuss the items found that relate to the day's theme or _____.
 Papers are dated and filed.

Recreational Reading and Storytime

For approximately 30 minutes all students read or look at books.

CONVERSATIONS
Check-In: Teacher moves among students, having 2- to 3-minute conversations with as many individuals as possible. If appropriate, discuss words that tell *when* and/or _____.

CLIPBOARD NOTES
Teacher notes titles or types of books chosen or _____.

BOOK SHARING
Each person tells another person something he or she has read about that day.

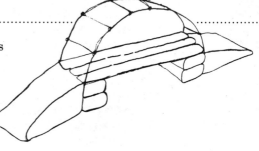

READ ALOUD
Madeline's Rescue by Ludwig Bemelmans or _____
 Discuss cause and effect. *What* happened and *why*?

ACTIVITY (Optional)
Make a bridge with clay and either toothpicks, popsicle sticks, or pipe cleaners.

Writing

MINI-LESSON
Teacher leads a 5- to 7-minute discussion about possible interpretations of the Writing Topic: Things That Have Similar Characteristics or _____.

COMPOSING
Each student writes on
■ the lesson's topic
■ a personally chosen topic
■ a topic begun previously

SHARING
Papers are read to a classmate or the teacher, dated, and filed.

Word Study

CHART DEVELOPMENT
Spelling Emphasis: *qu* and/or _____
 On the chart, the teacher writes any word clusters that contain the day's letters or _____.

WRITING
On their papers, students write
■ their favorite words from the chart
■ other words/clusters/sentences that would be appropriate for the chart
Papers are dated and filed.

Lesson 78

Research

LEAD-IN
Teacher introduces the Project Idea.
Theme: Characters or _____
Material: Magazines or _____
Reading Focus: Description or
_____

SEARCH & RECORD
Project Idea: Individually, students cut or tear from magazines pictures or words related to the lesson's theme. They paste or tape the pictures or words on their papers. Encourage discussion of findings with neighbors.
   Teachers check students for association of pictures/words with theme.

SHARING
Students discuss the items found that relate to the day's theme or _____.
   Papers are dated and filed.

Recreational Reading and Storytime

For approximately 30 minutes all students read or look at books.

CONVERSATIONS
Check-In: Teacher moves among students, having 2- to 3-minute conversations with as many individuals as possible. If appropriate, discuss words that tell *when* and/or _____.

CLIPBOARD NOTES
Teacher notes titles or types of books chosen or _____.

BOOK SHARING
Each person tells another person something he or she has read about that day.

READ ALOUD
Rotten Ralph by Jack Gantos or
_____
   Discuss which parts of the story are real and make-believe.

ACTIVITY (Optional)
Make a Rotten Ralph. Attach his arms and legs with brads, so that they move.

Writing

MINI-LESSON
Teacher leads a 5- to 7-minute discussion about possible interpretations of the Writing Topic: Draw and Label a Character in a Book or _____.

COMPOSING
Each student writes on
■ the lesson's topic
■ a personally chosen topic
■ a topic begun previously

SHARING
Papers are read to a classmate or the teacher, dated, and filed.

Word Study

CHART DEVELOPMENT
Spelling Emphasis: *wh* and/or
_____
   On the chart, the teacher writes any word clusters that contain the day's letters or _____.

WRITING
On their papers, students write
■ their favorite words from the chart
■ other words/clusters/sentences that would be appropriate for the chart
Papers are dated and filed.

Lesson 79

Research

LEAD-IN
Teacher introduces the Project Idea.
Theme: Characters or _____
Material: Library books or _____
Reading Focus: Description or
_____

SEARCH & RECORD
Project Idea: In teams of 2 or 3, students locate pictures in library books and discuss the characters in the pictures.

Team members should discuss ideas until all agree before recording the book's descriptions of the characters with drawing and/or developmental spelling.

SHARING
Two or three teams compare the pictures found and descriptions of the characters or _____.
Papers are dated and filed.

Recreational Reading and Storytime

For approximately 30 minutes all students read or look at books.

CONVERSATIONS
Check-In: Teacher moves among students, having 2- to 3-minute conversations with as many individuals as possible. If appropriate, discuss words that tell *where* and/or _____.

CLIPBOARD NOTES
Teacher notes who seems excited about books and reading or _____.

READ ALOUD
Any book written and illustrated by Helme Heine especially *The Most Wonderful Egg in the World* or
_____
Discuss *where* and *when* things happened in the story.

ACTIVITY (Optional)
Paint any picture using watercolors.

BOOK SHARING
Each person tells another person something he or she has read about that day.

Writing

MINI-LESSON
Teacher leads a 5- to 7-minute discussion about possible interpretations of the Writing Topic: Describe a Book Character or _____.

COMPOSING
Each student writes on
■ the lesson's topic
■ a personally chosen topic
■ a topic begun previously

SHARING
Papers are read to a classmate or the teacher, dated, and filed.

Word Study

CHART DEVELOPMENT
Spelling Emphasis: *ph* and/or
_____
On the chart, the teacher writes any word clusters that contain the day's letters or _____.

WRITING
On their papers, students write
■ their favorite words from the chart
■ other words/clusters/sentences that would be appropriate for the chart
Papers are dated and filed.

Research

LEAD-IN
Teacher introduces the Project Idea.
Theme: Characters or _____
Material: Library books or _____
Reading Focus: Description or
_____

SEARCH & RECORD
Project Idea: In teams of 2 or 3, students locate pictures in library books and discuss the characters in the pictures.

Team members should discuss ideas until all agree before recording descriptions of the characters in the book. Recording will be with drawing and/or developmental spelling.

SHARING
Two or three teams compare the pictures found and descriptions of the characters or _____.
Papers are dated and filed.

Recreational Reading

For approximately 30 minutes all students read or look at books.

CONVERSATIONS
Teacher Reads: For approximately 20 minutes the teacher reads silently with the class. During the last 10 minutes the teacher may choose to talk with some individuals about what they have read.

CLIPBOARD NOTES
Teacher notes who seems excited about books and reading or _____.

BOOK SHARING
Each person tells another person something he or she has read about that day.

your bugging ME!

and Storytime

READ ALOUD
Amelia Bedelia by Peggy Parish or
_____
Discuss figurative language.

ACTIVITY (Optional)
Make a class book of literal interpretations of idioms, such as dusting the furniture. They may or may not be from the story.

Writing

MINI-LESSON
Teacher leads a 5- to 7-minute discussion about possible interpretations of the Writing Topic: Write About an Incident Involving a Book Character or
_____.

COMPOSING
Each student writes on
■ the lesson's topic
■ a personally chosen topic
■ a topic begun previously

SHARING
Papers are read to a classmate or the teacher, dated, and filed.

Word Study

CHART DEVELOPMENT
Spelling Emphasis: *wr* and/or
_____
On the chart, the teacher writes any word clusters that contain the day's letters or _____.

WRITING
On their papers, students write
■ their favorite words from the chart
■ other words/clusters/sentences that would be appropriate for the chart
Papers are dated and filed.

Lesson 81

Research

LEAD-IN
Teacher introduces the Project Idea.
Theme: Details in pictures or

_____

Material: Newspapers or _____
Reading Focus: Details or

_____

SEARCH & RECORD
Project Idea: In groups of 3 or 4, students label details in a picture from

the newspaper. Teams paste or tape the picture on a piece of paper, write labels for details, and draw lines from the parts of the picture to the label. Recording will be with developmental spelling.

SHARING
Discuss pictures and labels with another team or _____.
  Papers are dated and filed.

Recreational Reading

For approximately 30 minutes all students read or look at books.

CONVERSATIONS
In-Depth: Teacher holds 7- to 10-minute conversations with 3 or 4 students (individually) discussing cause and effect, sequence, and/or _____.

CLIPBOARD NOTES
Teacher notes who seems excited about books and reading or _____.

BOOK SHARING
Each person tells another person something he or she has read about that day.

and Storytime

READ ALOUD
Any book about quilts such as *The Quilt Story* by Tony Johnston or *Sam Johnson and the Blue Ribbon Quilt* by Lisa Ernst or _____
  Reread parts of the story and discuss whom the pronouns refer to.

ACTIVITY (Optional)
Make a class quilt using construction paper.

Writing

MINI-LESSON
Teacher leads a 5- to 7-minute discussion about possible interpretations of the Writing Topic: Favorite Toys or

_____

COMPOSING
Each student writes on
- the lesson's topic
- a personally chosen topic
- a topic begun previously

SHARING
Papers are read to a classmate or the teacher, dated, and filed.

Word Study

CHART DEVELOPMENT
Spelling Emphasis: *nd* and/or

_____

  On the chart, the teacher writes sentences containing the day's letters or _____.

WRITING
On their papers, students write
- their favorite words from the chart
- other words/clusters/sentences that would be appropriate for the chart
Papers are dated and filed.

Lesson 82

Research

LEAD-IN
Teacher introduces the Project Idea.
Theme: Details in pictures or _____

Material: Newspapers or _____
Reading Focus: Details or _____

SEARCH & RECORD
Project Idea: In groups of 3 or 4, students label details in a picture from the newspaper. Teams paste or tape the picture on a piece of paper, write labels for details, and draw lines from the parts of the picture to the label. Recording will be with developmental spelling.

SHARING
Discuss pictures and labels with another team or _____.
　Papers are dated and filed.

Recreational Reading

For approximately 30 minutes all students read or look at books.

CONVERSATIONS
In-Depth: Teacher holds 7- to 10-minute conversations with 3 or 4 students (individually) discussing cause and effect, sequence, and/or _____.

CLIPBOARD NOTES
Teacher notes who stays seated and who walks around or _____.

BOOK SHARING
Each person tells another person something he or she has read about that day.

and Storytime

READ ALOUD
Alexander and the Wind-Up Mouse by Leo Lionni or _____
　Compare the characters in the story.

ACTIVITY (Optional)
Make wind-up keys that the students can wear. Parade around like wind-up toys.

Writing

MINI-LESSON
Teacher leads a 5- to 7-minute discussion about possible interpretations of the Writing Topic: Mechanical Toys or _____

COMPOSING
Each student writes on
- the lesson's topic
- a personally chosen topic
- a topic begun previously

SHARING
Papers are read to a classmate or the teacher, dated, and filed.

Word Study

CHART DEVELOPMENT
Spelling Emphasis: *mp* and/or _____

　On the chart, the teacher writes sentences containing the day's letters or _____.

WRITING
On their papers, students write
- their favorite words from the chart
- other words/clusters/sentences that would be appropriate for the chart
Papers are dated and filed.

Lesson 83

Research

LEAD-IN
Teacher introduces the Project Idea.
Theme: Noisy things or _____
Material: Science textbooks or nonfiction books or _____
Reading Focus: Classification

SEARCH & RECORD
Project Idea: In teams of 2 or 3, students explore science textbooks identifying noisy things or _____.

Team members should discuss their ideas until all agree before recording with drawing and/or developmental spelling.
   Teacher checks students for ideas associated with the text's content.

SHARING
Two or three teams compare the items found that are noisy. Discuss which is noisiest or _____.
   Papers are dated and filed.

Recreational Reading

For approximately 30 minutes all students read or look at books.

CONVERSATIONS
In-Depth: Teacher holds 7- to 10-minute conversations with 3 or 4 students (individually) discussing cause and effect, sequence, and/or _____.

CLIPBOARD NOTES
Teacher notes who stays seated and who walks around or _____.

BOOK SHARING
Each person tells another person something he or she has read about that day.

and Storytime

READ ALOUD
Too Much Noise by Ann McGovern *It's Too Noisy!* by Joanna Cole or *Noisy Nora* by Rosemary Wells or *The Quiet Mother and the Noisy Boy* by Charlotte Zolotow or _____
   Discuss causes and effects. What happened and why?

ACTIVITY (Optional)
Make props and act out the story.

Writing

MINI-LESSON
Teacher leads a 5- to 7-minute discussion about possible interpretations of the Writing Topic: Noisy Toys or _____.

COMPOSING
Each student writes (by drawing or developmental spelling) on
■ the lesson's topic
■ a personally chosen topic
■ a topic begun previously

SHARING
Papers are read to a classmate or the teacher, dated, and filed.

Word Study

CHART DEVELOPMENT
Spelling Emphasis: *ng* and/or
_____
   On the chart, the teacher writes sentences containing the day's letters or _____.

WRITING
On their papers, students write
■ their favorite words from the chart
■ other words/clusters/sentences that would be appropriate for the chart
   Papers are dated and filed.

Research

LEAD-IN
Teacher introduces the Project Idea.
Theme: Quiet things or _____
Material: Science textbooks or
_____

Reading Focus: Classification or
_____

SEARCH & RECORD
Project Idea: In teams of 2 or 3, students explore science textbooks identifying quiet things or _____.

Team members should discuss their ideas until all agree before recording with drawing and/or developmental spelling.
  Teachers check students for association of pictures/words with theme.

SHARING
Students meet in groups of 4 or 5 and discuss the items found that relate to the day's theme or _____.
  Papers are dated and filed.

Recreational Reading

For approximately 30 minutes all students read or look at books.

CONVERSATIONS
In-Depth: Teacher holds 7- to 10-minute conversations with 3 or 4 students (individually) discussing cause and effect, sequence, and/or _____.

CLIPBOARD NOTES
Teacher notes who stays seated and who walks around or _____.

BOOK SHARING
Each person tells another person something he or she has read about that day.

and Storytime

READ ALOUD
The City Noisy Book by Margaret Wise Brown or *The Indoor Noisy Book* by Margaret Wise Brown or _____
  Discuss *who* is in the story and *what* happened.

ACTIVITY (Optional)
Make a collage of noisy things using magazine pictures.

Writing

MINI-LESSON
Teacher leads a 5- to 7-minute discussion about possible interpretations of the Writing Topic: Quiet Toys or _____

COMPOSING
Each student writes on
■ the lesson's topic
■ a personally chosen topic
■ a topic begun previously

SHARING
Papers are read to a classmate or the teacher, dated, and filed.

Word Study

CHART DEVELOPMENT
Spelling Emphasis: *sw* and/or
_____
  On the chart, the teacher writes sentences containing the day's letters or _____.

WRITING
On their papers, students write
■ their favorite words from the chart
■ other words/clusters/sentences that would be appropriate for the chart
Papers are dated and filed.

Lesson 85

Research

LEAD-IN
Teacher introduces the Project Idea.
Theme: Noisy and quiet things or _____

Material: Magazines or _____
Reading Focus: Classification, opposites, or _____

SEARCH & RECORD
Project Idea: Individually, students cut or tear from magazines pictures or words related to the lesson's theme. They paste or tape the pictures or words on their papers. Encourage discussion of findings with neighbors.
  Teachers check students for association of pictures/words with theme.

SHARING
Students discuss the items found that relate to the day's theme or _____.
  Papers are dated and filed.

Recreational Reading and Storytime

For approximately 30 minutes all students read or look at books.

CONVERSATIONS
In-Depth: Teacher holds 7- to 10-minute conversations with 3 or 4 students (individually) discussing cause and effect, sequence, and/or _____.

CLIPBOARD NOTES
Teacher notes where students choose to read or _____.

BOOK SHARING
Each person tells another person something he or she has read about that day.

READ ALOUD
Ben's Trumpet by Rachel Isadora or _____
  Discuss the sequence of events.

ACTIVITY (Optional)
Cut out a musical instrument from construction paper or tagboard. Pretend to play it.

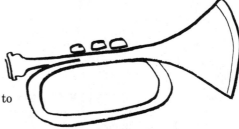

Writing

MINI-LESSON
Teacher leads a 5- to 7-minute discussion about possible interpretations of the Writing Topic: A Toy That Broke or Wouldn't Work or _____.

COMPOSING
Each student writes on
■ the lesson's topic
■ a personally chosen topic
■ a topic begun previously

SHARING
Papers are read to a classmate or the teacher, dated, and filed.

Word Study

CHART DEVELOPMENT
Spelling Emphasis: _cl_ and/or
_____
  On the chart, the teacher writes sentences containing the day's letters or _____.

WRITING
On their papers, students write
■ their favorite words from the chart
■ other words/clusters/sentences that would be appropriate for the chart
  Papers are dated and filed.

Lesson 86

Research

LEAD-IN
Teacher introduces the Project Idea.
Theme: Houses or _____
Material: Magazines or _____
Reading Focus: Association or
_____

SEARCH & RECORD
Project Idea: Individually, students cut or tear from magazines pictures or words related to the lesson's theme. They

paste or tape the pictures or words on their papers. Encourage discussion of findings with neighbors.
 Teachers check students for association of pictures/words with theme.

SHARING
Students discuss the items found that relate to the day's theme or _____.
 Papers are dated and filed.

Recreational Reading

For approximately 30 minutes all students read or look at books.

CONVERSATIONS
In-Depth: Teacher holds 7- to 10-minute conversations with 3 or 4 students (individually) discussing cause and effect, sequence, and/or _____.

CLIPBOARD NOTES
Teacher notes where students choose to read or _____.

BOOK SHARING
Each person tells another person something he or she has read about that day.

and Storytime

READ ALOUD
Ira Sleeps Over by Bernard Waber or *The Red Wool Blanket* by Bob Graham or
_____
 Relate the story to the students' experiences.

ACTIVITY (Optional)
Make a class book about sleeping over or favorite toys.

Writing

MINI-LESSON
Teacher leads a 5- to 7-minute discussion about possible interpretations of the Writing Topic: Security Objects or
_____.

COMPOSING
Each student writes (by drawing or developmental spelling) on
 ■ the lesson's topic
 ■ a personally chosen topic
 ■ a topic begun previously

SHARING
Papers are read to a classmate or the teacher, dated, and filed.

Word Study

CHART DEVELOPMENT
Spelling Emphasis: *er* and/or
_____
 On the chart, the teacher writes sentences containing the day's letters or
_____.

WRITING
On their papers, students write
 ■ their favorite words from the chart
 ■ other words/clusters/sentences that would be appropriate for the chart
Papers are dated and filed.

189

Lesson 87

Research

?

LEAD-IN
Teacher introduces the Project Idea.
Theme: Houses or _____
Material: Library books or _____
Reading Focus: Association or
_____

SEARCH & RECORD
Project Idea: In teams of 2 or 3, students locate pictures in library books and discuss houses in the pictures.

Team members should discuss ideas until all agree before recording information about houses in the book. Recording will be with drawing and/or developmental spelling.

SHARING
Two or three teams compare the pictures found and how they relate to houses or _____.
Papers are dated and filed.

Recreational Reading

For approximately 30 minutes all students read or look at books.

CONVERSATIONS
In-Depth: Teacher holds 7- to 10-minute conversations with 3 or 4 students (individually) discussing cause and effect, sequence, and/or _____.

CLIPBOARD NOTES
Teacher notes where students choose to read or _____.

BOOK SHARING
Each person tells another person something he or she has read about that day.

A mouth is a House for teeth

and Storytime

READ ALOUD
A House Is a House For Me by Mary Ann Hoberman *The Big Orange Splot* by Manus Pinkwater or _____
Discuss the places in the story.

ACTIVITY (Optional)
Design a house for something or design your dream house.

Writing

MINI-LESSON
Teacher leads a 5- to 7-minute discussion about possible interpretations of the Writing Topic: Sleeping Over at a Friend's House or _____.

COMPOSING
Each student writes on
■ the lesson's topic
■ a personally chosen topic
■ a topic begun previously

SHARING
Papers are read to a classmate or the teacher, dated, and filed.

Word Study

CHART DEVELOPMENT
Spelling Emphasis: *ir* and/or

_____
On the chart, the teacher writes sentences containing the day's letters or _____.

WRITING
On their papers, students write
■ their favorite words from the chart
■ other words/clusters/sentences that would be appropriate for the chart
Papers are dated and filed.

Research

LEAD-IN
Teacher introduces the Project Idea.
Theme: Houses or _____
Material: Library books or _____
Reading Focus: Description or
_____

SEARCH & RECORD
Project Idea: In teams of 2 or 3, students locate pictures of houses in library books and discuss descriptions of houses in the pictures.

Team members should discuss ideas until all agree before recording descriptions of houses in the book. Recording will be with drawing and/or developmental spelling.

SHARING
Two or three teams compare the pictures found and descriptions or _____.
Papers are dated and filed.

Recreational Reading

and

Storytime

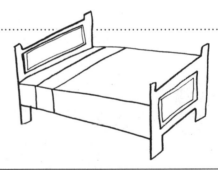

For approximately 30 minutes all students read or look at books.

CONVERSATIONS
Check-In: Teacher moves among students, having 2- to 3-minute conversations with as many individuals as possible. If appropriate, discuss words that tell *where* and/or _____.

CLIPBOARD NOTES
Teacher notes who studies or learns from pictures or _____.

READ ALOUD
The Napping House by Don and Audrey Wood or *The Bed Book* by Sylvia Plath or
_____
Discuss the pattern in the book.

ACTIVITY (Optional)
Make a bed out of construction paper. Make or draw what is in the bed.

BOOK SHARING
Each person tells another person something he or she has read about that day.

Writing

MINI-LESSON
Teacher leads a 5- to 7-minute discussion about possible interpretations of the Writing Topic: Places to Sleep; Types of Beds or _____.

COMPOSING
Each student writes on
- the lesson's topic
- a personally chosen topic
- a topic begun previously

SHARING
Papers are read to a classmate or the teacher, dated, and filed.

Word Study

CHART DEVELOPMENT
Spelling Emphasis: *ur* and/or
_____
On the chart, the teacher writes sentences containing the day's letters or
_____.

WRITING
On their papers, students write
- their favorite words from the chart
- other words/clusters/sentences that would be appropriate for the chart
Papers are dated and filed.

Lesson 89

Research

LEAD-IN
Teacher introduces the Project Idea.
Theme: Big/little or _____
Material: Catalogs or _____
Reading Focus: Functional reading
or _____

SEARCH & RECORD
Project Idea: Individually, students cut or tear from catalogs pictures or words of big and little items. They paste or tape the pictures or words on their papers. Encourage discussion of findings with neighbors.
    Teachers check students for association of pictures/words with theme.

SHARING
Students discuss the items found that relate to the day's theme or _____.
    Papers are dated and filed.

Recreational Reading

For approximately 30 minutes all students read or look at books.

CONVERSATIONS
Check-In: Teacher moves among students having 2- to 3-minute conversations with as many individuals as possible. If appropriate, discuss words that tell *when* and/or _____.

CLIPBOARD NOTES
Teacher notes who studies or learns from pictures or _____.

BOOK SHARING
Each person tells another person something he or she has read about that day.

and Storytime

READ ALOUD
Night in the Country by Cynthia Rylant or *Wait Till the Moon Is Full* by Margaret Wise Brown or *Nighttime Animals* by Joanna Cole or _____
    Discuss *why* things happened in the book.

ACTIVITY (Optional)
Draw a picture on black construction paper with crayons.

Writing

MINI-LESSON
Teacher leads a 5- to 7-minute discussion about possible interpretations of the Writing Topic: Unusual Places to Sleep or _____.

COMPOSING
Each student writes on
■ the lesson's topic
■ a personally chosen topic
■ a topic begun previously

SHARING
Papers are read to a classmate or the teacher, dated, and filed.

Word Study

CHART DEVELOPMENT
Spelling Emphasis: *or* and/or
_____
    On the chart, the teacher writes sentences containing the day's letters or _____.

WRITING
On their papers, students write
■ their favorite words from the chart
■ other words/clusters/sentences that would be appropriate for the chart
Papers are dated and filed.

Research

LEAD-IN
Teacher introduces the Project Idea.
Theme: Expensive/inexpensive or
_____

Material: Catalogs or _____
Reading Focus: Functional reading
or _____

SEARCH & RECORD
Project Idea: Individually, students
cut or tear from catalogs pictures or
words of expensive and inexpensive items.
They paste or tape the pictures or words
on their papers. Encourage discussion of
findings with neighbors.
  Teachers check students for association
of pictures/words with theme.

SHARING
Students discuss the items found that
relate to the day's theme or _____.
  Papers are dated and filed.

Recreational Reading

and Storytime

For approximately 30 minutes all
students read or look at books.

CONVERSATIONS
Teacher Reads: For approximately
20 minutes the teacher reads silently
with the class. During the last 10
minutes the teacher may choose to talk
with some individuals about what they
have read.

CLIPBOARD NOTES
Teacher notes who studies or learns from
pictures or _____.

BOOK SHARING
Each person tells another person
something he or she has read about that
day.

READ ALOUD
One Fine Day by Nonny Hogrogian or
Flossie and the Fox by Patricia McKissack
or _____
  Describe the characters.

ACTIVITY (Optional)
Make a large profile of a fox (the head
only). Cut slits to the left and right of his
eye. Draw an eyeball on a strip of paper.

Insert the strip throught the slits and
make the fox's eyes move back and forth.

Writing

MINI-LESSON
Teacher leads a 5- to 7-minute discussion
about possible interpretations of the
Writing Topic: Places Animals Sleep or
_____.

COMPOSING
Each student writes (by drawing or
developmental spelling) on
■ the lesson's topic
■ a personally chosen topic
■ a topic begun previously

SHARING
Papers are read to a classmate or the
teacher, dated, and filed.
  Each student chooses a composition
from his or her folder for the teacher to
display in the classroom. Students may
modify their writing and/or illustration as
they choose.

Word Study

CHART DEVELOPMENT
Spelling Emphasis: *dy* and/or

_____
  On the chart, the teacher writes
sentences containing the day's letters or
_____.

WRITING
On their papers, students write
■ their favorite words from the chart
■ other words/clusters/sentences that
  would be appropriate for the chart
  Papers are dated and filed.

Lesson **91**

Research

LEAD-IN
Teacher introduces the Project Idea.
Theme: Places or _____
Material: Newspapers or _____
Reading Focus: Reading
advertisements or _____

SEARCH & RECORD
Project Idea: Individually, students
cut or tear the lesson's letters or words
containing the letters from newspapers.
They paste or tape the letters or words on
their papers. Encourage discussion of
findings with neighbors.
  Teacher checks for letter recognition.

SHARING
Compare letters and words found with
another student or _____.
  Papers are dated and filed.

Recreational Reading

CONVERSATIONS
Check-In: Teacher moves among
students, having 2- to 3-minute
conversations with as many individuals
as possible. If appropriate, discuss
classification and/or _____.

CLIPBOARD NOTES
Teacher notes who is searching for
meaning or _____.

BOOK SHARING
Each person tells another person
something he or she has read about that
day.

and Storytime

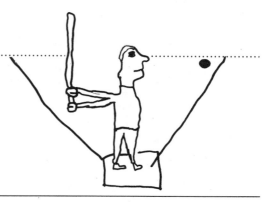

READ ALOUD
The Relatives Came by Cynthia Rylant or
_____
  Discuss the beginning, middle, and end
of the story.

ACTIVITY (Optional)
Make a class book about relatives. Each
student contributes one page.

Writing

MINI-LESSON
Teacher leads a 5- to 7-minute discussion
about possible interpretations of the
Writing Topic: A Time You Slept
Somewhere Other Than Your Bed or
_____.

COMPOSING
Each student writes on
■ the lesson's topic
■ a personally chosen topic
■ a topic begun previously

SHARING
Papers are read to a classmate or the
teacher, dated, and filed.

Word Study

CHART DEVELOPMENT
Spelling Emphasis: *oo* or 2 syllables
and/or _____
  On the chart, the teacher writes
sentences containing the day's letters or
number of syllables or _____.

WRITING
On their papers, students write
■ their favorite words from the chart
■ other words/clusters/sentences that
  would be appropriate for the chart
  Papers are dated and filed.

Lesson 92

Research

LEAD-IN
Teacher introduces the Project Idea.
Theme: Places or _____
Material: Newspapers or _____
Reading Focus: Words that tell where or _____

SEARCH & RECORD
Project Idea: Individually, students cut or tear the lesson's letters or words containing the letters from newspapers. They paste or tape the letters or words on their papers. Encourage discussion of findings with neighbors.
Teacher checks for letter recognition.

SHARING
Compare letters and words found with another student or _____.
Papers are dated and filed.

Recreational Reading

CONVERSATIONS
Check-In: Teacher moves among students, having 2- to 3-minute conversations with as many individuals as possible. If appropriate, discuss classification and/or _____.

CLIPBOARD NOTES
Teacher notes who is searching for meaning or _____.

BOOK SHARING
Each person tells another person something he or she has read about that day.

and Storytime

READ ALOUD
Time of Wonder by Robert McCloskey or _____
Discuss *where* and *when* things happened in the story.

ACTIVITY (Optional)
Make a crayon resist picture. Paint over a crayon drawing with a light grey wash of watercolor, making the scene look foggy.

Writing

MINI-LESSON
Teacher leads a 5- to 7-minute discussion about possible interpretations of the Writing Topic: A Vacation or _____.

COMPOSING
Each student writes on
■ the lesson's topic
■ a personally chosen topic
■ a topic begun previously

SHARING
Papers are read to a classmate or the teacher, dated, and filed.

Word Study

CHART DEVELOPMENT
Spelling Emphasis: *ew* or 2 syllables and/or _____
On the chart, the teacher writes sentences containing the day's letters or number of syllables or _____.

WRITING
On their papers, students write
■ their favorite words from the chart
■ other words/clusters/sentences that would be appropriate for the chart
Papers are dated and filed.

195

Lesson 93

Research

LEAD-IN
Teacher introduces the Project Idea.
Theme: Places or _____
Material: Social studies textbooks or _____

Reading Focus: Words that tell where or _____

SEARCH & RECORD
Project Idea: In teams of 2 or 3, students explore social studies textbooks identifying words or pictures which they can associate with places or _____.

Team members should discuss their ideas until all agree before recording with drawing and/or developmental spelling.
Teachers check students for association of pictures/words with theme.

SHARING
Students meet in groups of 4 or 5 and discuss the items found that relate to the day's theme or _____.
Papers are dated and filed.

Recreational Reading

CONVERSATIONS
Check-In: Teacher moves among students, having 2- to 3-minute conversations with as many individuals as possible. If appropriate, discuss classification and/or _____.

CLIPBOARD NOTES
On a clipboard teacher notes who is searching for meaning or _____.

BOOK SHARING
Each person tells another person something he or she has read about that day.

and Storytime

READ ALOUD
Guess Who My Favorite Person Is? by Byrd Baylor or _____
Relate the story to the students' experiences. Discuss favorite things.

ACTIVITY (Optional)
Play the game with a small group of students or the whole class. Students may

also draw a picture of a favorite thing to take home.

Writing

MINI-LESSON
Teacher leads a 5- to 7-minute discussion about possible interpretations of the Writing Topic: A Favorite Place of Yours or _____.

COMPOSING
Each student writes on
- the lesson's topic
- a personally chosen topic
- a topic begun previously

SHARING
Papers are read to a classmate or the teacher, dated, and filed.

Word Study

CHART DEVELOPMENT
Spelling Emphasis: *ss* or 2 syllables and/or _____
On the chart, the teacher writes sentences containing the day's letters or number of syllables or _____.

WRITING
On their papers, students write
- their favorite words from the chart
- other words/clusters/sentences that would be appropriate for the chart
Papers are dated and filed.

Lesson 94

Research

LEAD-IN
Teacher introduces the Project Idea.
Theme: Rural/urban/suburban areas or _____

Material: Social studies textbooks or _____

Reading Focus: Places or _____

SEARCH & RECORD
Project Idea: In teams of 2 or 3, students explore social studies textbooks identifying words or pictures which they associate with rural/urban/suburban areas or _____.

Team members should discuss their ideas until all agree before recording with drawing and/or developmental spelling.

Teachers check students for association of pictures/words with theme.

SHARING
Students meet in groups of 4 or 5 and discuss the items found that relate to the day's theme or _____.

Papers are dated and filed.

Recreational Reading

CONVERSATIONS
Check-In: Teacher moves among students, having 2- to 3-minute conversations with as many individuals as possible. If appropriate, discuss pronouns and their referents and/or _____.

CLIPBOARD NOTES
Teacher notes who is constantly seeking help decoding words or _____.

BOOK SHARING
Each person tells another person something he or she has read about that day.

and Storytime

READ ALOUD
Harold and the Purple Crayon by Crockett Johnson or *Blackboard Bear* by Martha Alexander or _____.
   Discuss *what* and *who* were in the story.

ACTIVITY (Optional)
Draw a picture with one color crayon or marker. Talk to your neighbors about what would happen if what you drew became real.

Writing

MINI-LESSON
Teacher leads a 5- to 7-minute discussion about possible interpretations of the Writing Topic: A Place You Like to Hide or _____.

COMPOSING
Each student writes on
■ the lesson's topic
■ a personally chosen topic
■ a topic begun previously

SHARING
Papers are read to a classmate or the teacher, dated, and filed.

Word Study

CHART DEVELOPMENT
Spelling Emphasis: *oi* or 2 syllables and/or _____
   On the chart, the teacher writes sentences containing the day's letters or number of syllables or _____.

WRITING
On their papers, students write
■ their favorite words from the chart
■ other words/clusters/sentences that would be appropriate for the chart
Papers are dated and filed.

Lesson 95

Research

LEAD-IN
Teacher introduces the Project Idea.
Theme: Rivers and lakes or _____
Material: Maps or _____
Reading Focus: Functional reading
or _____

SEARCH & RECORD
Project Idea: In teams of 2 or 3, students explore maps and record the names of lakes and rivers.

SHARING
Students discuss the items found that relate to the day's theme or _____.
 Papers are dated and filed.

Recreational Reading and Storytime

CONVERSATIONS
Teacher Reads: For approximately 20 minutes everyone, including the teacher, reads silently. During the last 10 minutes the teacher may choose to talk with some individuals about what they have read.

CLIPBOARD NOTES
Teacher notes who is constantly seeking help decoding words or _____.

BOOK SHARING
Each person tells another person something he or she has read about that day.

READ ALOUD
Any alphabet book such as *Alphabet Puzzle* by Jill Downie or *Anno's Alphabet* by Mitsumasa Anno or *All Butterflies* by M. Brown or _____
 Discuss words that begin with each letter of the alphabet.

ACTIVITY (Optional)
Make jigsaw puzzles out of paper or tag letters. Teachers may have the letters pre-cut or pre-drawn for the students to cut out and make into puzzles.

Writing

MINI-LESSON
Teacher leads a 5- to 7-minute discussion about possible interpretations of the Writing Topic: A Place You Hide Secret Things or _____.

COMPOSING
Each student writes on
■ the lesson's topic
■ a personally chosen topic
■ a topic begun previously

SHARING
Papers are read to a classmate or the teacher, dated, and filed.

Word Study

CHART DEVELOPMENT
Spelling Emphasis: *oy* or 2 syllables and/or _____
 On the chart, the teacher writes sentences containing the day's letters or number of syllables or _____.

WRITING
On their papers, students write
■ their favorite words from the chart
■ other words/clusters/sentences that would be appropriate for the chart
 Papers are dated and filed.

Research

LEAD-IN
Teacher introduces the Project Idea.
Theme: Big cities and little towns or _____

Material: Maps or _____
Reading Focus: Functional reading or _____

SEARCH & RECORD
Project Idea: In teams of 2 or 3, students explore maps and record the names of big cities and little towns.

SHARING
Students discuss the items found that relate to the day's theme or _____.
Papers are dated and filed.

Recreational Reading

CONVERSATIONS
Check-In: Teacher moves among students, having 2- to 3-minute conversations with as many individuals as possible. If appropriate, discuss pronouns and their referents and/or _____.

CLIPBOARD NOTES
Teacher notes who is constantly seeking help decoding words or _____.

BOOK SHARING
Each person tells another person something he or she has read about that day.

and Storytime

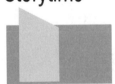

READ ALOUD
Where the Wild Things Are by Maurice Sendak or _____
Discuss real and make-believe in the story.

ACTIVITY (Optional)
Make a "wild thing" paper bag or stick puppet.

Writing

MINI-LESSON
Teacher leads a 5- to 7-minute discussion about possible interpretations of the Writing Topic: Monsters or _____.

COMPOSING
Each student writes (by drawing or developmental spelling) on
- the lesson's topic
- a personally chosen topic
- a topic begun previously

SHARING
Papers are read to a classmate or the teacher, dated, and filed.

Word Study

CHART DEVELOPMENT
Spelling Emphasis: *ll* or 2 syllables and/or _____
On the chart, the teacher writes sentences containing the day's letters or number of syllables or _____.

WRITING
On their papers, students write
- their favorite words from the chart
- other words/clusters/sentences that would be appropriate for the chart
Papers are dated and filed.

Lesson 97

Research

LEAD-IN
Teacher introduces the Project Idea.
Theme: Rural/urban/suburban areas or _____

Material: Magazines or _____
Reading Focus: Places or _____

SEARCH & RECORD
Project Idea: Individually, students cut or tear from magazines pictures or words related to the lesson's theme. They

paste or tape the pictures or words on their papers. Encourage discussion of findings with neighbors.
   Teachers check students for association of pictures/words with theme.

SHARING
Students discuss the items found that relate to the day's theme or _____.
   Papers are dated and filed.

Recreational Reading

CONVERSATIONS
Check-In: Teacher moves among students having 2- to 3-minute conversations with as many individuals as possible. If appropriate, discuss pronouns and their referents and/or _____.

CLIPBOARD NOTES
Teacher notes who reads books written by students or class books or _____.

BOOK SHARING
Each person tells another person something he or she has read about that day.

and Storytime

READ ALOUD
A Dark, Dark Tale by Ruth Brown or _____

   Discuss *why* things happened in the story.

ACTIVITY (Optional)
Make a construction paper or tag box. Tell a friend what is in your magic box.

Writing

MINI-LESSON
Teacher leads a 5- to 7-minute discussion about possible interpretations of the Writing Topic: Something Invisible or _____.

COMPOSING
Each student writes on
■ the lesson's topic
■ a personally chosen topic
■ a topic begun previously

SHARING
Papers are read to a classmate or the teacher, dated, and filed.

Word Study

CHART DEVELOPMENT
Spelling Emphasis: *al* or 2 syllables and/or _____
   On the chart, the teacher writes sentences containing the day's letters or number of syllables or _____.

WRITING
On their papers, students write
■ their favorite words from the chart
■ other words/clusters/sentences that would be appropriate for the chart
Papers are dated and filed.

Research

LEAD-IN
Teacher introduces the Project Idea.
Theme: Real and make-believe or
_____

Material: Magazines or _____
Reading Focus: Real and make-believe or _____

SEARCH & RECORD
Project Idea: Individually, students cut or tear from magazines pictures or

words related to the lesson's theme. They paste or tape the letters or words on their papers. Encourage discussion of findings with neighbors.
   Teachers check students for association of pictures/words with theme.

SHARING
Students discuss the items found that relate to the day's theme or _____.
   Papers are dated and filed.

Recreational Reading

CONVERSATIONS
Check-In: Teacher moves among students, having 2- to 3-minute conversations with as many individuals as possible. If appropriate, discuss connotations of the words chosen by the author and/or _____.

CLIPBOARD NOTES
Teacher notes who reads books written by students or class books or _____.

BOOK SHARING
Each person tells another person something he or she has read about that day.

and Storytime

READ ALOUD
Arrow to the Sun by Gerald McDermott or _____
   Discuss the sequence of events in the story.

ACTIVITY (Optional)
Using colored paper, make a picture in the manner of the illustrations in the book. Teacher may pre-cut many small

triangles and squares out of colored paper for students to assemble into a picture.

Writing

MINI-LESSON
Teacher leads a 5- to 7-minute discussion about possible interpretations of the Writing Topic: An Imaginary Friend or _____

COMPOSING
Each student writes (by drawing or developmental spelling) on
■ the lesson's topic
■ a personally chosen topic
■ a topic begun previously

SHARING
Papers are read to a classmate or the teacher, dated, and filed.

Word Study

CHART DEVELOPMENT
Spelling Emphasis: *au* or 2 syllables and/or _____
   On the chart, the teacher writes sentences containing the day's letters or number of syllables or _____.

WRITING
On their papers, students write
■ their favorite words from the chart
■ other words/clusters/sentences that would be appropriate for the chart
Papers are dated and filed.

Lesson 99

Research

LEAD-IN
Teacher introduces the Project Idea.
Theme: Real and make-believe or _____

Material: Library books or _____
Reading Focus: Real and make-believe or _____

SEARCH & RECORD
Project Idea: In teams of 2 or 3, students locate pictures in library books and discuss things that are real and make-believe in the pictures.

Team members should discuss ideas until all agree before recording what is real and make-believe in the book. with drawing and/or developmental spelling.

SHARING
Two or three teams compare the pictures that are real and make-believe or _____

Papers are dated and filed.

Recreational Reading

CONVERSATIONS
Check-In: Teacher moves among students having 2- to 3-minute conversations with as many individuals as possible. If appropriate, discuss connotations of the words chosen by the author and/or _____.

CLIPBOARD NOTES
Teacher notes who reads books written by students or class books or _____.

BOOK SHARING
Each person tells another person something he or she has read about that day.

and Storytime

READ ALOUD
Space Case by Edward Marshall or _____

Compare the characters in the book.

ACTIVITY (Optional)
Design a costume for yourself as an alien.

Writing

MINI-LESSON
Teacher leads a 5- to 7-minute discussion about possible interpretations of the Writing Topic: A Space Creature or _____.

COMPOSING
Each student writes on
■ the lesson's topic
■ a personally chosen topic
■ a topic begun previously

SHARING
Papers are read to a classmate or the teacher, dated, and filed.

Word Study

CHART DEVELOPMENT
Spelling Emphasis: _aw_ or 2 syllables and/or _____
On the chart, the teacher writes sentences containing the day's letters or number of syllables or _____.

WRITING
On their papers, students write
■ their favorite words from the chart
■ other words/clusters/sentences that would be appropriate for the chart
Papers are dated and filed.

Research

LEAD-IN
Teacher introduces the Project Idea.
Theme: Feelings or _____
Material: Library books or _____
Reading Focus: Inference or
_____

SEARCH & RECORD
Project Idea: In teams of 2 or 3, students locate pictures in library books and discuss feelings in the pictures.

Team members should discuss ideas until all agree before recording feelings in the book. with drawing and/or developmental spelling.

SHARING
Two or three teams compare the pictures found and the feelings represented or
_____.
Papers are dated and filed.

Recreational Reading

CONVERSATIONS
Teacher Reads: For approximately 20 minutes everyone, including the teacher, reads silently. During the last 10 minutes the teacher may choose to talk with some individuals about what they have read.

CLIPBOARD NOTES
Teacher notes who reads a book previously read or introduced by the teacher or _____.

BOOK SHARING
Each person tells another person something he or she has read about that day.

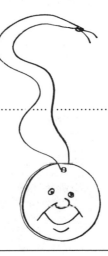

and Storytime

READ ALOUD
Many Moons by James Thurber or
_____
Discuss *who* was in the story and *what* each solution was.

ACTIVITY (Optional)
Make moon necklaces and wear them.

Writing

MINI-LESSON
Teacher leads a 5- to 7-minute discussion about possible interpretations of the Writing Topic: A Magic Potion or
_____

COMPOSING
Each student writes on
■ the lesson's topic
■ a personally chosen topic
■ a topic begun previously

SHARING
Papers are read to a classmate or the teacher, dated, and filed.

Word Study

CHART DEVELOPMENT
Spelling Emphasis: *un* or 2 syllables and/or _____
On the chart, the teacher writes sentences containing the day's letters or number of syllables or _____.

WRITING
On their papers, students write
■ their favorite words from the chart
■ other words/clusters/sentences that would be appropriate for the chart
Papers are dated and filed.

Lesson 101

Research

LEAD-IN
Teacher introduces the Project Idea.
Theme: Feelings or _____
Material: Art prints or _____
Reading Focus: Functional reading
or _____

SEARCH & RECORD
Project Idea: In teams of 2 or 3,
students look at a variety of art prints

and identify feelings represented in the
pictures.

SHARING
Students discuss the items found that
relate to the day's theme or _____.
    Papers are dated and filed.

Recreational Reading

CONVERSATIONS
Check-In: Teacher moves among
students, having 2- to 3-minute
conversations with as many individuals
as possible. If appropriate, discuss
connotations of the words chosen by the
author and/or _____.

CLIPBOARD NOTES
Teacher notes who reads a book
previously read or introduced by the
teacher or _____.

BOOK SHARING
Each person tells another person
something he or she has read about that
day.

and Storytime

READ ALOUD
Any book about art or artists such as Any
artist, *Getting to Know the World's
Greatest Artists*, series by Mike Venezia
or Any Artist, *Art for Children*, series by
Ernest Raboff or _____
    Describe the art in the book.

ACTIVITY (Optional)
Draw or paint a picture in the style of the
artist.

Writing

MINI-LESSON
Teacher leads a 5- to 7-minute discussion
about possible interpretations of the
Writing Topic: A Time You Were Afraid
or _____.

COMPOSING
Each student writes on
■ the lesson's topic
■ a personally chosen topic
■ a topic begun previously

SHARING
Papers are read to a classmate or the
teacher, dated, and filed.

Word Study

CHART DEVELOPMENT
Spelling Emphasis: *ing* or 2
syllables and/or _____
    On the chart, the teacher writes
sentences containing the day's letters or
number of syllables or _____.

WRITING
On their papers, students write
■ their favorite words from the chart
■ other words/clusters/sentences that
would be appropriate for the chart
Papers are dated and filed.

Lesson 102

Research

LEAD-IN
Teacher introduces the Project Idea.
Theme: Comparison or _____
Material: Art prints or _____
Reading Focus: Functional reading
or _____

SEARCH & RECORD
Project Idea: In teams of 3 or 4,
students compare a variety of art prints.

They record how the prints are alike and
how they are different.

SHARING
Students discuss the items found that
relate to the day's theme or _____.
    Papers are dated and filed.

Recreational Reading

CONVERSATIONS
Check-In: Teacher moves among
students, having 2- to 3-minute
conversations with as many individuals
as possible. If appropriate, discuss
synonyms and/or _____.

CLIPBOARD NOTES
Teacher notes who reads a book
previously read or introduced by the
teacher or _____.

BOOK SHARING
Each person tells another person
something he or she has read about that
day.

and Storytime

READ ALOUD
Any other book about art or artists such
as any in the *Getting to Know the World's
Greatest Artists* series by Mike Venezia or
the *Art for Children,* series by Ernest
Raboff or _____
    Compare today's artist with the one
discussed yesterday and the art prints
used in Research.

ACTIVITY (Optional)
Draw or paint a picture in the style of the
artist.

Writing

MINI-LESSON
Teacher leads a 5- to 7-minute discussion
about possible interpretations of the
Writing Topic: A Time You Were Excited
or _____.

COMPOSING
Each student writes (by drawing or
developmental spelling) on
- the lesson's topic
- a personally chosen topic
- a topic begun previously

SHARING
Papers are read to a classmate or the
teacher, dated, and filed.

Word Study

CHART DEVELOPMENT
Spelling Emphasis: *ow* or 2 syllables
and/or _____
    On the chart, the teacher writes
sentences containing the day's letters or
number of syllables or _____.

WRITING
On their papers, students write
- their favorite words from the chart
- other words/clusters/sentences that
  would be appropriate for the chart
  Papers are dated and filed.

Lesson 103

Research

LEAD-IN
Teacher introduces the Project Idea.
Theme: Sports or _____
Material: Newspapers or _____
Reading Focus: Main idea or
_____

SEARCH & RECORD
Project Idea: In teams of 2 or 3, students determine which sport is being reported on in different articles in the

sports section. They also write any further information they can learn about the article, such as terms or names that prove it is a particular sport.

SHARING
Two or more teams that find articles about the same sport compare the words or other information found or _____.
    Papers are dated and filed.

Recreational Reading

CONVERSATIONS
Small Group: For approximately 10 to 15 minutes the teacher meets with a small group of students who have all read the same story or portion of a book. The other students read quietly in books of their choice.

CLIPBOARD NOTES
Teacher notes who compares books by author, by topic, or by different versions of the same story or _____.

BOOK SHARING
Each person tells another person something he or she has read about that day.

and Storytime

READ ALOUD
The Dallas Titans Get Ready for Bed by Karla Kuskin or _____
    Discuss the details of what the players wore and did.

ACTIVITY (Optional)
Make a football helmet out of a cylinder of construction paper. The cylinder must be large enough in diameter to go over

the student's head. Cut out an opening for the face. Add paper strips for a face mask.

Writing

MINI-LESSON
Teacher leads a 5- to 7-minute discussion about possible interpretations of the Writing Topic: A Time You Were Sad or
_____.

COMPOSING
Each student writes on
■ the lesson's topic
■ a personally chosen topic
■ a topic begun previously

SHARING
Papers are read to a classmate or the teacher, dated, and filed.

Word Study

CHART DEVELOPMENT
Spelling Emphasis: *pp* or 2 syllables and/or _____
    On the chart, the teacher writes sentences containing the day's letters or number of syllables or _____.

WRITING
On their papers, students write
■ their favorite words from the chart
■ other words/clusters/sentences that would be appropriate for the chart
Papers are dated and filed.

Research

LEAD-IN
Teacher introduces the Project Idea.
Theme: Words that sell in advertisements or _____
Material: Newspapers or _____
Reading Focus: Word connotations or _____

SEARCH & RECORD
Project Idea: In teams of 2 or 3, students highlight or record words in advertisements that are intended to make people want to buy the items for sale.

SHARING
Two or more teams compare their findings or _____.
   Papers are dated and filed.

Recreational Reading

CONVERSATIONS
Check-In: Teacher moves among students having 2- to 3-minute conversations with as many individuals as possible. If appropriate, discuss synonyms and/or _____.

CLIPBOARD NOTES
Teacher notes who compares books by author, by topic, or by different versions of the same story or _____.

BOOK SHARING
Each person tells another person something he or she has read about that day.

and Storytime

READ ALOUD
Rain Makes Applesauce by Julian Scheer or _____
   Reread so that the class can join in on the repeating phrase.

ACTIVITY (Optional)
Make (or at least eat) applesauce. Talk silly.

Writing

MINI-LESSON
Teacher leads a 5- to 7-minute discussion about possible interpretations of the Writing Topic: A Time You Were Silly or _____.

COMPOSING
Each student writes on
■ the lesson's topic
■ a personally chosen topic
■ a topic begun previously

SHARING
Papers are read to a classmate or the teacher, dated, and filed.

Word Study

CHART DEVELOPMENT
Spelling Emphasis: _en_ or 2 syllables and/or _____
   On the chart, the teacher writes sentences containing the day's letters or number of syllables or _____.

WRITING
On their papers, students write
■ their favorite words from the chart
■ other words/clusters/sentences that would be appropriate for the chart
Papers are dated and filed.

Lesson 105

Research

LEAD-IN
Teacher introduces the Project Idea.
Theme: Direction words or _____
Material: Math textbooks or nonfiction books or _____
Reading Focus: Specialized vocabulary

SEARCH & RECORD
Project Idea: In teams of 2 or 3, students list direction words found in math textbooks.

SHARING
Two or three teams compare the words found and explain their reasoning or _____.

Papers are dated and filed.

Recreational Reading

CONVERSATIONS
Check-In: Teacher moves among students, having 2- to 3-minute conversations with as many individuals as possible. If appropriate, discuss synonyms and/or _____.

CLIPBOARD NOTES
Teacher notes who compares books by author, by topic, or by different versions of the same story or _____.

BOOK SHARING
Each person tells another person something he or she has read about that day.

and Storytime

READ ALOUD
Let's Be Enemies by Janice M. Udry or _____
Compare the characters in the story.

ACTIVITY (Optional)
Draw or paint a picture of an argument you and a friend had once.

Writing

MINI-LESSON
Teacher leads a 5- to 7-minute discussion about possible interpretations of the Writing Topic: A Time You Were Angry or _____.

COMPOSING
Each student writes (by drawing or developmental spelling) on
- the lesson's topic
- a personally chosen topic
- a topic begun previously

SHARING
Papers are read to a classmate or the teacher, dated, and filed.

Word Study

CHART DEVELOPMENT
Spelling Emphasis: *ed* or 2 syllables and/or _____
On the chart, the teacher writes sentences containing the day's letters or number of syllables or _____.

WRITING
On their papers, students write
- their favorite words from the chart
- other words/clusters/sentences that would be appropriate for the chart

Papers are dated and filed.
Each student chooses a composition from his or her folder for the teacher to display in the classroom. Students may modify their writing and/or illustration as they choose.

Research

LEAD-IN
Teacher introduces the Project Idea.
Theme: Addition and subtraction
problems or _____
Material: Math textbooks or
_____

Reading Focus: Main idea and
supporting detail or _____

SEARCH & RECORD
Project Idea: In teams of 2 or 3,
students explore math textbooks

identifying addition and subtraction word
problems. Record the words or groups of
words that indicate whether the problems
are addition or subtraction or _____.
   Team members should discuss their
ideas until all agree before recording

SHARING
Students meet in groups of 4 or 5 and
discuss the items found that relate to the
day's theme or _____.
   Papers are dated and filed.

Recreational Reading

CONVERSATIONS
In-Depth: Teacher holds 7- to 10-
minute conversations with 3 or 4 students
(individually) discussing general things
about a book such as the author and/or
illustrator or parts of the book,
description, and/or _____.

CLIPBOARD NOTES
Teacher notes who moves lips or uses
hand to guide their reading or
_____.

BOOK SHARING
Each person tells another person
something he or she has read about that
day.

There were 96 panda and 4 came along and
they all are in line to go to the bamboo shop to eat
lunch. How many were there all together?

96 + 4 = 100

and Storytime

READ ALOUD
Anno's Counting House by Mitsumasa
Anno or *Anno's Counting Book* by
Mitsumasa Anno or *Arthur's Funny
Money* by Lillian Hoban or _____
   Discuss similarities and differences in
items in the story.

ACTIVITY (Optional)
Make individual story-problem books.

Writing

MINI-LESSON
Teacher leads a 5- to 7-minute discussion
about possible interpretations of the
Writing Topic: Describe a Snake or
_____.

COMPOSING
Each student writes on
■ the lesson's topic
■ a personally chosen topic
■ a topic begun previously

SHARING
Papers are read to a classmate or the
teacher, dated, and filed.

Word Study

CHART DEVELOPMENT
Spelling Emphasis: *ar* or 2 syllables
and/or _____
   On the chart, the teacher writes
sentences containing the day's letters or
number of syllables or _____.

WRITING
On their papers, students write
■ their favorite words from the chart
■ other words/clusters/sentences that
   would be appropriate for the chart
Papers are dated and filed.

Lesson **107**

Research

LEAD-IN
Teacher introduces the Project Idea.
Theme: White pages or _____
Material: Telephone books or
_____

Reading Focus: Functional reading
or _____

SEARCH & RECORD
Project Idea: In teams of 2 or 3,
students explore the white pages of

telephone books looking for numbers of
people they know. Teams record the
names and telephone numbers.

SHARING
Two or more teams compare the names
and numbers found or _____.
   Papers are dated and filed.

Recreational Reading

CONVERSATIONS
In-Depth: Teacher holds 7- to 10-
minute conversations with 3 or 4 students
(individually) discussing general things
about a book such as the author and/or
illustrator or parts of the book,
description, and/or _____.

CLIPBOARD NOTES
Teacher notes who moves lips or uses
hand to guide their reading or
_____.

BOOK SHARING
Each person tells another person
something he or she has read about that
day.

and Storytime

READ ALOUD
Snakes Are Hunters by Patricia Lauber or
A Snake's Body by Joanna Cole or
_____
   Discuss words that describe snakes.

ACTIVITY (Optional)
Make string paintings of snake tracks.
Dip strings or yarn in different colors of
paints. Place them in interesting patterns

on your paper and pick them up. "Snake
tracks" will be left.

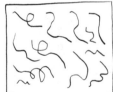

Writing

MINI-LESSON
Teacher leads a 5- to 7-minute discussion
about possible interpretations of the
Writing Topic: Write about an Incident
Involving a Snake or _____.

COMPOSING
Each student writes on
■ the lesson's topic
■ a personally chosen topic
■ a topic begun previously

SHARING
Papers are read to a classmate or the
teacher, dated, and filed.

Word Study

CHART DEVELOPMENT
Spelling Emphasis: *kn* or 2 syllables
and/or _____
   On the chart, the teacher writes
sentences containing the day's letters or
number of syllables or _____.

WRITING
On their papers, students write
■ their favorite words from the chart
■ other words/clusters/sentences that
   would be appropriate for the chart
   Papers are dated and filed.

Research

LEAD-IN
Teacher introduces the Project Idea.
Theme: Emergency numbers or
_____

Material: Telephone books or
_____

Reading Focus: Functional reading
or _____

SEARCH & RECORD
Project Idea: In teams of 2 or 3,
students explore telephone books looking

for emergency numbers. They record the
numbers and type of emergency for which
each would be used.

SHARING
Two or more teams compare the numbers
found and reasons for using them or
_____.
   Papers are dated and filed.

Recreational Reading

CONVERSATIONS
In-Depth: Teacher holds 7- to 10-
minute conversations with 3 or 4 students
(individually) discussing general things
about a book such as the author and/or
illustrator or parts of the book,
description, and/or _____.

CLIPBOARD NOTES
Teacher notes who moves lips or uses
hand to guide their reading or
_____.

BOOK SHARING
Each person tells another person
something he or she has read about that
day.

and Storytime

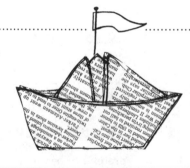

READ ALOUD
Curious George Rides a Bike by H. A. Rey
or _____
   Teacher stops occasionally while
reading the story for students to predict
what will happen next.

ACTIVITY (Optional)
Make paper boats out of newspaper like
George did.

Writing

MINI-LESSON
Teacher leads a 5- to 7-minute discussion
about possible interpretations of the
Writing Topic: Describe a Monkey or
_____.

COMPOSING
Each student writes (by drawing or
developmental spelling) on
■ the lesson's topic
■ a personally chosen topic
■ a topic begun previously

SHARING
Papers are read to a classmate or the
teacher, dated, and filed.

Word Study

CHART DEVELOPMENT
Spelling Emphasis: *ly* or 2 syllables
and/or _____
   On the chart, the teacher writes
sentences containing the day's letters or
number of syllables or _____.

WRITING
On their papers, students write
■ their favorite words from the chart
■ other words/clusters/sentences that
   would be appropriate for the chart
Papers are dated and filed.

Lesson 109

Research

LEAD-IN
Teacher introduces the Project Idea.
Theme: Slithery, slimy things or
_____

Material: Magazines or _____
Reading Focus: Association or
_____

SEARCH & RECORD
Project Idea: In teams of 3 or 4, students explore magazines looking for pictures and words related to the lesson's theme. They paste or tape them on their papers. Each team saves 1 or 2 items to put on the class chart.
Teacher checks students for association of pictures/words with theme.

SHARING
Each team pastes 1 or 2 items on a class chart and explains how it relates to the day's theme or _____.
Papers are dated and filed.

Recreational Reading

CONVERSATIONS
In-Depth: Teacher holds 7- to 10-minute conversations with 3 or 4 students (individually) discussing general things about a book such as the author and/or illustrator or parts of the book, description, and/or _____.

CLIPBOARD NOTES
Teacher notes who talks spontaneously about books or _____.

BOOK SHARING
Each person tells another person something he or she has read about that day.

and Storytime

READ ALOUD
Crocodile Beat by Gail Jorgensen or *Thump, Thump, Rat-a-Tat-Tat* by Gene Baer or _____
Read a second time so that students can join in. Discuss the pattern.

ACTIVITY (Optional)
Have a parade. Make costumes first or pretend to be a character from the book.

Writing

MINI-LESSON
Teacher leads a 5- to 7-minute discussion about possible interpretations of the Writing Topic: Write About an Incident Involving a Monkey or _____.

COMPOSING
Each student writes on
- the lesson's topic
- a personally chosen topic
- a topic begun previously

SHARING
Papers are read to a classmate or the teacher, dated, and filed.

Word Study

CHART DEVELOPMENT
Spelling Emphasis: *n't* or 2 syllables and/or _____
On the chart, the teacher writes sentences containing the day's letters or number of syllables or _____.

WRITING
On their papers, students write
- their favorite words from the chart
- other words/clusters/sentences that would be appropriate for the chart
Papers are dated and filed.

Lesson **110**

Research

LEAD-IN
Teacher introduces the Project Idea.
Theme: Soft, furry things or
_____

Material: Magazines or _____
Reading Focus: Association or
_____

SEARCH & RECORD
Project Idea: In teams of 2 or 3, students explore magazines looking for pictures and words related to the lesson's

theme. They paste or tape the pictures or words on their papers. Each team saves 1 or 2 items to put on the class chart.

Teachers check students for association of pictures/words with theme.

SHARING
Each team pastes 1 or 2 items on a class chart and explains how it relates to the theme or _____.

Papers are dated and filed.

Recreational Reading

CONVERSATIONS
In-Depth: Teacher holds 7- to 10-minute conversations with 3 or 4 students (individually) discussing general things about a book such as the author and/or illustrator or parts of the book, description, and/or _____.

CLIPBOARD NOTES
Teacher notes who talks spontaneously about books or _____.

BOOK SHARING
Each person tells another person something he or she has read about that day.

and Storytime

READ ALOUD
Millions of Cats by Wanda Gág or
_____

Have students retell the story. Discuss the plot.

ACTIVITY (Optional)
Make a cat or cat face by tearing shapes of paper and gluing them onto a second piece of paper.

Writing

MINI-LESSON
Teacher leads a 5- to 7-minute discussion about possible interpretations of the Writing Topic: Describe an Insect or Any Small Animal or _____.

COMPOSING
Each student writes (by drawing or developmental spelling) on
■ the lesson's topic
■ a personally chosen topic
■ a topic begun previously

SHARING
Papers are read to a classmate or the teacher, dated, and filed.

Word Study

CHART DEVELOPMENT
Spelling Emphasis: *tion* or 2 syllables and/or _____
On the chart, the teacher writes sentences containing the day's letters or number of syllables or _____.

WRITING
On their papers, students write
■ their favorite words from the chart
■ other words/clusters/sentences that would be appropriate for the chart
Papers are dated and filed.

213

Lesson 111

Research

LEAD-IN
Teacher introduces the Project Idea.
Theme: Little things or _____
Material: Library books or _____
Reading Focus: Association or
_____

SEARCH & RECORD
Project Idea: In teams of 2 or 3, students look at pictures and words in

library books and discuss and record little things found.

SHARING
Two or three teams compare their findings or _____.
   Papers are dated and filed.

Recreational Reading

CONVERSATIONS
In-Depth: Teacher holds 7- to 10-minute conversations with 3 or 4 students (individually) discussing general things about a book such as the author and/or illustrator or parts of the book, description, and/or _____.

CLIPBOARD NOTES
Teacher notes students who watch the teacher or daydream or _____.

BOOK SHARING
Each person tells another person something he or she has read about that day.

and Storytime

READ ALOUD
Anansi the Spider by Gerald McDermott or *The Grouchy Ladybug* by Eric Carle or
_____
   Compare the characters in the story.

ACTIVITY (Optional)
Glue yarn on paper. Make a spider web (or a ladybug).

Writing

MINI-LESSON
Teacher leads a 5- to 7-minute discussion about possible interpretations of the Writing Topic:
   Write About an Incident Involving an Insect or Small Animal or _____.

COMPOSING
Each student writes on
■ the lesson's topic
■ a personally chosen topic
■ a topic begun previously

SHARING
Papers are read to a classmate or the teacher, dated, and filed.

Word Study

CHART DEVELOPMENT
Spelling Emphasis: *ing* or 2 syllables and/or _____
   On the chart, the teacher writes sentences containing the day's letters or number of syllables or _____.

WRITING
On their papers, students write
■ their favorite words from the chart
■ other words/clusters/sentences that would be appropriate for the chart
   Papers are dated and filed.

Research

LEAD-IN
Teacher introduces the Project Idea.
Theme: Big things or _____
Material: Library books or _____
Reading Focus: Association or
_____

SEARCH & RECORD
Project Idea: In teams of 2 or 3,
students look at pictures and words in
library books and discuss and record big
things found.

SHARING
Two or three teams compare their
findings or _____.
   Papers are dated and filed.

Recreational Reading

CONVERSATIONS
In-Depth: Teacher holds 7- to 10-
minute conversations with 3 or 4 students
(individually) discussing general things
about a book such as the author and/or
illustrator or parts of the book,
description, and/or _____.

CLIPBOARD NOTES
Teacher notes who prefers what type of
book or _____.

BOOK SHARING
Each person tells another person
something he or she has read about that
day.

and Storytime

READ ALOUD
Dinosaur Bones by Aliki or *Bones, Bones,
Dinosaur Bones* by Byron Barton or
_____
   Discuss similarities and differences of
dinosaur skeletons and human skeletons.

ACTIVITY (Optional)
Make paper bones and assemble a
skeleton.

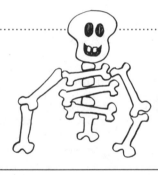

Writing

MINI-LESSON
Teacher leads a 5- to 7-minute discussion
about possible interpretations of the
Writing Topic: Big Things or _____.

COMPOSING
Each student writes on
■ the lesson's topic
■ a personally chosen topic
■ a topic begun previously

SHARING
Papers are read to a classmate or the
teacher, dated, and filed.

Word Study

CHART DEVELOPMENT
Spelling Emphasis: *ble* or 2 syllables
and/or _____
   On the chart, the teacher writes
sentences containing the day's letters or
number of syllables or _____.

WRITING
On their papers, students write
■ their favorite words from the chart
■ other words/clusters/sentences that
   would be appropriate for the chart
Papers are dated and filed.

Lesson 113

Research

LEAD-IN
Teacher introduces the Project Idea.
Theme: Relative size or _____
Material: Catalogs or _____
Reading Focus: Functional reading or _____

SEARCH & RECORD
Project Idea: In teams of 2 or 3, students explore catalogs. They cut or tear out big and little items. They paste or tape the items on their papers under the headings Big and Little. (Some students may choose to have three or more headings.)

SHARING
Students share with the class the largest and smallest items they found or _____.

Papers are dated and filed.

Recreational Reading and Storytime

CONVERSATIONS
Small Group: For approximately 10 to 15 minutes, teacher meets with a small group of students who have all read the same story or portion of a book. The other students read quietly in books of their choice.

CLIPBOARD NOTES
Teacher notes who prefers what type of book or _____.

BOOK SHARING
Each person tells another person something he or she has read about that day.

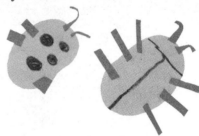

READ ALOUD
Any nonfiction book about bugs or insects such as *Big on Bugs* by Edith Fine & Judith Josephson or *When It Comes to Bugs* by Aileen Fisher or *My First Insects, Spiders & Crawlers* by Cecelia Fitzsimons or *Bugs!* by Patricia & Frederick McKissack or _____
Describe the animals in the book.

ACTIVITY (Optional)
Make potato print bugs. Cut one potato lengthwise making two "bodies," and cut another crosswise nearer one end making "heads." Apply a thin layer of paint with a brayer to a shallow pan or flat surface. Dip the potatoes in the paint and print bodies and heads. Draw or add colored paper appendages.

Writing

MINI-LESSON
Teacher leads a 5- to 7-minute discussion about possible interpretations of the Writing Topic: Little Things or _____.

COMPOSING
Each student writes on
■ the lesson's topic
■ a personally chosen topic
■ a topic begun previously

SHARING
Papers are read to a classmate or the teacher, dated, and filed.

Word Study

CHART DEVELOPMENT
Spelling Emphasis: *ee* or 2 syllables and/or _____
On the chart, the teacher writes sentences containing the day's letters or number of syllables or _____.

WRITING
On their papers, students write
■ their favorite words from the chart
■ other words/clusters/sentences that would be appropriate for the chart
Papers are dated and filed.

Research

LEAD-IN
Teacher introduces the Project Idea.
Theme: Relative cost or _____
Material: Catalogs or _____
Reading Focus: Functional reading or _____

SEARCH & RECORD
Project Idea: In teams of 2 or 3, students explore catalogs. They cut or tear out big and little items. They paste or tape the items on their papers under the headings Big and Little. (Some students may choose to have three or more headings.)

SHARING
Students share with the class the largest and smallest items they found or _____.

Papers are dated and filed.

Recreational Reading

CONVERSATIONS
Check-In: Teacher moves among students, having 2- to 3-minute conversations with as many individuals as possible. If appropriate, discuss opposites and/or _____.

CLIPBOARD NOTES
Teacher notes who prefers what type of book or _____.

BOOK SHARING
Each person tells another person something he or she has read about that day.

and Storytime

READ ALOUD
Any story about a big and little animal such as *Andy and the Lion* by James Daugherty or *Androcles and the Lion* by Janet Stevens or _____
   Discuss *why* things happened in the story.

ACTIVITY (Optional)
Draw a picture of your favorite part of the story.

Writing

MINI-LESSON
Teacher leads a 5- to 7-minute discussion about possible interpretations of the Writing Topic: Compare or Write a Story About a Big and a Little Thing or

_____.

COMPOSING
Each student writes (by drawing or developmental spelling) on
- the lesson's topic
- a personally chosen topic
- a topic begun previously

SHARING
Papers are read to a classmate or the teacher, dated, and filed.

Word Study

CHART DEVELOPMENT
Spelling Emphasis: *gh* or 2 syllables and/or _____
   On the chart, the teacher writes sentences containing the day's letters or number of syllables or _____.

WRITING
On their papers, students write
- their favorite words from the chart
- other words/clusters/sentences that would be appropriate for the chart
Papers are dated and filed.

Lesson 115

Research

LEAD-IN
Teacher introduces the Project Idea.
Theme: Big and little words or _____

Material: Newspapers or _____
Reading Focus: Classification or _____

SEARCH & RECORD
Project Idea: In teams of 2 or 3, students cut or tear big and little words from newspapers. They paste or tape the items on their papers.

SHARING
Students share with the class their largest and smallest words or _____.
　Papers are dated and filed.

Recreational Reading

CONVERSATIONS
Check-In: Teacher moves among students, having 2- to 3-minute conversations with as many individuals as possible. If appropriate, discuss opposites and/or _____.

CLIPBOARD NOTES
Teacher notes which students are continuing to read the same book more than one day or _____.

BOOK SHARING
Each person tells another person something he or she has read about that day.

and Storytime

READ ALOUD
Corduroy by Don Freeman or _____
　Discuss *where* and *when* events in the story happened.

ACTIVITY (Optional)
Sew a button on paper or cloth overalls that are precut by the teacher.

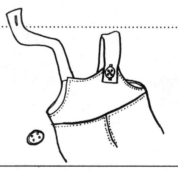

Writing

MINI-LESSON
Teacher leads a 5- to 7-minute discussion about possible interpretations of the Writing Topic: Something that Changes Its Appearance, Such as Shape or _____.

COMPOSING
Each student writes on
■ the lesson's topic
■ a personally chosen topic
■ a topic begun previously

SHARING
Papers are read to a classmate or the teacher, dated, and filed.

Word Study

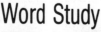

CHART DEVELOPMENT
Spelling Emphasis: *el* or 2 syllables and/or _____
　On the chart, the teacher writes sentences containing the day's letters or number of syllables or _____.

WRITING
On their papers, students write
■ their favorite words from the chart
■ other words/clusters/sentences that would be appropriate for the chart
　Papers are dated and filed.

Lesson 116

Research

LEAD-IN
Teacher introduces the Project Idea.
Theme: Changes or _____
Material: Newspapers or _____
Reading Focus: Prediction or
_____

SEARCH & RECORD
Project Idea: In teams of 2 or 3, students explore newspapers looking for things that have changed or could change.

SHARING
Two or more teams compare their findings. Share one item with the entire class or _____.
Papers are dated and filed.

Recreational Reading and Storytime

CONVERSATIONS
Check-In: Teacher moves among students, having 2- to 3-minute conversations with as many individuals as possible. If appropriate, discuss opposites and/or _____.

CLIPBOARD NOTES
Teacher notes which students are continuing to read the same book more than one day or _____.

BOOK SHARING
Each person tells another person something he or she has read about that day.

READ ALOUD
Little Blue and Little Yellow by Leo Lionni or *The Great Blueness* by Arnold Lobel or *Mouse Paint* by Ellen S. Walsh or _____
Discuss causes and their effects, especially as they pertain to mixing paints.

ACTIVITY (Optional)
Paint a picture using red, yellow, and green paints.

Writing

MINI-LESSON
Teacher leads a 5- to 7-minute discussion about possible interpretations of the Writing Topic: Something That Changes Color or _____.

COMPOSING
Each student writes on
■ the lesson's topic
■ a personally chosen topic
■ a topic begun previously

SHARING
Papers are read to a classmate or the teacher, dated, and filed.

Word Study

CHART DEVELOPMENT
Spelling Emphasis: *ld* or 2 syllables and/or _____
On the chart, the teacher writes sentences containing the day's letters or number of syllables or _____.

WRITING
On their papers, students write
■ their favorite words from the chart
■ other words/clusters/sentences that would be appropriate for the chart
Papers are dated and filed.

219

Lesson **117**

Research

LEAD-IN
Teacher introduces the Project Idea.
Theme: Changes or _____
Material: Science textbooks or nonfiction books or _____
Reading Focus: Words or pictures with certain letters

SEARCH & RECORD
Project Idea: In teams of 2 or 3, students explore science textbooks or nonfiction books looking for things that have changed or could change.

SHARING
Two or more teams compare their findings. Share one item with the entire class or _____.
    Papers are dated and filed.

Recreational Reading

CONVERSATIONS
Check-In: Teacher moves among students, having 2- to 3-minute conversations with as many individuals as possible. If appropriate, discuss how a passage in the book could be paraphrased and/or _____.

CLIPBOARD NOTES
Teacher notes which students are continuing to read the same book more than one day or _____.

BOOK SHARING
Each person tells another person something he or she has read about that day.

and Storytime

READ ALOUD
A version of The Three Bears such as *The Three Bears* by Paul Galdone or
_____
    Discuss the beginning, middle, and end of the story.

ACTIVITY (Optional)
Students work in groups of four to prepare props for acting out the story.

Students will work on these for two days and present their skits on the third day (Lesson 119). Teacher assists, but student groups each decide what they will need and how to make them.

Writing

MINI-LESSON
Teacher leads a 5- to 7-minute discussion about possible interpretations of the Writing Topic: Something That Changes Taste or _____.

COMPOSING
Each student writes (by drawing or developmental spelling) on
■ the lesson's topic
■ a personally chosen topic
■ a topic begun previously

SHARING
Papers are read to a classmate or the teacher, dated, and filed.

Word Study

CHART DEVELOPMENT
Spelling Emphasis: *ry* or 2 syllables and/or _____
    On the chart, the teacher writes sentences containing the day's letters or number of syllables or _____.

WRITING
On their papers, students write
■ their favorite words from the chart
■ other words/clusters/sentences that would be appropriate for the chart
    Papers are dated and filed.

Research

LEAD-IN
Teacher introduces the Project Idea.
Theme: Changes or _____
Material: Science textbooks or nonfiction books or _____
Reading Focus: Words or pictures with certain letters

SEARCH & RECORD
Project Idea: In teams of 2 or 3, students explore science textbooks or

nonfiction books looking for things that have changed or could change.

SHARING
Two or more teams compare their findings. Share one item with the entire class or _____.
Papers are dated and filed.

Recreational Reading

CONVERSATIONS
Check-In: Teacher moves among students, having 2- to 3-minute conversations with as many individuals as possible. If appropriate, discuss how a passage in the book could be paraphrased and/or _____.

CLIPBOARD NOTES
Teacher notes titles of books being read or _____.

BOOK SHARING
Each person tells another person something he or she has read about that day.

and Storytime

READ ALOUD
A second version of The Three Bears such as *Goldilocks and the Three Bears* by James Marshall or _____
Compare this version of the story with the one read in Lesson 117.

ACTIVITY (Optional)
Students continue working in groups of four to prepare props for acting out the

story. Students will present their skits in Lesson 119.

Writing

MINI-LESSON
Teacher leads a 5- to 7-minute discussion about possible interpretations of the Writing Topic: Something That Changes Smell or _____.

COMPOSING
Each student writes on
■ the lesson's topic
■ a personally chosen topic
■ a topic begun previously

SHARING
Papers are read to a classmate or the teacher, dated, and filed.

Word Study

CHART DEVELOPMENT
Spelling Emphasis: *bb* or 2 syllables and/or _____
On the chart, the teacher writes sentences containing the day's letters or number of syllables or _____.

WRITING
On their papers, students write
■ their favorite words from the chart
■ other words/clusters/sentences that would be appropriate for the chart
Papers are dated and filed.

Lesson **119**

Research

LEAD-IN
Teacher introduces the Project Idea.
Theme: Senses: tasting, hearing, or
_____

Material: Catalogs or _____
Reading Focus: Functional reading
or _____

SEARCH & RECORD
Project Idea: In teams of 2 or 3,
students explore catalogs looking for

things that could be heard or tasted. Cut
or tear out items and paste or tape them
on a paper. Save one from each category
to display on a class chart. Write how
some of the things sound or taste.

SHARING
Each team adds one picture from each
category to the class chart or _____.
    Papers are dated and filed.

Recreational Reading

CONVERSATIONS
Check-In: Teacher moves among
students having 2- to 3-minute
conversations with as many individuals
as possible. If appropriate, discuss how a
passage in the book could be paraphrased
and/or _____.

CLIPBOARD NOTES
Teacher notes which students are
continuing to read the same book more
than one day or _____.

BOOK SHARING
Each person tells another person
something he or she has read about that
day.

and Storytime

READ ALOUD
The Jolly Postman by Janet & Allen
Ahlberg or _____
    Read any of the mail, especially the
letter to the three bears from Goldilocks.
Discuss the humor.

ACTIVITY (Optional)
Students present their skits of *The Three
Bears.* Each should be different.

Writing

MINI-LESSON
Teacher leads a 5- to 7-minute discussion
about possible interpretations of the
Writing Topic: Something That Changes
The Way It Feels or _____.

COMPOSING
Each student writes on
■ the lesson's topic
■ a personally chosen topic
■ a topic begun previously

SHARING
Papers are read to a classmate or the
teacher, dated, and filed.

Word Study

CHART DEVELOPMENT
Spelling Emphasis: *rr* or 2 syllables
and/or _____
    On the chart, the teacher writes
sentences containing the day's letters or
number of syllables or _____.

WRITING
On their papers, students write
■ their favorite words from the chart
■ other words/clusters/sentences that
    would be appropriate for the chart
    Papers are dated and filed.

Lesson 120

Research

LEAD-IN
Teacher introduces the Project Idea.
Theme: Senses: smelling, feeling, or _____

Material: Catalogs or _____
Reading Focus: Functional reading or _____

SEARCH & RECORD
Project Idea: In teams of 2 or 3, students explore catalogs looking for

things that could be heard or tasted. Cut or tear out items and paste or tape them on a paper. Save one from each category to display on a class chart. Write how some of the things sound or taste.

SHARING
Each team adds one picture from each category to the class chart or _____.
  Papers are dated and filed.

Recreational Reading

CONVERSATIONS
Teacher Reads: For approximately 20 minutes everyone, including the teacher, reads silently. During the last 10 minutes the teacher may choose to talk with some individuals about what they have read.

CLIPBOARD NOTES
Teacher notes titles of books being read or _____.

BOOK SHARING
Each person tells another person something he or she has read about that day.

and Storytime

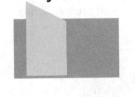

READ ALOUD
Any book of sounds such as *City Sounds* by Rebecca Emberly or _____
  Discuss words that describe sounds.

ACTIVITY (Optional)
Fold a piece of paper in half and open it. Label one side "Daytime Sounds" and the other "Nighttime Sounds." Cut out of magazines pictures of things that make

sounds and glue them on the appropriate side.

Writing

MINI-LESSON
Teacher leads a 5- to 7-minute discussion about possible interpretations of the Writing Topic: Something That Changes Sound or _____.

COMPOSING
Each student writes (by drawing or developmental spelling) on
■ the lesson's topic
■ a personally chosen topic
■ a topic begun previously

SHARING
Papers are read to a classmate or the teacher, dated, and filed.

Word Study

CHART DEVELOPMENT
Spelling Emphasis: *dge* or 2 syllables and/or _____
  On the chart, the teacher writes sentences containing the day's letters or number of syllables or _____.

WRITING
On their papers, students write
■ their favorite words from the chart
■ other words/clusters/sentences that would be appropriate for the chart

Papers are dated and filed.
  Each student chooses a composition from his or her folder for the teacher to display in the classroom. Students may modify their writing and/or illustration as they choose.

Lesson 121

Research

LEAD-IN
Teacher introduces the Project Idea.
Theme: Shapes or _____
Material: Magazines or _____
Reading Focus: Classification or _____

SEARCH & RECORD
Project Idea: In teams of 3 to 5, students explore magazines looking for circular, triangular, and other shaped objects. Team members classify the items before attaching them to their paper. Label each classification.

SHARING
Two or more teams compare their findings or _____.
Papers are dated and filed.

Recreational Reading

CONVERSATIONS
Check-In: Teacher moves among students, having 2- to 3-minute conversations with as many individuals as possible. If appropriate, discuss problem-solving techniques used by the characters in the book and/or _____.

CLIPBOARD NOTES
Teacher notes who seems to be excited about books and reading or _____.

BOOK SHARING
Each person tells another person something he or she has read about that day.

and Storytime

READ ALOUD
Playing Marbles by Julie Brinckloe or *The Klutz Book of Marbles* by Klutz Press or *Games (and How to Play Them)* by Anne Rockwell or *1 2 3 Play With Me* by Karen Gundersheimer or _____
Discuss games you play either alone or with one other person.

ACTIVITY (Optional)
Teacher duplicates instructions for several different games and students play them in small groups.

Writing

MINI-LESSON
Teacher leads a 5- to 7-minute discussion about possible interpretations of the Writing Topic: Games You Play With One Other Person or _____.

COMPOSING
Each student writes on
■ the lesson's topic
■ a personally chosen topic
■ a topic begun previously

SHARING
Papers are read to a classmate or the teacher, dated, and filed.

Word Study

CHART DEVELOPMENT
Spelling Emphasis: *al* or 2 syllables and/or _____
On the chart, the teacher writes sentences containing the day's letters or number of syllables or _____.

WRITING
On their papers, students write
■ their favorite words from the chart
■ other words/clusters/sentences that would be appropriate for the chart
Papers are dated and filed.

Research

LEAD-IN
Teacher introduces the Project Idea.
Theme: Similar and different or
_____
Material: Magazines or _____
Reading Focus: Comparison or
_____

SEARCH & RECORD
Project Idea: In teams of 2 or 3, students explore magazines looking for items that are similar or different. Cut or tear out words or pictures and label them according to how they are either similar or different.

SHARING
Two or more teams compare their findings and report one finding to the entire class or _____.
Papers are dated and filed.

Recreational Reading

CONVERSATIONS
Check-In: Teacher moves among students, having 2- to 3-minute conversations with as many individuals as possible. If appropriate, discuss problem-solving techniques used by the characters in the book and/or _____.

CLIPBOARD NOTES
Teacher notes who seems to be excited about books and reading or _____.

BOOK SHARING
Each person tells another person something he or she has read about that day.

and Storytime

READ ALOUD
Will's Mammoth by Rafe Martin or
_____
Discuss real and make-believe pets you would like to have.

ACTIVITY (Optional)
Make bubble prints over a drawing. Students draw a picture of a real or imaginary pet. Teacher puts food color and soap in a small amount of water in a shallow pan and stirs to make bubbles. Place students' drawings carefully on the colored bubbles.

Writing

MINI-LESSON
Teacher leads a 5- to 7-minute discussion about possible interpretations of the Writing Topic: Games You Play Alone or
_____.

COMPOSING
Each student writes (by drawing or developmental spelling) on
■ the lesson's topic
■ a personally chosen topic
■ a topic begun previously

SHARING
Papers are read to a classmate or the teacher, dated, and filed.

Word Study

CHART DEVELOPMENT
Spelling Emphasis: *le* or 2 syllables and/or _____
On the chart, the teacher writes sentences containing the day's letters or number of syllables or _____.

WRITING
On their papers, students write
■ their favorite words from the chart
■ other words/clusters/sentences that would be appropriate for the chart
Papers are dated and filed.

Lesson 123

Research

LEAD-IN
Teacher introduces the Project Idea.
Theme: Similar and different or _____

Material: Library books or _____
Reading Focus: Comparison or _____

SEARCH & RECORD
Project Idea: In teams of 2 or 3, students explore library books looking for items that are similar or different. Record findings in developmental spelling or by drawing. Label them according to how they are either similar or different.

SHARING
Two or more teams compare their findings and report one finding to the entire class or _____.
 Papers are dated and filed.

Recreational Reading

and

Storytime

CONVERSATIONS
Small Group: For approximately 10 to 15 minutes teacher meets with a small group of students who have all read the same story or portion of a book. The other students read quietly in books of their choice.

CLIPBOARD NOTES
Teacher notes who seems to be excited about books and reading or _____.

READ ALOUD
The Ghost-Eye Tree by Bill Martin, Jr., and John Archambault or _____
 Discuss times students have been afraid.

ACTIVITY (Optional)
Draw a picture of the Ghost-Eye tree or something else that is scary.

BOOK SHARING
Each person tells another person something he or she has read about that day.

Writing

MINI-LESSON
Teacher leads a 5- to 7-minute discussion about possible interpretations of the Writing Topic: Games You Play on a Team or _____.

COMPOSING
Each student writes on
■ the lesson's topic
■ a personally chosen topic
■ a topic begun previously

SHARING
Papers are read to a classmate or the teacher, dated, and filed.

Word Study

CHART DEVELOPMENT
Spelling Emphasis: *ai* or 2 syllables and/or _____
 On the chart, the teacher writes sentences containing the day's letters or number of syllables or _____.

WRITING
On their papers, students write
■ their favorite words from the chart
■ other words/clusters/sentences that would be appropriate for the chart
 Papers are dated and filed.

Lesson 124

Research

LEAD-IN
Teacher introduces the Project Idea.
Theme: Money or _____
Material: Library books or _____
Reading Focus: Association or
_____

SEARCH & RECORD
Project Idea: In teams of 2 or 3, students locate pictures or words of objects that could be purchased in library books and discuss the relative cost of the items found.

Team members should discuss the relative cost and star those that are less expensive. Put a different symbol beside the most expensive items.

SHARING
Two or more teams compare their findings or _____.
Papers are dated and filed.

Recreational Reading

CONVERSATIONS
Check-In: Teacher moves among students, having 2- to 3-minute conversations with as many individuals as possible. If appropriate, discuss problem-solving techniques used by the characters in the book and/or _____.

CLIPBOARD NOTES
Teacher notes who is constantly seeking help decoding words or _____.

BOOK SHARING
Each person tells another person something he or she has read about that day.

and Storytime

READ ALOUD
Everybody Needs a Rock by Byrd Baylor or _____
When the class returns from their walk, discuss the appealing aspects of the rocks collected.

ACTIVITY (Optional)
Class goes for a walk, looking for special rocks. Each student keeps one rock.

Writing

MINI-LESSON
Teacher leads a 5- to 7-minute discussion about possible interpretations of the Writing Topic: Games That Require Special Clothes or Equipment or
_____.

COMPOSING
Each student writes on
- the lesson's topic
- a personally chosen topic
- a topic begun previously

SHARING
Papers are read to a classmate or the teacher, dated, and filed.

Word Study

CHART DEVELOPMENT
Spelling Emphasis: *ea* or 2 syllables and/or _____
On the chart, the teacher writes sentences containing the day's letters or number of syllables or _____.

WRITING
On their papers, students write
- their favorite words from the chart
- other words/clusters/sentences that would be appropriate for the chart
Papers are dated and filed.

Lesson 125

Research

LEAD-IN
Teacher introduces the Project Idea.
Theme: Cost of food items or
_____

Material: Menus or _____
Reading Focus: Functional reading
or _____

SEARCH & RECORD
Project Idea: In teams of 3 or 4, students explore menus looking for things

they like to eat. Record items and their cost.

SHARING
Class decides on one item from each section of the menu and totals the cost of the meal.
  Papers are dated and filed.

Recreational Reading

CONVERSATIONS
Check-In: Teacher moves among students, having 2- to 3-minute conversations with as many individuals as possible. If appropriate, discuss main ideas and/or _____.

CLIPBOARD NOTES
Teacher notes who is constantly seeking help decoding words or _____.

BOOK SHARING
Each person tells another person something he or she has read about that day.

and Storytime

READ ALOUD
Jumanji by Chris Van Allsburg or *Cat in the Hat* by Dr. Seuss or _____
  Class discusses things that happened to them when they did not do as their parents told them to do.

ACTIVITY (Optional)
Teacher provides a blank game board. Students work with partners to make up a game.

Writing

MINI-LESSON
Teacher leads a 5- to 7-minute discussion about possible interpretations of the Writing Topic: Playing With a Friend or _____

COMPOSING
Each student writes on
■ the lesson's topic
■ a personally chosen topic
■ a topic begun previously

SHARING
Papers are read to a classmate or the teacher, dated, and filed.

Word Study

CHART DEVELOPMENT
Spelling Emphasis: *te* or 2 syllables and/or _____
  On the chart, the teacher writes sentences containing the day's letters or number of syllables or _____.

WRITING
On their papers, students write
■ their favorite words from the chart
■ other words/clusters/sentences that would be appropriate for the chart
Papers are dated and filed.

Lesson 126

Research

LEAD-IN
Teacher introduces the Project Idea.
Theme: Colors of food or _____
Material: Menus or _____
Reading Focus: Functional reading or _____

SEARCH & RECORD
Project Idea: In teams of 2 or 3, students explore menus looking for foods of different colors. Record the name of the food under the color heading.

SHARING
Two or more teams compare their findings or _____.
    Papers are dated and filed.

Recreational Reading

CONVERSATIONS
In-Depth: Teacher holds 7- to 10-minute conversations with 3 or 4 students (individually) discussing real and make-believe, how the book relates to the reader's experience, and/or _____.

CLIPBOARD NOTES
Teacher notes who is constantly seeking help decoding words or _____.

BOOK SHARING
Each person tells another person something he or she has read about that day.

and Storytime

READ ALOUD
Today is Tana Hoban Day. Teacher reads or shows students several books by Tana Hoban, such as *26 Letters and 99 Cents* or *Of Colors and Things* or *I Read Symbols* or *Take Another Look* or *Is it Larger? Is It Smaller?* or *Shapes, Shapes, Shapes* or *Shapes and Things* or _____
    Students explore the books in groups of 3 or 4.

ACTIVITY (Optional)
Using photographs from magazines, students create books that are similar to Tana Hoban's.

Writing

MINI-LESSON
Teacher leads a 5- to 7-minute discussion about possible interpretations of the Writing Topic: A Famous Athlete or _____.

COMPOSING
Each student writes (by drawing or developmental spelling) on
■ the lesson's topic
■ a personally chosen topic
■ a topic begun previously

SHARING
Papers are read to a classmate or the teacher, dated, and filed.

Word Study

CHART DEVELOPMENT
Spelling Emphasis: *nt* or 2 syllables and/or _____
    On the chart, the teacher writes words, word clusters, or sentences (Teacher's Choice) containing the day's letters or number of syllables or _____.

WRITING
On their papers, students write
■ their favorite words from the chart
■ other words/clusters/sentences that would be appropriate for the chart
Papers are dated and filed.

Lesson 127

Research

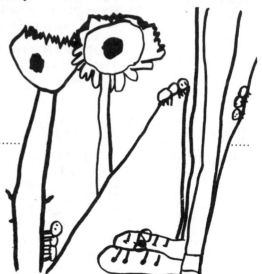

LEAD-IN
Teacher introduces the Project Idea.
Theme: Colors of items or _____
Material: Newspapers or _____
Reading Focus: Association or _____

SEARCH & RECORD
Project Idea: Individually, students locate words or pictures of items that they associate with particular colors, and cut or tear them out. They paste the items on a piece of paper and label them with the color. Encourage discussion with neighbors.

SHARING
Compare items or words found and their colors with another student or _____.

Papers are dated and filed.

Recreational Reading

CONVERSATIONS
In-Depth: Teacher holds 7- to 10-minute conversations with 3 or 4 students (individually) discussing real and make-believe, how the book relates to the reader's experience, and/or _____.

CLIPBOARD NOTES
Teacher notes who seeks recommendations from others or _____.

BOOK SHARING
Each person tells another person something he or she has read about that day.

and Storytime

READ ALOUD
Two Bad Ants by Chris Van Allsburg or *George Shrinks* by William Joyce or _____

Discuss what it would be like to be very small and live in this world.

ACTIVITY (Optional)
Draw a picture from the ants' or George's point of view.

Writing

MINI-LESSON
Teacher leads a 5- to 7-minute discussion about possible interpretations of the Writing Topic: Furniture in a Bedroom or _____.

COMPOSING
Each student writes on
- the lesson's topic
- a personally chosen topic
- a topic begun previously

SHARING
Papers are read to a classmate or the teacher, dated, and filed.

Word Study

CHART DEVELOPMENT
Spelling Emphasis: *igh* or 2 syllables and/or _____
On the chart, the teacher writes words, word clusters, or sentences (Teacher's Choice) containing the day's letters or number of syllables or _____.

WRITING
On their papers, students write
- their favorite words from the chart
- other words/clusters/sentences that would be appropriate for the chart
Papers are dated and filed.

Lesson 128

Research

LEAD-IN
Teacher introduces the Project Idea.
Theme: Comics or _____
Material: Newspapers or _____
Reading Focus: Sequence of events or _____

SEARCH & RECORD
Project Idea: In teams of 2 or 3, students look at comic strips in the newspaper. Record a series of events for as many strips as there is time.

SHARING
Compare letters and words found with another student or _____. Papers are dated and filed.

Recreational Reading

CONVERSATIONS
In-Depth: Teacher holds 7- to 10-minute conversations with 3 or 4 students (individually) discussing real and make-believe, how the book relates to the reader's experience, and/or _____.

CLIPBOARD NOTES
Teacher notes who seeks recommendations from others or _____.

BOOK SHARING
Each person tells another person something he or she has read about that day.

and Storytime

READ ALOUD
Chair for My Mother by Vera B. Williams or _____
  Discuss the sequence of events that happened in the story.

ACTIVITY (Optional)
Make a bank out of a can, jar, or box and decorate it. Decide what you would like to save money to buy.

Writing

MINI-LESSON
Teacher leads a 5- to 7-minute discussion about possible interpretations of the Writing Topic: Furniture in Another Room or _____.

COMPOSING
Each student writes on
- the lesson's topic
- a personally chosen topic
- a topic begun previously

SHARING
Papers are read to a classmate or the teacher, dated, and filed.

Word Study

CHART DEVELOPMENT
Spelling Emphasis: *ad* or 2 syllables and/or _____
  On the chart, the teacher writes words, word clusters, or sentences (Teacher's Choice) containing the day's letters or number of syllables or _____.

WRITING
On their papers, students write
- their favorite words from the chart
- other words/clusters/sentences that would be appropriate for the chart Papers are dated and filed.

Lesson **129**

Research

LEAD-IN
Teacher introduces the Project Idea.
Theme: Sequence of events or

Material: Social studies textbooks or nonfiction books or _____
Reading Focus: Sequence of events

SEARCH & RECORD
Project Idea: In teams of 2 or 3, students explore social studies textbooks

for a sequence of events. Record what is happening in any event or picture in the social studies text. Also record what happened before and after _____.

SHARING
Two or more teams compare their findings or _____.
   Papers are dated and filed.

Recreational Reading

CONVERSATIONS
In-Depth: Teacher holds 7- to 10-minute conversations with 3 or 4 students (individually) discussing real and make-believe, how the book relates to the reader's experience, and/or _____.

CLIPBOARD NOTES
Teacher notes who seeks recommendations from others or _____.

BOOK SHARING
Each person tells another person something he or she has read about that day.

and Storytime

READ ALOUD
A variety of alphabet books such as *Alphabatics* by Suse Macdonald or *ABC The Museum of Modern Art, New York* by Florence C. Mayers or *A-B-Cing* by Janet Beller or *Arlene Alda's ABC Book* by Arlene Alda or *A My Name is Alice* by Jane Bayer or _____
   Compare the words for different letters in the various books.

ACTIVITY (Optional)
Make a class alphabet book about clothes. Each student can make one page.

Writing

MINI-LESSON
Teacher leads a 5- to 7-minute discussion about possible interpretations of the Writing Topic: Rules About Furniture or _____.

COMPOSING
Each student writes (by drawing or developmental spelling) on
■ the lesson's topic
■ a personally chosen topic
■ a topic begun previously

SHARING
Papers are read to a classmate or the teacher, dated, and filed.

Word Study

CHART DEVELOPMENT
Spelling Emphasis: *ck* or 2 syllables and/or _____
   On the chart, the teacher writes words, word clusters, or sentences (Teacher's Choice) containing the day's letters or number of syllables or _____.

WRITING
On their papers, students write
■ their favorite words from the chart
■ other words/clusters/sentences that would be appropriate for the chart
Papers are dated and filed.

Research

LEAD-IN
Teacher introduces the Project Idea.
Theme: Clothing or _____
Material: Social studies textbooks or _____

Reading Focus: Association or _____

SEARCH & RECORD
Project Idea: In teams of 2 or 3, students explore social studies textbooks identifying words or pictures which they can associate with clothing or _____.

SHARING
Students meet in groups of 4 or 5 and discuss the items found that relate to the day's theme or _____.
Papers are dated and filed.

Recreational Reading

CONVERSATIONS
In-Depth: Teacher holds 7- to 10-minute conversations with 3 or 4 students (individually) discussing real and make-believe, how the book relates to the reader's experience, and/or _____.

CLIPBOARD NOTES
Teacher notes who recommends books to others or _____.

BOOK SHARING
Each person tells another person something he or she has read about that day.

and Storytime

READ ALOUD
Pelle's New Suit by Elsa Beskow or *Thomas' Snow Suit* by Robert Munsch or _____
Discuss *why* things happened in the story.

ACTIVITY (Optional)
Make a paper doll and paper-doll clothes.

Writing

MINI-LESSON
Teacher leads a 5- to 7-minute discussion about possible interpretations of the Writing Topic: Clothing in Different Seasons or _____.

COMPOSING
Each student writes on
- the lesson's topic
- a personally chosen topic
- a topic begun previously

SHARING
Papers are read to a classmate or the teacher, dated, and filed.

Word Study

CHART DEVELOPMENT
Spelling Emphasis: *ow* or 2 syllables and/or _____
On the chart, the teacher writes words, word clusters, or sentences (Teacher's Choice) containing the day's letters or number of syllables or _____.

WRITING
On their papers, students write
- their favorite words from the chart
- other words/clusters/sentences that would be appropriate for the chart
Papers are dated and filed.

Lesson **131**

Research

LEAD-IN
Teacher introduces the Project Idea.
Theme: Clothing or _____
Material: Art prints or _____
Reading Focus: Functional reading or _____

SEARCH & RECORD
Project Idea: In teams of 2 or 3, students explore a variety of art prints

looking particularly at the clothing worn by people in the prints. Describe the clothing and/or compare it to today's clothing.

SHARING
Students meet in groups of 4 or 5 and discuss the clothing found or _____.
Papers are dated and filed.

Recreational Reading

CONVERSATIONS
In-Depth: Teacher holds 7- to 10-minute conversations with 3 or 4 students (individually) discussing real and make-believe, how the book relates to the reader's experience, and/or _____.

CLIPBOARD NOTES
Teacher notes who recommends books to others or _____.

BOOK SHARING
Each person tells another person something he or she has read about that day.

and Storytime

READ ALOUD
Going Up by Peter Sis or _____
Discuss *when* and *where* things happened in the story.

ACTIVITY (Optional)
Make elevator doors that open onto your favorite floor in a big building. Cut large doors in one piece of construction paper. They will open like a cupboard's doors,

not like an elevator's. On another piece of paper, draw what you would see when the elevator doors open. Glue the "elevator" over the picture of the floor. Open the doors and see the floor.

Writing

MINI-LESSON
Teacher leads a 5- to 7-minute discussion about possible interpretations of the Writing Topic: Costumes or _____.

COMPOSING
Each student writes on
- the lesson's topic
- a personally chosen topic
- a topic begun previously

SHARING
Papers are read to a classmate or the teacher, dated, and filed.

Word Study

CHART DEVELOPMENT
Spelling Emphasis: *b* or 3 syllables and/or _____
On the chart, the teacher writes words, word clusters, or sentences (Teacher's Choice) containing the day's letters or number of syllables or _____.

WRITING
On their papers, students write
- their favorite words from the chart
- other words/clusters/sentences that would be appropriate for the chart
Papers are dated and filed.

Lesson 132

Research

LEAD-IN
Teacher introduces the Project Idea.
Theme: Main idea or _____
Material: Art prints or _____
Reading Focus: Functional reading or _____

SEARCH & RECORD
Project Idea: In teams of 2 or 3, students explore a variety of art prints.

Discuss and record what each picture is about. What is the main idea the artist is trying to show?

SHARING
Students discuss the titles of the pictures and how the titles relate to the main idea of the picture or _____.
    Papers are dated and filed.

Recreational Reading

CONVERSATIONS
In-Depth: Teacher holds 7- to 10-minute conversations with 3 or 4 students (individually) discussing real and make-believe, how the book relates to the reader's experience, and/or _____.

CLIPBOARD NOTES
Teacher notes who reads books written by students or class books or _____.

BOOK SHARING
Each person tells another person something he or she has read about that day.

and Storytime

READ ALOUD
Drummer Hoff by Rebecca Emberley or _____

    Discuss *who* is in the story and *what* each person did.

ACTIVITY (Optional)
Design a soldier's hat out of paper. Attach a ring of paper for a neckband so that the children can wear the hats.

Writing

MINI-LESSON
Teacher leads a 5- to 7-minute discussion about possible interpretations of the Writing Topic: Uniforms or _____.

COMPOSING
Each student writes (by drawing or developmental spelling) on
■ the lesson's topic
■ a personally chosen topic
■ a topic begun previously

SHARING
Papers are read to a classmate or the teacher, dated, and filed.

Word Study

CHART DEVELOPMENT
Spelling Emphasis: *c* or 3 syllables and/or _____
    On the chart, the teacher writes words, word clusters, or sentences (Teacher's Choice) containing the day's letters or number of syllables or _____.

WRITING
On their papers, students write
■ their favorite words from the chart
■ other words/clusters/sentences that would be appropriate for the chart
Papers are dated and filed.

Lesson 133

Research

LEAD-IN
Teacher introduces the Project Idea.
Theme: Main idea or _____
Material: Magazines or _____
Reading Focus: Main idea or _____

SEARCH & RECORD
Project Idea: In teams of 2 or 3, students look at magazine pictures and articles. Record the main idea of pictures and/or articles. What are they about?

SHARING
Two or more teams compare their findings or _____.
   Papers are dated and filed.

Recreational Reading

CONVERSATIONS
Small Group: For approximately 10 to 15 minutes teacher meets with a small group of students who have all read the same story or portion of a book. The other students read quietly in books of their choice.

CLIPBOARD NOTES
Teacher notes who reads books written by students or class books or _____.

BOOK SHARING
Each person tells another person something he or she has read about that day.

and

Storytime

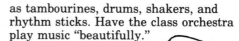

READ ALOUD
The Philharmonic Gets Dressed by Karla Kuskin or _____
   Discuss groups of things or people in the story.

ACTIVITY (Optional)
Make musical instruments. They may be "pretend" instruments made out of paper or tagboard or rhythm instruments such as tambourines, drums, shakers, and rhythm sticks. Have the class orchestra play music "beautifully."

Writing

MINI-LESSON
Teacher leads a 5- to 7-minute discussion about possible interpretations of the Writing Topic: Clothing for Special Occasions or _____.

COMPOSING
Each student writes on
■ the lesson's topic
■ a personally chosen topic
■ a topic begun previously

SHARING
Papers are read to a classmate or the teacher, dated, and filed.

Word Study

CHART DEVELOPMENT
Spelling Emphasis: *d* or 3 syllables and/or _____
   On the chart, the teacher writes words, word clusters, or sentences (Teacher's Choice) containing the day's letters or number of syllables or _____.

WRITING
On their papers, students write
■ their favorite words from the chart
■ other words/clusters/sentences that would be appropriate for the chart
Papers are dated and filed.

Lesson 134

Research

LEAD-IN
Teacher introduces the Project Idea.
Theme: Details or _____
Material: Magazines or _____
Reading Focus: Details or _____

SEARCH & RECORD
Project Idea: In teams of 2 or 3, students locate a picture in a magazine, tape it to a larger piece of paper, and label as many details as possible in the picture. Draw lines from the items to the words labeling them.

SHARING
Students discuss the items found that relate to the day's theme or _____.
   Papers are dated and filed.

Recreational Reading

CONVERSATIONS
Check-In: Teacher moves among students, having 2- to 3-minute conversations with as many individuals as possible. If appropriate, discuss main ideas and/or _____.

CLIPBOARD NOTES
Teacher notes who reads books written by students or class books or _____.

BOOK SHARING
Each person tells another person something he or she has read about that day.

and Storytime

READ ALOUD
Getting Dressed by Vicki Cobb or _____

   Discuss other names for articles of clothing, e.g., coat, jacket, parka, etc.

ACTIVITY (Optional)
Cut or tear out magazine pictures of clothes. Arrange them by groups or types and in the order that a person would put them on.

Writing

MINI-LESSON
Teacher leads a 5- to 7-minute discussion about possible interpretations of the Writing Topic: Safety and Clothing or _____.

COMPOSING
Each student writes (by drawing or developmental spelling) on
■ the lesson's topic
■ a personally chosen topic
■ a topic begun previously

SHARING
Papers are read to a classmate or the teacher, dated, and filed.

Word Study

CHART DEVELOPMENT
Spelling Emphasis: *f* or 3 syllables and/or _____
   On the chart, the teacher writes words, word clusters, or sentences (Teacher's Choice) containing the day's letters or number of syllables or _____.

WRITING
On their papers, students write
■ their favorite words from the chart
■ other words/clusters/sentences that would be appropriate for the chart
Papers are dated and filed.

Lesson 135

Research

LEAD-IN
Teacher introduces the Project Idea.
Theme: Details or _____
Material: Library books or _____
Reading Focus: Details or
_____

SEARCH & RECORD
Project Idea: In teams of 2 or 3, students locate pictures in library books,

discuss, and record the details in the pictures.

SHARING
Two or three teams compare the details found or _____. Papers are dated and filed.

Recreational Reading

CONVERSATIONS
Check-In: Teacher moves among students, having 2- to 3-minute conversations with as many individuals as possible. If appropriate, discuss detail and/or _____.

CLIPBOARD NOTES
Teacher notes who reads books written by students or class books or _____.

BOOK SHARING
Each person tells another person something he or she has read about that day.

and Storytime

READ ALOUD
Do You Want to be My Friend? by Eric Carle or _____
   Before beginning to read the book, have the class predict what it will be about. Then have them predict each page. Reread without stopping for discussion.

ACTIVITY (Optional)
Make a class book in the manner of the read-aloud book.

Writing

MINI-LESSON
Teacher leads a 5- to 7-minute discussion about possible interpretations of the Writing Topic: Memo for Refrigerator Door (e.g., Gone Out) or _____.

COMPOSING
Each student writes on
■ the lesson's topic
■ a personally chosen topic
■ a topic begun previously

SHARING
Papers are read to a classmate or the teacher, dated, and filed.

Word Study

CHART DEVELOPMENT
Spelling Emphasis: *g* or 3 syllables and/or _____
   On the chart, the teacher writes words, word clusters, or sentences (Teacher's Choice) containing the day's letters or number of syllables or _____.

WRITING
On their papers, students write
■ their favorite words from the chart
■ other words/clusters/sentences that would be appropriate for the chart

Papers are dated and filed.
   Each student chooses a composition from his or her folder for the teacher to display in the classroom. Students may modify their writing and/or illustrations as they choose.

Research

LEAD-IN
Teacher introduces the Project Idea.
Theme: Businesses or _____
Material: Library books or _____
Reading Focus: Association or _____

SEARCH & RECORD
Project Idea: In teams of 2 or 3, students locate pictures, words, or symbols in library books that they can associate with businesses.

SHARING
Two or three teams compare the lists of businesses and discuss what each team found that they associated with the businesses or _____.
   Papers are dated and filed.

Recreational Reading

CONVERSATIONS
Check-In: Teacher moves among students, having 2- to 3-minute conversations with as many individuals as possible. If appropriate, discuss detail and/or _____.

CLIPBOARD NOTES
Teacher notes who is not an independent reader or _____.

BOOK SHARING
Each person tells another person something he or she has read about that day.

and Storytime

READ ALOUD
The Josefina Story Quilt by Eleanor Coerr or *The Keeping Quilt* by Patricia Polacco or *The Quilt* by Ann Jonas or _____
   Teacher rereads parts of the story and the class discusses referents to pronouns.

ACTIVITY (Optional)
Make a class quilt out of paper or wallpaper.

Writing

MINI-LESSON
Teacher leads a 5- to 7-minute discussion about possible interpretations of the Writing Topic: Memo: Phone Message or _____.

COMPOSING
Each student writes on
■ the lesson's topic
■ a personally chosen topic
■ a topic begun previously

SHARING
Papers are read to a classmate or the teacher, dated, and filed.

Word Study

CHART DEVELOPMENT
Spelling Emphasis: *h* or 3 syllables and/or _____
   On the chart, the teacher writes words, word clusters, or sentences (Teacher's Choice) containing the day's letters or number of syllables or _____.

WRITING
On their papers, students write
■ their favorite words from the chart
■ other words/clusters/sentences that would be appropriate for the chart
   Papers are dated and filed.

Lesson 137

Research

LEAD-IN
Teacher introduces the Project Idea.
Theme: What businesses sell or
_____

Material: Yellow pages or _____
Reading Focus: Functional reading
or _____

SEARCH & RECORD
Project Idea: In teams of 2 or 3,
students explore the yellow pages of

telephone books listing the names of
businesses and what they sell.

SHARING
Students discuss the items found that
relate to the day's theme or _____.
   Papers are dated and filed.

Recreational Reading

CONVERSATIONS
Check-In: Teacher moves among
students, having 2- to 3-minute
conversations with as many individuals
as possible. If appropriate, discuss
prediction or inference and/or _____.

CLIPBOARD NOTES
Teacher notes who is not an independent
reader or _____.

BOOK SHARING
Each person tells another person
something he or she has read about that
day.

and Storytime

READ ALOUD
Delphine by Molly Bang or _____
   Discuss the illustrations.

ACTIVITY (Optional)
Make a bicycle by gluing yarn onto paper
or make it out of pipe cleaners.

Writing

MINI-LESSON
Teacher leads a 5- to 7-minute discussion
about possible interpretations of the
Writing Topic: Memo: Reminder or
_____.

COMPOSING
Each student writes on
■ the lesson's topic
■ a personally chosen topic
■ a topic begun previously

SHARING
Papers are read to a classmate or the
teacher, dated, and filed.

Word Study

CHART DEVELOPMENT
Spelling Emphasis: *j* or 3 syllables
and/or _____
   On the chart, the teacher writes words,
word clusters, or sentences (Teacher's
Choice) containing the day's letters or
number of syllables or _____.

WRITING
On their papers, students write
■ their favorite words from the chart
■ other words/clusters/sentences that
   would be appropriate for the chart
   Papers are dated and filed.

Research

LEAD-IN
Teacher introduces the Project Idea.
Theme: Phone numbers of businesses
or _____
Material: Yellow pages or _____
Reading Focus: Functional reading
or _____

SEARCH & RECORD
Project Idea: In teams of 2 or 3, students explore the yellow pages of telephone books listing the names of businesses and their telephone numbers.

SHARING
Students discuss the items found that relate to the day's theme or _____.
Papers are dated and filed.

Recreational Reading and Storytime

CONVERSATIONS
Check-In: Teacher moves among students, having 2- to 3-minute conversations with as many individuals as possible. If appropriate, discuss prediction or inference and/or _____.

CLIPBOARD NOTES
Teacher notes who is not an independent reader or _____.

BOOK SHARING
Each person tells another person something he or she has read about that day.

READ ALOUD
May I Bring a Friend? by Beatrice Schenk de Regniers or *Little Bear's Friend* by Else Minarik or _____
Discuss *who* is in the story and *what* happened.

ACTIVITY (Optional)
Make an invitation to a tea party.

Writing

MINI-LESSON
Teacher leads a 5- to 7-minute discussion about possible interpretations of the Writing Topic: Party Invitation or _____.

COMPOSING
Each student writes (by drawing or developmental spelling) on
■ the lesson's topic
■ a personally chosen topic
■ a topic begun previously

SHARING
Papers are read to a classmate or the teacher, dated, and filed.

Word Study

CHART DEVELOPMENT
Spelling Emphasis: *k* or 3 syllables and/or _____
On the chart, the teacher writes words, word clusters, or sentences (Teacher's Choice) containing the day's letters or number of syllables or _____.

WRITING
On their papers, students write
■ their favorite words from the chart
■ other words/clusters/sentences that would be appropriate for the chart
Papers are dated and filed.

Lesson 139

Research

LEAD-IN
Teacher introduces the Project Idea.
Theme: Names of businesses or _____

Material: Newspapers or _____
Reading Focus: Locating specific information or _____

SEARCH & RECORD
Project Idea: In teams of 2 or 3, students explore newspapers to locate and record the names of businesses. Write a fact about some of the businesses.

SHARING
Two or more teams compare their findings or _____.
Papers are dated and filed.

Recreational Reading

CONVERSATIONS
Check-In: Teacher moves among students, having 2- to 3-minute conversations with as many individuals as possible. If appropriate, discuss comparison and/or _____.

CLIPBOARD NOTES
Teacher notes titles being read or _____.

BOOK SHARING
Each person tells another person something he or she has read about that day.

and Storytime

READ ALOUD
"Eeyore Has a Birthday and Gets Two Presents" in *Winnie-the-Pooh* by A. A. Milne or _____
Discuss the humor in the story.

ACTIVITY (Optional)
Make party hats.

Writing

MINI-LESSON
Teacher leads a 5- to 7-minute discussion about possible interpretations of the Writing Topic: List of Supplies for a Party or _____.

COMPOSING
Each student writes on
■ the lesson's topic
■ a personally chosen topic
■ a topic begun previously

SHARING
Papers are read to a classmate or the teacher, dated, and filed.

Word Study

CHART DEVELOPMENT
Spelling Emphasis: *l* or 3 syllables and/or _____
On the chart, the teacher writes words, word clusters, or sentences (Teacher's Choice) containing the day's letters or number of syllables or _____.

WRITING
On their papers, students write
■ their favorite words from the chart
■ other words/clusters/sentences that would be appropriate for the chart
Papers are dated and filed.

Research

LEAD-IN
Teacher introduces the Project Idea.
Theme: Symbols of businesses or
_____

Material: Newspapers or _____
Reading Focus: Symbols or
_____

SEARCH & RECORD
Project Idea: In teams of 2 or 3, students explore newspapers looking for

and recording symbols for businesses. Write the name beside the symbol.

SHARING
Two or more teams compare their findings or _____.
Papers are dated and filed.

Recreational Reading

CONVERSATIONS
Teacher Reads: For approximately 20 minutes everyone, including the teacher, reads silently. During the last 10 minutes the teacher may choose to talk with some individuals about what they have read.

CLIPBOARD NOTES
Teacher notes titles being read or
_____.

BOOK SHARING
Each person tells another person something he or she has read about that day.

Lift flap

and Storytime

READ ALOUD
Lyle and the Birthday Party by Bernard Waber or _____
Discuss _where_ and _when_ events happened in the story.

ACTIVITY (Optional)
Cut out a picture in a magazine or catalog of a present you would like to give or receive. Glue or tape it onto a

piece of paper. Then cut a rectangle out of colored or decorated paper that will represent the top of a gift box. Place the rectangle on the first paper so that it covers the "present." Attach only the top or one side, so that the box top will lift and you can see the present.

Writing

MINI-LESSON
Teacher leads a 5- to 7-minute discussion about possible interpretations of the Writing Topic: Schedule of Activities for a Party or _____.

COMPOSING
Each student writes on
■ the lesson's topic
■ a personally chosen topic
■ a topic begun previously

SHARING
Papers are read to a classmate or the teacher, dated, and filed.

Word Study

CHART DEVELOPMENT
Spelling Emphasis: _m_ or 3 syllables and/or _____
On the chart, the teacher writes words, word clusters, or sentences (Teacher's Choice) containing the day's letters or number of syllables or _____.

WRITING
On their papers, students write
■ their favorite words from the chart
■ other words/clusters/sentences that would be appropriate for the chart
Papers are dated and filed.

Lesson 141

Research

LEAD-IN
Teacher introduces the Project Idea.
Theme: Things that are made or manufactured or _____
Material: Math textbooks or _____

Reading Focus: Association or _____

SEARCH & RECORD
Project Idea: In teams of 2 or 3, students explore math textbooks identifying words or pictures which they associate with things that are made or manufactured or _____.

SHARING
Students meet in groups of 4 or 5 and discuss the items found that relate to the day's theme or _____.
Papers are dated and filed.

Recreational Reading

CONVERSATIONS
Check-In: Teacher moves among students, having 2- to 3-minute conversations with as many individuals as possible. If appropriate, discuss comparison and/or _____.

CLIPBOARD NOTES
Teacher notes titles being read or _____.

BOOK SHARING
Each person tells another person something he or she has read about that day.

and Storytime

READ ALOUD
Any book about manners such as *What Do You Say, Dear?* by Sesyle Joslin or *Perfect Pigs* by Marc Brown and Stephen Krensky or _____
Relate the incidents in the story to the students' own experiences. Make a class list of things that are good manners.

ACTIVITY (Optional)
Make a class book of manners. Each student chooses something to illustrate from the class list.

Writing

MINI-LESSON
Teacher leads a 5- to 7-minute discussion about possible interpretations of the Writing Topic: Write a Thank-you Note or _____.

COMPOSING
Each student writes on
- the lesson's topic
- a personally chosen topic
- a topic begun previously

SHARING
Papers are read to a classmate or the teacher, dated, and filed.

Word Study

CHART DEVELOPMENT
Spelling Emphasis: *n* or 3 syllables and/or _____
On the chart, the teacher writes words, word clusters, or sentences (Teacher's Choice) containing the day's letters or number of syllables or _____.

WRITING
On their papers, students write
- their favorite words from the chart
- other words/clusters/sentences that would be appropriate for the chart
Papers are dated and filed.

Research

LEAD-IN
Teacher introduces the Project Idea.
Theme: Things that are not made or _____

Material: Math textbooks or _____

Reading Focus: Association or _____

SEARCH & RECORD
Project Idea: In teams of 2 or 3, students explore math textbooks identifying words or pictures of things that are not manufactured or made or _____.

SHARING
Students meet in groups of 4 or 5 and discuss the items found that relate to the day's theme or _____.
    Papers are dated and filed.

Recreational Reading and Storytime

CONVERSATIONS
Check-In: Teacher moves among students, having 2- to 3-minute conversations with as many individuals as possible. If appropriate, discuss cause and effect and/or _____.

CLIPBOARD NOTES
Teacher notes which students are continuing to read the same book on more than one day or _____.

BOOK SHARING
Each person tells another person something he or she has read about that day.

READ ALOUD
Sam, Bangs, and Moonshine by Evaline Ness or _____
    Discuss a time you teased someone or told a lie and were sorry about it later.

ACTIVITY (Optional)
Make a cat out of clay.

Writing

MINI-LESSON
Teacher leads a 5- to 7-minute discussion about possible interpretations of the Writing Topic: Write a Business Letter to Request Something or _____.

COMPOSING
Each student writes on
■ the lesson's topic
■ a personally chosen topic
■ a topic begun previously

SHARING
Papers are read to a classmate or the teacher, dated, and filed.

Word Study

CHART DEVELOPMENT
Spelling Emphasis: *p* or 3 syllables and/or _____
    On the chart, the teacher writes words, word clusters, or sentences (Teacher's Choice) containing the day's letters or number of syllables or _____.

WRITING
On their papers, students write
■ their favorite words from the chart
■ other words/clusters/sentences that would be appropriate for the chart
Papers are dated and filed.

Lesson **143**

Research

LEAD-IN
Teacher introduces the Project Idea.
Theme: Addresses or _____
Material: Forms or _____
Reading Focus: Functional reading or _____

SEARCH & RECORD
Project Idea: In teams of 2 or 3, each student locates forms in magazines and completes it with his or her address. Each should check his or her partner's form for completeness and accuracy.

SHARING
Students discuss the information requested and written on their forms or _____.

Papers are dated and filed.

Recreational Reading

CONVERSATIONS
Small Group: For approximately 10 to 15 minutes teacher meets with a small group of students who have all read the same story or portion of a book. The other students read quietly in books of their choice.

CLIPBOARD NOTES
Teacher notes which students are continuing to read the same book on more than one day or _____.

BOOK SHARING
Each person tells another person something he or she has read about that day.

and

Storytime

READ ALOUD
Song and Dance Man by Karen Ackerman or _____
  Discuss parents and grandparents and things they used to do when they were younger.

ACTIVITY (Optional)
Make top hats out of black construction paper.

Writing

MINI-LESSON
Teacher leads a 5- to 7-minute discussion about possible interpretations of the Writing Topic: Write a Business Letter to Praise or Complain or _____.

COMPOSING
Each student writes on
■ the lesson's topic
■ a personally chosen topic
■ a topic begun previously

SHARING
Papers are read to a classmate or the teacher, dated, and filed.

Word Study

CHART DEVELOPMENT
Spelling Emphasis: *q* or 3 syllables and/or _____
  On the chart, the teacher writes words, word clusters, or sentences (Teacher's Choice) containing the day's letters or number of syllables or _____.

WRITING
On their papers, students write
■ their favorite words from the chart
■ other words/clusters/sentences that would be appropriate for the chart
Papers are dated and filed.

Research

LEAD-IN
Teacher introduces the Project Idea.
Theme: Ordering information or _____

Material: Forms or _____
Reading Focus: Functional reading or _____

SEARCH & RECORD
Project Idea: The teacher leads a brief discussion about how this is just an activity and that no one should mail an order without permission from the person who will pay the bill.

In teams of 3 or 4, students complete the ordering information for something they would like to buy.

SHARING
Students discuss the items they "ordered" and the types of information requested or _____.

Papers are dated and filed.

Recreational Reading

CONVERSATIONS
Check-In: Teacher moves among students, having 2- to 3-minute conversations with as many individuals as possible. If appropriate, discuss cause and effect and/or _____.

CLIPBOARD NOTES
Teacher notes which students are continuing to read the same book more than one day or _____.

BOOK SHARING
Each person tells another person something he or she has read about that day.

and Storytime

READ ALOUD
A Penguin's Tale by B. Cooney *Angus and the Ducks* by Marjorie Flack or _____

Discuss a time you or someone you know were so curious that it almost got you in trouble.

ACTIVITY (Optional)
Make a penguin or duck out of paper. Attach the wings with brads so that they move.

Writing

MINI-LESSON
Teacher leads a 5- to 7-minute discussion about possible interpretations of the Writing Topic: Write a Letter to a Celebrity or _____.

COMPOSING
Each student writes (by drawing or developmental spelling) on
- the lesson's topic
- a personally chosen topic
- a topic begun previously

SHARING
Papers are read to a classmate or the teacher, dated, and filed.

Word Study

CHART DEVELOPMENT
Spelling Emphasis: *r* or 3 syllables and/or _____
On the chart, the teacher writes words, word clusters, or sentences (Teacher's Choice) containing the day's letters or number of syllables or _____.

WRITING
On their papers, students write
- their favorite words from the chart
- other words/clusters/sentences that would be appropriate for the chart
Papers are dated and filed.

247

Lesson 145

Research

LEAD-IN
Teacher introduces the Project Idea.
Theme: Main idea or _____
Material: Magazines or _____
Reading Focus: Main idea or
_____

SEARCH & RECORD
Project Idea: In teams of 2 or 3, students explore magazines. Team

members discuss and record the main idea of pictures, advertisements, and/or articles in the magazine.

SHARING
Two or more teams compare their findings or _____.
  Papers are dated and filed.

Recreational Reading

CONVERSATIONS
Check-In: Teacher moves among students, having 2- to 3-minute conversations with as many individuals as possible. If appropriate, discuss sequence of events and/or _____.

CLIPBOARD NOTES
Teacher notes students who watch the teacher or daydream or _____.

BOOK SHARING
Each person tells another person something he or she has read about that day.

and Storytime

READ ALOUD
Any biography such as *Benjamin Franklin* or *Abraham Lincoln* or others by Edgar P. & Ingri d'Aulaire or *A Picture Book of Benjamin Franklin* or *A Picture Book of George Washington* or others by David Adler or _____.
  Discuss *where* and *when* things happened in this person's life.

ACTIVITY (Optional)
Draw a picture of an incident you remember from the biography.

Writing

MINI-LESSON
Teacher leads a 5- to 7-minute discussion about possible interpretations of the Writing Topic: Write a Letter to a Political Figure or _____.

COMPOSING
Each student writes (by drawing or developmental spelling) on
■ the lesson's topic
■ a personally chosen topic
■ a topic begun previously

SHARING
Papers are read to a classmate or the teacher, dated, and filed.

Word Study

CHART DEVELOPMENT
Spelling Emphasis: *s* or 3 syllables and/or _____
  On the chart, the teacher writes words, word clusters, or sentences (Teacher's Choice) containing the day's letters or number of syllables or _____.

WRITING
On their papers, students write
■ their favorite words from the chart
■ other words/clusters/sentences that would be appropriate for the chart
Papers are dated and filed.

248

Research

LEAD-IN
Teacher introduces the Project Idea.
Theme: Details or _____
Material: Magazines or _____
Reading Focus: Details or
_____

SEARCH & RECORD
Project Idea: In teams of 2 or 3,
students label as many details in a

magazine picture as they can. Teams title
their pictures.

SHARING
Students show and tell about their
picture(s) to a group of 4 to 6 students or
_____.
    Papers are dated and filed.

Recreational Reading

CONVERSATIONS
Check-In: Teacher moves among
students, having 2- to 3-minute
conversations with as many individuals
as possible. If appropriate, discuss
sequence of events and/or _____.

CLIPBOARD NOTES
Teacher notes students who watch the
teacher or daydream or _____.

BOOK SHARING
Each person tells another person
something he or she has read about that
day.

and Storytime

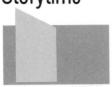

READ ALOUD
Cherries and Cherry Pits by Vera B.
Williams or _____
    Discuss the colors Bidemmi used to
draw her pictures.

ACTIVITY (Optional)
Use bright colored markers or crayons to
draw the kind of tree you would like to
have in your yard.

Writing

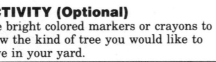

MINI-LESSON
Teacher leads a 5- to 7-minute discussion
about possible interpretations of the
Writing Topic: Write a Letter to a Family
Member or Friend or _____.

COMPOSING
Each student writes (by drawing or
developmental spelling) on
■ the lesson's topic
■ a personally chosen topic
■ a topic begun previously

SHARING
Papers are read to a classmate or the
teacher, dated, and filed.

Word Study

CHART DEVELOPMENT
Spelling Emphasis: *t* or 3 syllables
and/or _____
    On the chart, the teacher writes words,
word clusters, or sentences (Teacher's
Choice) containing the day's letters or
number of syllables or _____.

WRITING
On their papers, students write
■ their favorite words from the chart
■ other words/clusters/sentences that
    would be appropriate for the chart
    Papers are dated and filed.

Lesson 147

Research

LEAD-IN
Teacher introduces the Project Idea.
Theme: Details or _____
Material: Library books or _____
Reading Focus: Details or
_____

SEARCH & RECORD
Project Idea: In teams of 2 or 3, students explore library books discussing and recording as many details as possible in some of the illustrations. Determine a title or main idea for each illustration for which details are listed.

SHARING
Two or more teams compare their findings or _____.
    Papers are dated and filed.

Recreational Reading

CONVERSATIONS
Check-In: Teacher moves among students, having 2- to 3-minute conversations with as many individuals as possible. If appropriate, discuss general things about a book such as the author and/or illustrator or parts of the book and/or _____.

CLIPBOARD NOTES
Teacher notes students who watch the teacher or daydream or _____.

BOOK SHARING
Each person tells another person something he or she has read about that day.

and Storytime

READ ALOUD
Inch by Inch by Leo Lionni or _____
    Discuss how the inchworm solved his problem.

ACTIVITY (Optional)
Make an inchworm ruler out of a strip of paper. Measure different objects.

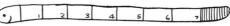

Writing

MINI-LESSON
Teacher leads a 5- to 7-minute discussion about possible interpretations of the Writing Topic: Measure Things in the Classroom. Record data or _____.

COMPOSING
Each student writes (by drawing or developmental spelling) on
- the lesson's topic
- a personally chosen topic
- a topic begun previously

SHARING
Papers are read to a classmate or the teacher, dated, and filed.

Word Study

CHART DEVELOPMENT
Spelling Emphasis: *v* or 3 syllables and/or _____
    On the chart, the teacher writes words, word clusters, or sentences (Teacher's Choice) containing the day's letters or number of syllables or _____.

WRITING
On their papers, students write
- their favorite words from the chart
- other words/clusters/sentences that would be appropriate for the chart
Papers are dated and filed.

Research

LEAD-IN
Teacher introduces the Project Idea.
Theme: Animal babies or _____
Material: Newspapers or _____
Reading Focus: Association or
_____

SEARCH & RECORD
Project Idea: In teams of 2 or 3, students locate information they can associate with birds. Record the information in word clusters of two or more words.

SHARING
Two or more teams compare their findings or _____.
    Papers are dated and filed.

Recreational Reading

CONVERSATIONS
Check-In: Teacher moves among students, having 2- to 3-minute conversations with as many individuals as possible. If appropriate, discuss general things about a book such as the author and/or illustrator or parts of the book and/or _____.

CLIPBOARD NOTES
Teacher notes who prefers what type of book or _____.

BOOK SHARING
Each person tells another person something he or she has read about that day.

and Storytime

READ ALOUD
The Line-up Book by Marisabina Russo or
_____
    Discuss ways to order or sequence things.

ACTIVITY (Optional)
Cut or tear pictures of objects from magazines that show an order or sequence.

Writing

MINI-LESSON
Teacher leads a 5- to 7-minute discussion about possible interpretations of the Writing Topic: Measure Things in the Classroom with a Different Measuring Device Than Yesterday. Record data or

COMPOSING
Each student writes on
■ the lesson's topic
■ a personally chosen topic
■ a topic begun previously

SHARING
Papers are read to a classmate or the teacher, dated, and filed.

Word Study

CHART DEVELOPMENT
Spelling Emphasis: *w, x* or 3 syllables and/or _____
    On the chart, the teacher writes words, word clusters, or sentences (Teacher's Choice) containing the day's letters or number of syllables or _____.

WRITING
On their papers, students write
■ their favorite words from the chart
■ other words/clusters/sentences that would be appropriate for the chart
Papers are dated and filed.

Lesson 149

Research

LEAD-IN
Teacher introduces the Project Idea.
Theme: Animal babies or _____
Material: Science textbooks or

_____

Reading Focus: Association or

_____

SEARCH & RECORD
Project Idea: In teams of 2 or 3, students locate information they can associate with birds. Record the information in word clusters of two or more words.

SHARING
Students discuss the items found that relate to the day's theme or _____.
    Papers are dated and filed.

Recreational Reading

CONVERSATIONS
Check-In: Teacher moves among students, having 2- to 3-minute conversations with as many individuals as possible. If appropriate, discuss connotations of the words chosen by the author and/or _____.

CLIPBOARD NOTES
Teacher notes who prefers what type of book or _____.

BOOK SHARING
Each person tells another person something he or she has read about that day.

---

and Storytime

READ ALOUD
Flat Stanley by Jeff Brown or _____
    Discuss things that Flat Stanley could do and things he could not do.

ACTIVITY (Optional)
Make a Flat Stanley out of construction paper. Write on him some things he can do and other things he cannot do.

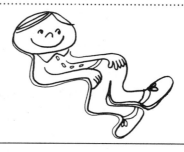

Writing

MINI-LESSON
Teacher leads a 5- to 7-minute discussion about possible interpretations of the Writing Topic: A Time When You Went Out to Eat or _____.

COMPOSING
Each student writes (by drawing or developmental spelling) on
- the lesson's topic
- a personally chosen topic
- a topic begun previously

SHARING
Papers are read to a classmate or the teacher, dated, and filed.

Word Study

CHART DEVELOPMENT
Spelling Emphasis: *y, z* or 3 syllables and/or _____
    On the chart, the teacher writes words, word clusters, or sentences (Teacher's Choice) containing the day's letters or number of syllables or _____.

WRITING
On their papers, students write
- their favorite words from the chart
- other words/clusters/sentences that would be appropriate for the chart
Papers are dated and filed.

Research

LEAD-IN
Teacher introduces the Project Idea.
Theme: Symbols or _____
Material: Science textbooks or
_____

Reading Focus: Association or
_____

SEARCH & RECORD
Project Idea: In teams of 2 or 3, students explore science textbooks looking

for symbols. They record the symbol and what it represents.

SHARING
Two or more teams compare their findings or _____.
    Papers are dated and filed.

Recreational Reading

CONVERSATIONS
In-Depth: Teacher holds 7- to 10-minute conversations with 3 or 4 students (individually) discussing humor, words that tell *when*, words that tell *where*, and/or _____.

CLIPBOARD NOTES
Teacher notes who prefers what type of book or _____.

BOOK SHARING
Each person tells another person something he or she has read about that day.

and Storytime

READ ALOUD
Frank and Ernest by Alexandra Day or
_____
    Discuss the book's figurative language.

ACTIVITY (Optional)
Draw what you might order at a diner or cut pictures out of a magazine. Try to write what some parts of the picture might be called in diner talk.

Writing

MINI-LESSON
Teacher leads a 5- to 7-minute discussion about possible interpretations of the Writing Topic: Waiters or Waitresses or
_____.

COMPOSING
Each student writes on
■ the lesson's topic
■ a personally chosen topic
■ a topic begun previously

SHARING
Papers are read to a classmate or the teacher, dated, and filed.

Word Study

CHART DEVELOPMENT
Spelling Emphasis: *er* or 3 syllables and/or _____
    On the chart, the teacher writes words, word clusters, or sentences (Teacher's Choice) containing the day's letters or number of syllables or _____.

WRITING
On their papers, students write
■ their favorite words from the chart
■ other words/clusters/sentences that would be appropriate for the chart

Papers are dated and filed.
    Each student chooses a composition from his or her folder for the teacher to display in the classroom. Students may modify their writing and/or illustration as they choose.

253

Lesson 151

Research

LEAD-IN
Teacher introduces the Project Idea.
Theme: Symbols or _____
Material: Maps or _____
Reading Focus: Functional reading or _____

SEARCH & RECORD
Project Idea: In teams of 2 or 3, students explore maps looking for symbols and what they represent. Students record symbols found, what they mean, and a nearby town or city.

SHARING
Two or more teams compare their findings or _____.
    Papers are dated and filed.

Recreational Reading

NOTE TO THE TEACHER: Students will be studying fairy tales in Lessons 156–60. It will be a good idea to have many fairy tales available for the next two weeks

CONVERSATIONS
In-Depth: Teacher holds 7- to 10-minute conversations with three or four students (individually) discussing humor, words that tell *when,* words that tell *where,* and/or _____.

CLIPBOARD NOTES
Teacher notes who prefers which authors or _____.

BOOK SHARING
Each person tells another person something he or she has read about that day.

and Storytime

READ ALOUD
Sylvester and the Magic Pebble by William Steig or _____
    Class makes a list of wishes and discusses the advantages and disadvantages of each.

ACTIVITY (Optional)
Make a class wish book. Each student chooses a wish to illustrate.

Writing

MINI-LESSON
Teacher leads a 5- to 7-minute discussion about possible interpretations of the Writing Topic: Picnics or _____.

COMPOSING
Each student writes on
■ the lesson's topic
■ a personally chosen topic
■ a topic begun previously

SHARING
Papers are read to a classmate or the teacher, dated, and filed.

Word Study

CHART DEVELOPMENT
Spelling Emphasis: *er* or 3 syllables and/or _____
    On the chart, the teacher writes words, word clusters, or sentences (Teacher's Choice) containing the day's letters or number of syllables or _____.

WRITING
On their papers, students write
■ their favorite words from the chart
■ other words/clusters/sentences that would be appropriate for the chart
Papers are dated and filed.

254

Research

LEAD-IN
Teacher introduces the Project Idea.
Theme: Landmarks or _____
Material: Maps or _____
Reading Focus: Functional reading
or _____

SEARCH & RECORD
Project Idea: In teams of 2 or 3,
students explore maps looking for any
historical or physical landmarks. Students
record the name or type of landmarks and
a nearby town or city.

SHARING
Two or more teams compare their findings
or _____.
   Papers are dated and filed.

Recreational Reading

CONVERSATIONS
In-Depth: Teacher holds 7- to 10-
minute conversations with 3 or 4 students
(individually) discussing humor, words
that tell *when*, words that tell *where*, and/
or _____.

CLIPBOARD NOTES
Teacher notes who prefers which authors
or _____.

BOOK SHARING
Each person tells another person
something he or she has read about that
day.

and Storytime

READ ALOUD
Where Do Birds Live? by Ron Hirschi or
_____
   Compare different bird nests or houses.
Discuss what birds need to make nests.

ACTIVITY (Optional)
Make nests out of clay. Add straw, twigs,
and/or other items that birds use in
making nests.

Writing

MINI-LESSON
Teacher leads a 5- to 7-minute discussion
about possible interpretations of the
Writing Topic: Bird Houses or
_____.

COMPOSING
Each student writes (by drawing or
developmental spelling) on
■ the lesson's topic
■ a personally chosen topic
■ a topic begun previously

SHARING
Papers are read to a classmate or the
teacher, dated, and filed.

Word Study

CHART DEVELOPMENT
Spelling Emphasis: *tr* or 3 syllables
and/or _____
   On the chart, the teacher writes words,
word clusters, or sentences (Teacher's
Choice) containing the day's letters or
number of syllables or _____.

WRITING
On their papers, students write
■ their favorite words from the chart
■ other words/clusters/sentences that
   would be appropriate for the chart
   Papers are dated and filed.

Lesson **153**

Research

LEAD-IN
Teacher introduces the Project Idea.
Theme: Birds or _____
Material: Any or _____
Reading Focus: Picture Report—
Day 1 or _____

SEARCH & RECORD
Project Idea: Teacher presents
material in the form of a filmstrip, video,
or nonfiction book about the theme.

Students draw one or more pictures
related to the information presented by
the teacher.
   Teacher assists students in recording
some information about their picture(s).

SHARING
Students show and tell about their
picture(s) to a group of 4 to 6 students or
_____.
   Papers are dated and filed.

Recreational Reading

CONVERSATIONS
In-Depth: Teacher holds 7- to 10-
minute conversations with 3 or 4 students
(individually) discussing humor, words
that tell *when,* words that tell *where,* and/
or _____.

CLIPBOARD NOTES
Teacher notes who prefers which authors
or _____.

BOOK SHARING
Each person tells another person
something he or she has read about that
day.

and Storytime

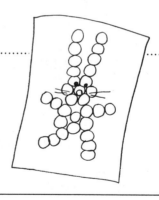

READ ALOUD
Marshmallow by Clare T. Newberry or
_____
   Compare the two animals. How are
they alike? How are they different?

ACTIVITY (Optional)
Make pictures of animals by gluing
miniature marshmallows onto paper.

Writing

MINI-LESSON
Teacher leads a 5- to 7-minute discussion
about possible interpretations of the
Writing Topic: Types of Birds and the
Places They Live or _____.

COMPOSING
Each student writes (by drawing or
developmental spelling) on
■ the lesson's topic
■ a personally chosen topic
■ a topic begun previously

SHARING
Papers are read to a classmate or the
teacher, dated, and filed.

Word Study

CHART DEVELOPMENT
Spelling Emphasis: *ing* or 3
syllables and/or _____
   On the chart, the teacher writes words,
word clusters, or sentences (Teacher's
Choice) containing the day's letters or
number of syllables or _____.

WRITING
On their papers, students write
■ their favorite words from the chart
■ other words/clusters/sentences that
   would be appropriate for the chart
   Papers are dated and filed.

Research

LEAD-IN
Teacher introduces the Project Idea.
Theme: Birds or _____
Material: Any or _____
Reading Focus: Picture Report—
Day 2 or _____

SEARCH & RECORD
Project Idea: Teacher presents
additional material in the form of a
filmstrip, video, or nonfiction book about
the theme. Students draw one or more
pictures related to the information
presented by the teacher. They may
create a new picture(s) or add to
yesterday's picture.
  Teacher assists students in recording
some information about their picture(s).

SHARING
Students show and tell about their
picture(s) to a group of 4 to 6 students or
_____.
  Papers are dated and filed.

Recreational Reading

CONVERSATIONS
In-Depth: Teacher holds 7- to 10-
minute conversations with 3 or 4 students
(individually) discussing humor, words
that tell *when,* words that tell *where,* and/
or _____.

CLIPBOARD NOTES
Teacher notes who studies and/or learns
from the pictures or _____.

BOOK SHARING
Each person tells another person
something he or she has read about that
day.

and Storytime

READ ALOUD
Horton Hatches the Egg by Dr. Seuss or
_____
  Discuss ways of showing loyalty to a
friend.

ACTIVITY (Optional)
Draw a picture of your favorite part of
the story.

Writing

MINI-LESSON
Teacher leads a 5- to 7-minute discussion
about possible interpretations of the
Writing Topic: Migration of Birds or
_____.

COMPOSING
Each student writes (by drawing or
developmental spelling) on
■ the lesson's topic
■ a personally chosen topic
■ a topic begun previously

SHARING
Papers are read to a classmate or the
teacher, dated, and filed.

Word Study

CHART DEVELOPMENT
Spelling Emphasis: *ch* or 3 syllables
and/or _____
  On the chart, the teacher writes words,
word clusters, or sentences (Teacher's
Choice) containing the day's letters or
number of syllables or _____.

WRITING
On their papers, students write
■ their favorite words from the chart
■ other words/clusters/sentences that
  would be appropriate for the chart
Papers are dated and filed.

Lesson 155

Research

LEAD-IN
Teacher introduces the Project Idea.
Theme: Birds or _____
Material: Any or _____
Reading Focus: Picture Report—
Day 3 or _____

SEARCH & RECORD
Project Idea: Teacher presents
additional material in the form of a
filmstrip, video, or nonfiction book about
the theme. Students draw one or more

pictures related to the information
presented by the teacher. They may
create a new picture(s) or add to a
previous picture.
   Teacher assists students in recording
some information about their picture(s).

SHARING
Students show and tell the class about
their favorite picture(s) or _____.
   Papers are dated and filed.

Recreational Reading

CONVERSATIONS
In-Depth: Teacher holds 7- to 10-
minute conversations with 3 or 4 students
(individually) discussing humor, words
that tell *when*, words that tell *where*, and/
or _____.

CLIPBOARD NOTES
Teacher notes who studies and/or learns
from the pictures or _____.

BOOK SHARING
Each person tells another person
something he or she has read about that
day.

and Storytime

READ ALOUD
Hey, Al by Arthur Yorinks or _____
   Discuss the beginning, middle, and end
of the story.

ACTIVITY (Optional)
Make brooms out of straws and fringed
paper.

Writing

MINI-LESSON
Teacher leads a 5- to 7-minute discussion
about possible interpretations of the
Writing Topic: Talking Birds or

_____.

COMPOSING
Each student writes on
■ the lesson's topic
■ a personally chosen topic
■ a topic begun previously

SHARING
Papers are read to a classmate or the
teacher, dated, and filed.

Word Study

CHART DEVELOPMENT
Spelling Emphasis: *on* or 3 syllables
and/or _____
   On the chart, the teacher writes words,
word clusters, or sentences (Teacher's
Choice) containing the day's letters or
number of syllables or _____.

WRITING
On their papers, students write
■ their favorite words from the chart
■ other words/clusters/sentences that
   would be appropriate for the chart
Papers are dated and filed.

Research

LEAD-IN
Teacher introduces the Project Idea.
Theme: Places or _____
Material: Newspapers or _____
Reading Focus: Word(s) that tell *where* or _____

SEARCH & RECORD
Project Idea: In teams of 2 or 3, students explore newspapers looking for references to places. They list words that tell *where* things are happening in the news and what event is taking place there.

SHARING
Two or more teams compare their findings or _____.
    Papers are dated and filed.

Recreational Reading

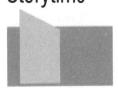

CONVERSATIONS
In-Depth: Teacher holds 7- to 10-minute conversations with 3 or 4 students (individually) discussing humor, words that tell *when,* words that tell *where,* and/or _____.

CLIPBOARD NOTES
Teacher notes who studies and/or learns from the pictures or _____.

BOOK SHARING
Each person tells another person something he or she has read about that day.

and Storytime

READ ALOUD
Book Sharing Day
    Instead of the teacher reading aloud, students work with partners and choose a book to present to the class. The presentations will be brief and not elaborate. They will be similar to book commercials. If announced ahead of time, students can come to school dressed as a book character or make a poster or _____.

Writing

MINI-LESSON
Teacher leads a 5- to 7-minute discussion about possible interpretations of the Writing Topic: Describe a Character in a Fairy Tale or _____.

COMPOSING
Each student writes (by drawing or developmental spelling) on
■ the lesson's topic
■ a personally chosen topic
■ a topic begun previously

SHARING
Papers are read to a classmate or the teacher, dated, and filed.

Word Study

CHART DEVELOPMENT
Spelling Emphasis: *ly* or 3 syllables and/or _____
    On the chart, the teacher writes words, word clusters, or sentences (Teacher's Choice) containing the day's letters or number of syllables or _____.

WRITING
On their papers, students write
■ their favorite words from the chart
■ other words/clusters/sentences that would be appropriate for the chart
Papers are dated and filed.

259

Lesson 157

Research

LEAD-IN
Teacher introduces the Project Idea.
Theme: Places or _____
Material: Magazines or _____
Reading Focus: Word(s) that tell *where* or _____

SEARCH & RECORD
Project Idea: In teams of 2 or 3, students explore magazines looking for references to places. They list words that tell *where* things are happening and what event is taking place there.

SHARING
Two or more teams compare their findings or _____.
   Papers are dated and filed.

Recreational Reading

CONVERSATIONS
Check-In: Teacher moves among students, having 2- to 3-minute conversations with as many individuals as possible. If appropriate, discuss connotations of the words chosen by the author and/or _____.

CLIPBOARD NOTES
Teacher notes who tries new books or _____.

BOOK SHARING
Each person tells another person something he or she has read about that day.

and Storytime

READ ALOUD
Any fairy tale or _____
   Describe the role of magic in the fairy tale.

ACTIVITY (Optional)
Students work together in groups of 4 to 6 to prepare a puppet show about the fairy tale of the group's choice. The puppets may be stick puppets, paper bag puppets, or any other kind. The students will work on their presentation for three days during this time and present the show to the class on the fourth day.

Writing

MINI-LESSON
Teacher leads a 5- to 7-minute discussion about possible interpretations of the Writing Topic: Describe a Place in a Fairy Tale or _____.

COMPOSING
Each student writes on
■ the lesson's topic
■ a personally chosen topic
■ a topic begun previously

SHARING
Papers are read to a classmate or the teacher, dated, and filed.

Word Study

CHART DEVELOPMENT
Spelling Emphasis: *ba* or 3 syllables and/or _____
   On the chart, the teacher writes words, word clusters, or sentences (Teacher's Choice) containing the day's letters or number of syllables or _____.

WRITING
On their papers, students write
■ their favorite words from the chart
■ other words/clusters/sentences that would be appropriate for the chart
Papers are dated and filed.

Research

LEAD-IN
Teacher introduces the Project Idea.
Theme: Fairy tale or _____
Material: Magazines or _____
Reading Focus: Retelling or _____

SEARCH & RECORD
Project Idea: Teams of 4 or 5, select a fairy tale and look through magazines for pictures and/or words that relate to their fairy tale. On a large piece of paper they display the item found in a way that retells all or part of the fairy tale.

SHARING
Teams display and tell the class about their posters.

Recreational Reading

CONVERSATIONS
Check-In: Teacher moves among students, having 2- to 3-minute conversations with as many individuals as possible. If appropriate, discuss synonyms and/or _____.

CLIPBOARD NOTES
Teacher notes who tries new books or _____.

BOOK SHARING
Each person tells another person something he or she has read about that day.

and Storytime

READ ALOUD
Any fairy tale or _____
   Describe the characters in the fairy tale.

ACTIVITY (Optional)
Students continue working in groups of 4 to 6 to prepare a puppet show about the fairy tale of the group's choice. The students will work on their presentation today and tomorrow and present the show to the class on the following day.

Writing

MINI-LESSON
Teacher leads a 5- to 7-minute discussion about possible interpretations of the Writing Topic: Describe an Event in a Fairy Tale or _____.

COMPOSING
Each student writes (by drawing or developmental spelling) on
■ the lesson's topic
■ a personally chosen topic
■ a topic begun previously

SHARING
Papers are read to a classmate or the teacher, dated, and filed.

Word Study

CHART DEVELOPMENT
Spelling Emphasis: *bl* or 3 syllables and/or _____
   On the chart, the teacher writes words, word clusters, or sentences (Teacher's Choice) containing the day's letters or number of syllables or _____.

WRITING
On their papers, students write
■ their favorite words from the chart
■ other words/clusters/sentences that would be appropriate for the chart
Papers are dated and filed.

261

Lesson 159

Research

LEAD-IN
Teacher introduces the Project Idea.
Theme: Fairy tales or _____
Material: Library books or _____
Reading Focus: Characters or
_____

SEARCH & RECORD
Project Idea: In teams of 2 or 3, students read parts of fairy tales and record descriptions of the characters.

SHARING
Two or more teams compare their findings or _____.
    Papers are dated and filed.

Recreational Reading

CONVERSATIONS
Check-In: Teacher moves among students, having 2- to 3-minute conversations with as many individuals as possible. If appropriate, discuss synonyms and/or _____.

CLIPBOARD NOTES
Teacher notes who tries new books or
_____.

BOOK SHARING
Each person tells another person something he or she has read about that day.

and Storytime

READ ALOUD
Two versions of any fairy tale or
_____
    Compare the similarities and differences in the two versions of the same tale.

ACTIVITY (Optional)
Students continue working in groups of 4 to 6 to prepare a puppet show about the

fairy tale of the group's choice. The students will present their fairy tale puppet show to the class tomorrow during this time.

Writing

MINI-LESSON
Teacher leads a 5- to 7-minute discussion about possible interpretations of the Writing Topic: Compare Two Characters or Places in a Fairy Tale(s) or
_____.

COMPOSING
Each student writes on
■ the lesson's topic
■ a personally chosen topic
■ a topic begun previously

SHARING
Papers are read to a classmate or the teacher, dated, and filed.

Word Study

CHART DEVELOPMENT
Spelling Emphasis: *gr* or 3 syllables and/or _____
    On the chart, the teacher writes words, word clusters, or sentences (Teacher's Choice) containing the day's letters or number of syllables or _____.

WRITING
On their papers, students write
■ their favorite words from the chart
■ other words/clusters/sentences that would be appropriate for the chart
    Papers are dated and filed.

Lesson 160

Research

LEAD-IN
Teacher introduces the Project Idea.
Theme: Fairy tales or _____
Material: Library books or _____
Reading Focus: Magic or _____

SEARCH & RECORD
Project Idea: All fairy tales involve magic. In teams of 2 or 3, students explore various fairy tales looking for the magical moment(s). Record what magic produced or caused to happen.

SHARING
Teams report their findings to the class and compare notes with others who read the same fairy tales or _____.
Papers are dated and filed.

Recreational Reading

CONVERSATIONS
Teacher Reads: For approximately 20 minutes everyone, including the teacher, reads silently. During the last 10 minutes the teacher may choose to talk with some individuals about what they have read.

CLIPBOARD NOTES
Teacher notes who rereads the same book or _____.

BOOK SHARING
Each person tells another person something he or she has read about that day.

and Storytime

READ ALOUD
Any fairy tale or _____
Describe the different places or settings in the fairy tale.

ACTIVITY (Optional)
The student groups present their puppet shows to the class.

Writing

MINI-LESSON
Teacher leads a brief discussion of possible topics students may write on. Students make a personal list of potential Writing Topics that they may choose from in the next few weeks to write on. This list should be added to continually as students think of further writing topics.

COMPOSING
Each student writes on
- the teacher's topic
- a personally chosen topic
- a topic begun previously

SHARING
Papers are read to a classmate or the teacher, dated, and filed.

Word Study

CHART DEVELOPMENT
Spelling Emphasis: *dy* or 3 syllables and/or _____
On the chart, the teacher writes words, word clusters, or sentences (Teacher's Choice) containing the day's letters or number of syllables or _____.

WRITING
On their papers, students write
- their favorite words from the chart
- other words/clusters/sentences that would be appropriate for the chart
Papers are dated and filed.

Lesson **161**

Research

LEAD-IN
Teacher introduces the Project Idea.
Theme: Tables of Contents or
_____

Material: Science textbooks or
_____

Reading Focus: Functional reading
or _____

SEARCH & RECORD
Project Idea: In teams of 2 or 3, students explore science textbooks looking at the table of contents and finding information in the text. Teams record interesting information found.

SHARING
Two or more teams compare their findings or _____.
  Papers are dated and filed.
  Teachers check students for association of pictures/words with theme.

Recreational Reading and Storytime

CONVERSATIONS
Check-In: Teacher moves among students, having 2- to 3-minute conversations with as many individuals as possible. If appropriate, discuss opposites and/or _____.

CLIPBOARD NOTES
Teacher notes who rereads the same book or _____.

BOOK SHARING
Each person tells another person something he or she has read about that day.

READ ALOUD
Partner Reading
  Students read with another student any book(s) or _____.

ACTIVITY (Optional)
Two or more teams meet and present a brief "commercial" about the book(s) they have been reading.

Writing

MINI-LESSON
Teacher helps students select a Writing Topic from their personal list or the teacher introduces a topic of his or her choice.

COMPOSING
Each student writes on
■ the teacher's topic
■ a personally chosen topic
■ a topic begun previously

SHARING
Papers are read to a classmate or the teacher, dated, and filed.

Word Study

CHART DEVELOPMENT
Spelling Emphasis: *bi* or 3 syllables and/or _____
  On the chart, the teacher writes words, word clusters, or sentences (Teacher's Choice) containing the day's letters or number of syllables or _____.

WRITING
On their papers, students write
■ their favorite words from the chart
■ other words/clusters/sentences that would be appropriate for the chart
  Papers are dated and filed.

Lesson 162

Research

LEAD-IN
Teacher introduces the Project Idea.
Theme: Tables of Contents or
_____

Material: Magazines or _____
Reading Focus: Functional reading
or _____

SEARCH & RECORD
Project Idea: In teams of 2 or 3,
students explore magazines looking at the
table of contents and finding information
listed there in the magazine. Teams
record interesting information found.

SHARING
Two or more teams compare their findings
or _____.
   Papers are dated and filed.

Recreational Reading

CONVERSATIONS
Check-In: Teacher moves among
students, having 2- to 3-minute
conversations with as many individuals
as possible. If appropriate, discuss
opposites and/or _____.

CLIPBOARD NOTES
Teacher notes who rereads the same book
or _____.

BOOK SHARING
Each person tells another person
something he or she has read about that
day.

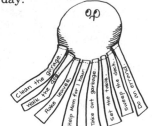

and Storytime

READ ALOUD
Herman the Helper by Robert Kraus or
_____

   List ways students can help their
parents.

ACTIVITY (Optional)
Make or draw an octopus. On each of its
eight legs, the student writes one thing
he or she can do for his parents to be
helpful. The student can take home the
octopus and give it to the parents. Each
leg functions like a coupon that can be
"cashed in."

Writing

MINI-LESSON
Teacher helps students select a Writing
Topic from their personal list or
introduces a topic of the teacher's choice.

COMPOSING
Each student writes on
■ the teacher's topic
■ a personally chosen topic
■ a topic begun previously

SHARING
Papers are read to a classmate or the
teacher, dated, and filed.

Word Study

CHART DEVELOPMENT
Spelling Emphasis: *tion* or 3
syllables and/or _____
   On the chart, the teacher writes words,
word clusters, or sentences (Teacher's
Choice) containing the day's letters or
number of syllables or _____.

WRITING
On their papers, students write
■ their favorite words from the chart
■ other words/clusters/sentences that
   would be appropriate for the chart
Papers are dated and filed.

Lesson **163**

Research

LEAD-IN
Teacher introduces the Project Idea.
Theme: Dinosaurs or _____
Material: Any or _____
Reading Focus: Individual Written Report—Day 1 or _____

SEARCH & RECORD
Project Idea: Class brainstorms two subtopics related to dinosaurs. Four-page notetaking booklets are assembled. Pages are labeled: Introduction, one page for each subtopic in the order determined by the class, and Conclusion. Students gather materials to be used for researching the topic for the next four days.

SHARING
Students discuss what they want to know about the general topic as well as tomorrow's subtopic or _____.

Recreational Reading

CONVERSATIONS
Small Group: For approximately 10 to 15 minutes teacher meets with a small group of students who have all read the same story or portion of a book. The other students read quietly in books of their choice.

CLIPBOARD NOTES
Teacher notes who compares books by author, by topic, or by different versions of the same story or _____.

BOOK SHARING
Each person tells another person something he or she has read about that day.

and
Storytime

READ ALOUD
Look What I Can Do by Jose Aruego or
We Hide, You Seek by Jose Aruego or
_____
  Discuss how the author tells a story with very few words. Also talk about the joke or humor in the book.

ACTIVITY (Optional)
Design your own book with few words. It can tell a joke or a story.

Writing

MINI-LESSON
Teacher helps students select a Writing Topic from their personal list or introduces a topic of the teacher's choice.

COMPOSING
Each student writes on
■ the teacher's topic
■ a personally chosen topic
■ a topic begun previously

SHARING
Papers are read to a classmate or the teacher, dated, and filed.

Word Study

CHART DEVELOPMENT
Spelling Emphasis: _bl_ or 3 syllables and/or _____
  On the chart, the teacher writes words, word clusters, or sentences (Teacher's Choice) containing the day's letters or number of syllables or _____.

WRITING
On their papers, students write
■ their favorite words from the chart
■ other words/clusters/sentences that would be appropriate for the chart Papers are dated and filed.

Research

LEAD-IN
Teacher introduces the Project Idea.
Theme: Dinosaurs or _____
Material: Any or _____
Reading Focus: Individual Written Report—Day 2 or _____

SEARCH & RECORD
Project Idea: Students work in teams of 2 or 3 exploring materials looking for information related to the day's subtopic. As they locate information, they raise their hands and tell the teacher what they have found. The teacher records the information volunteered on a piece of chart paper in notetaking form.

After 10 to 15 minutes, each student selects what he or she wishes to record in his or her notetaking packet.

SHARING
Students show and tell about their notes to a group of 4 to 6 students or _____.

Booklets are dated and filed.

Recreational Reading

CONVERSATIONS
Check-In: Teacher moves among students, having 2- to 3-minute conversations with as many individuals as possible. If appropriate, discuss how a passage in the book could be paraphrased and/or _____.

CLIPBOARD NOTES
Teacher notes who compares books by author, by topic, or by different versions of the same story or _____.

BOOK SHARING
Each person tells another person something he or she has read about that day.

and Storytime

READ ALOUD
Crocodile's Tale by Jose Aruego with A. Aruego or *Rockabye Crocodile* by Jose Aruego with A. Dewey or _____
Discuss the title. Why did the authors name the book what they did?

ACTIVITY (Optional)
Paint a crocodile or paint your favorite part of the story.

Writing

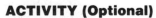

MINI-LESSON
Teacher helps students select a Writing Topic from their personal list or introduces a topic of the teacher's choice.

COMPOSING
Each student writes on
- the teacher's topic
- a personally chosen topic
- a topic begun previously

SHARING
Papers are read to a classmate or the teacher, dated, and filed.

Word Study

CHART DEVELOPMENT
Spelling Emphasis: *ed* or 3 syllables and/or _____
On the chart, the teacher writes words, word clusters, or sentences (Teacher's Choice) containing the day's letters or number of syllables or _____.

WRITING
On their papers, students write
- their favorite words from the chart
- other words/clusters/sentences that would be appropriate for the chart
Papers are dated and filed.

Lesson **165**

Research

LEAD-IN
Teacher introduces the Project Idea.
Theme: Dinosaurs or _____
Material: Any or _____
Reading Focus: Individual Written Report—Day 3 or _____

SEARCH & RECORD
Project Idea: Students work in teams of 2 or 3 exploring materials looking for information related to the day's subtopic. As they locate information, they raise their hands and tell the teacher what they have found. The teacher records the information volunteered on a piece of chart paper in notetaking form.

After 10 to 15 minutes, each student selects what he or she wishes to record in his or her notetaking packet.

SHARING
Students show and tell about their notes to a group of 4 to 6 students or _____.

Booklets are dated and filed.

Recreational Reading

CONVERSATIONS
Check-in: Teacher moves among students, having 2- to 3-minute conversations with as many individuals as possible. If appropriate, discuss how a passage in the book could be paraphrased and/or _____.

CLIPBOARD NOTES
Teacher notes who compares books by author, by topic, or by different versions of the same story or _____.

BOOK SHARING
Each person tells another person something he or she has read about that day.

and Storytime

READ ALOUD
Whose Mouse Are You? by Robert Kraus, illustrated by Jose Aruego or *Another Mouse to Feed* by Robert Kraus, illustrated by Jose Aruego or _____
Students pretend to *be* a mouse. Have them answer, "Whose mouse are you?"

ACTIVITY (Optional)
Make mice out of rocks or nutshells. Add paper or felt ears, tail, etc.

Writing

MINI-LESSON
Teacher helps students select a Writing Topic from their personal list or introduces a topic of the teacher's choice.

COMPOSING
Each student writes on
- the teacher's topic
- a personally chosen topic
- a topic begun previously

SHARING
Papers are read to a classmate or the teacher, dated, and filed.

Word Study

CHART DEVELOPMENT
Spelling Emphasis: *or* or 3 syllables and/or _____
On the chart, the teacher writes words, word clusters, or sentences (Teacher's Choice) containing the day's letters or number of syllables or _____.

WRITING
On their papers, students write
- their favorite words from the chart
- other words/clusters/sentences that would be appropriate for the chart

Papers are dated and filed.
Each student chooses a composition from his or her folder for the teacher to display in the classroom. Students may modify their writing and/or illustration as they choose.

Lesson 166

Research

LEAD-IN
Teacher introduces the Project Idea.
Theme: Dinosaurs or _____
Material: Any or _____
Reading Focus: Individual Written
Report—Day 4 or _____

SEARCH & RECORD
Project Idea: Using the notes
gathered over the last four days, students
begin writing their reports. Notes may be

made first about what should be included
in the introduction and conclusion.
Writing may continue during the Writing
module.

SHARING
Students read their rough drafts to a
small group of students and discuss what
else they need to add or _____.
   Booklets and rough drafts are dated
and filed.

Recreational Reading

CONVERSATIONS
Check-In: Teacher moves among
students, having 2- to 3-minute
conversations with as many individuals
as possible. If appropriate, discuss
problem-solving techniques used by the
characters in the book and/or _____.

CLIPBOARD NOTES
Teacher notes who is constantly seeking
help decoding words or _____.

BOOK SHARING
Each person tells another person
something he or she has read about that
day.

and Storytime

READ ALOUD
Book Groups Meet
   Students meet in groups of 4 or 5 and
discuss favorite books. Alone or with a
partner, students introduce the rest of the
group to a favorite book. Some may
choose to read aloud or act out parts of
their books.

Writing

MINI-LESSON
Teacher helps students select a Writing
Topic from their personal list or
introduces a topic of the teacher's choice.

COMPOSING
Each student writes on
■ the teacher's topic
■ a personally chosen topic
■ a topic begun previously

SHARING
Papers are read to a classmate or the
teacher, dated, and filed.

Word Study

CHART DEVELOPMENT
Spelling Emphasis: *b, c* or 4
syllables and/or _____
   On the chart, the teacher writes words,
word clusters, or sentences (Teacher's
Choice) containing the day's letters or
number of syllables or _____.

WRITING
On their papers, students write
■ their favorite words from the chart
■ other words/clusters/sentences that
   would be appropriate for the chart
Papers are dated and filed.

Lesson 167

Research

LEAD-IN
Teacher introduces the Project Idea.
Theme: Dinosaurs or _____
Material: Any or _____
Reading Focus: Individual Written
Report—Day 5 or _____

SEARCH & RECORD
Project Idea: Students complete their
reports and prepare them for publication.

SHARING
Class is divided into three large groups.
Student present their reports to their
groups.
   Reports are displayed in the room for
all to see.

Recreational Reading

CONVERSATIONS
Check-In: Teacher moves among
students, having 2- to 3-minute
conversations with as many individuals
as possible. If appropriate, discuss
problem-solving techniques used by the
characters in the book and/or _____.

CLIPBOARD NOTES
Teacher notes who is constantly seeking
help decoding words or _____.

BOOK SHARING
Each person tells another person
something he or she has read about that
day.

and Storytime

READ ALOUD
Why Mosquitoes Buzz in People's Ears by
Verna Aardema or _____
   Discuss the pattern in the book. Also
discuss the award-winning illustrations
by Leo and Diane Dillon.

ACTIVITY (Optional)
Students trace around their hands. Then
they draw or cut out of paper and glue a
smashed mosquito on the hand.

Writing

MINI-LESSON
Teacher helps students select a Writing
Topic from their personal list or
introduces a topic of the teacher's choice.

COMPOSING
Each student writes on
■ the teacher's topic
■ a personally chosen topic
■ a topic begun previously

SHARING
Papers are read to a classmate or the
teacher, dated, and filed.

Word Study

CHART DEVELOPMENT
Spelling Emphasis: *d, f* or 4
syllables and/or _____
   On the chart, the teacher writes words,
word clusters, or sentences (Teacher's
Choice) containing the day's letters or
number of syllables or _____.

WRITING
On their papers, students write
■ their favorite words from the chart
■ other words/clusters/sentences that
   would be appropriate for the chart
   Papers are dated and filed.

Lesson 168

Research

LEAD-IN
Teacher introduces the Project Idea.
Theme: Science words or _____
Material: Science textbooks or _____

Reading Focus: Specialized vocabulary or _____

SEARCH & RECORD
Project Idea: In teams of 2 or 3, students explore science textbooks identifying words or pictures which they associate with science or _____. Record the words found and how they relate to science.
   Teachers check students for association of pictures/words with theme.

SHARING
Students meet in groups of 4 or 5 and discuss the items found that relate to the day's theme or _____.
   Papers are dated and filed.

Recreational Reading

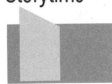

CONVERSATIONS
Check-In: Teacher moves among students, having 2- to 3-minute conversations with as many individuals as possible. If appropriate, discuss main ideas and/or _____.

CLIPBOARD NOTES
Teacher notes who is constantly seeking help decoding words or _____.

BOOK SHARING
Each person tells another person something he or she has read about that day.

and Storytime

READ ALOUD
Get to Know an Author/Illustrator Series: Gail Gibbons
   The Post Office Book: Mail and How It Moves or _____
   Discuss the sequence of events when a letter is mailed.

ACTIVITY (Optional)
Write a note to someone in your family and mail it. See how long it takes. Notice the postmark.

Writing

MINI-LESSON
Teacher helps students select a Writing Topic from their personal list or the teacher introduces a topic of his or her choice.

COMPOSING
Each student writes on
■ the lesson's topic
■ a personally chosen topic
■ a topic begun previously

SHARING
Papers are read to a classmate or the teacher, dated, and filed.

Word Study

CHART DEVELOPMENT
Spelling Emphasis: *g, h* or 4 syllables and/or _____
   On the chart, the teacher writes words, word clusters, or sentences (Teacher's Choice) containing the day's letters or number of syllables or _____.

WRITING
On their papers, students write
■ their favorite words from the chart
■ other words/clusters/sentences that would be appropriate for the chart
Papers are dated and filed.

Lesson 169

Research

LEAD-IN
Teacher introduces the Project Idea.
Theme: Using indexes or _____
Material: Science textbooks or

_____

Reading Focus: Locating specific
information or _____

SEARCH & RECORD
Project Idea: In teams of 2 or 3,
students explore indexes in science

textbooks. Teams look for information
about topics listed in the index and record
information found about some of the
entries or _____.

SHARING
Two or more teams compare their findings
or _____.
Papers are dated and filed.

Recreational Reading

CONVERSATIONS
Check-In: Teacher moves among
students, having 2- to 3-minute
conversations with as many individuals
as possible. If appropriate, discuss main
ideas and/or _____.

CLIPBOARD NOTES
Teacher notes who seems to be excited
about books and reading or _____.

BOOK SHARING
Each person tells another person
something he or she has read about that
day.

and Storytime

READ ALOUD
Trucks by Gail Gibbons or _____
Make a list of many types of trucks.
Put a star beside those mentioned in the
book.

ACTIVITY (Optional)
Make a dump truck. Teacher leads class
in a following directions activity. Have
the students cut their papers according to

teacher's directions and example, without
telling them what kind of truck they are
making. Cut a piece of 9″ × 12″
construction paper or tagboard according
to the diagram. Attach the dumping part
of the truck with a brad so that it will
move.

Writing

MINI-LESSON
Teacher helps students select a Writing
Topic from their personal list or the
teacher introduces a topic of his or her
choice.

COMPOSING
Each student writes on
■ the lesson's topic
■ a personally chosen topic
■ a topic begun previously

SHARING
Papers are read to a classmate or the
teacher, dated, and filed.

Word Study

CHART DEVELOPMENT
Spelling Emphasis: *j, k* or 4
syllables and/or _____
On the chart, the teacher writes words,
word clusters, or sentences (Teacher's
Choice) containing the day's letters or
number of syllables or _____.

WRITING
On their papers, students write
■ their favorite words from the chart
■ other words/clusters/sentences that
would be appropriate for the chart
Papers are dated and filed.

Research

LEAD-IN
Teacher introduces the Project Idea.
Theme: Using indexes or _____
Material: Newspapers or _____
Reading Focus: Locating specific information or _____

SEARCH & RECORD
Project Idea: In teams of 2 or 3, students explore newspapers finding information listed in the index on page 1. Teams record something about the information found.

SHARING
Two or more teams compare their findings or _____.
   Papers are dated and filed.

Recreational Reading

CONVERSATIONS
Teacher Reads: For approximately 20 minutes everyone, including the teacher, reads silently. During the last 10 minutes the teacher may choose to talk with some individuals about what they have read.

CLIPBOARD NOTES
Teacher notes who seems to be excited about books and reading or _____.

BOOK SHARING
Each person tells another person something he or she has read about that day.

and Storytime

READ ALOUD
Farming by Gail Gibbons or _____
   Discuss the times in the book and how the farm changes at the different times.

ACTIVITY (Optional)
Students cut out of magazines things they associate with farming and then make a collage.

Writing

MINI-LESSON
Teacher helps students select a Writing Topic from their personal list or the teacher introduces a topic of his or her choice.

COMPOSING
Each student writes on
■ the lesson's topic
■ a personally chosen topic
■ a topic begun previously

SHARING
Papers are read to a classmate or the teacher, dated, and filed.

Word Study

CHART DEVELOPMENT
Spelling Emphasis: *l, m* or 4 syllables and/or _____
   On the chart, the teacher writes words, word clusters, or sentences (Teacher's Choice) containing the day's letters or number of syllables or _____.

WRITING
On their papers, students write
■ their favorite words from the chart
■ other words/clusters/sentences that would be appropriate for the chart
Papers are dated and filed.

Lesson 171

Research

LEAD-IN
Teacher introduces the Project Idea.
Theme: People in the news or
_____

Material: Newspapers or _____
Reading Focus: Word(s) telling *who*
or _____

SEARCH & RECORD
Project Idea: In teams of 2 or 3,
students explore newspapers looking for

references to people. They list *who* is in
the newspaper and why some of the
people found are in the news.

SHARING
Two or more teams compare their findings
or _____.
     Papers are dated and filed.

Recreational Reading

CONVERSATIONS
In-Depth: Teacher holds 7- to 10-
minute conversations with 3 or 4 students
(individually) discussing classification,
pronouns and their referents,
connotations of the words chosen by the
author, and/or _____.

CLIPBOARD NOTES
Teacher notes who seems to be excited
about books and reading or _____.

BOOK SHARING
Each person tells another person
something he or she has read about that
day.

and Storytime

READ ALOUD
*Lights! Camera! Action!: How a Movie Is
Made* by Gail Gibbons or _____
     Discuss *who* is involved in making a
movie and *what* each person's job is.

ACTIVITY (Optional)
Make simple props and pretend to make a
movie. The story should be a simple one
that everyone in the class is familiar

with. You will need actors, a director,
camera operators, etc.

Writing

MINI-LESSON
Teacher helps students select a Writing
Topic from their personal list or the
teacher introduces a topic of his or her
choice.

COMPOSING
Each student writes on
- the lesson's topic
- a personally chosen topic
- a topic begun previously

SHARING
Papers are read to a classmate or the
teacher, dated, and filed.

Word Study

CHART DEVELOPMENT
Spelling Emphasis: *n, p* or 4
syllables and/or _____
     On the chart, the teacher writes words,
word clusters, or sentences (Teacher's
Choice) containing the day's letters or
number of syllables or _____.

WRITING
On their papers, students write
- their favorite words from the chart
- other words/clusters/sentences that
  would be appropriate for the chart
  Papers are dated and filed.

Lesson 172

Research

LEAD-IN
Teacher introduces the Project Idea.
Theme: (class decides) or _____
Material: Any or _____
Reading Focus: Individual Written Report—Day 1 or _____

SEARCH & RECORD
Project Idea: Class decides on a report topic and brainstorms four subtopics related to the report topic. Six-page notetaking booklets are assembled.

Pages are labeled: Introduction, one page for each subtopic in the order determined by the class, and Conclusion. Students gather materials to be used for researching the topic for the next four days.

SHARING
Students discuss what they want to know about the general topic as well as tomorrow's subtopic or _____.

Recreational Reading

CONVERSATIONS
In-Depth: Teacher holds 7- to 10-minute conversations with 3 or 4 students (individually) discussing classification, pronouns and their referents, connotations of the words chosen by the author, and/or _____.

CLIPBOARD NOTES
Teacher notes titles being read or _____.

BOOK SHARING
Each person tells another person something he or she has read about that day.

and Storytime

READ ALOUD
Partner Reading: Students read together with another student any book(s) of their choosing or _____.

ACTIVITY (Optional)
Two or more teams meet and present a brief "commercial" about the book(s) they have been reading.

Writing

MINI-LESSON
Teacher helps students select a Writing Topic from their personal list or the teacher introduces a topic of his or her choice.

COMPOSING
Each student writes (by drawing or developmental spelling) on
- the lesson's topic
- a personally chosen topic
- a topic begun previously

SHARING
Papers are read to a classmate or the teacher, dated, and filed.

Word Study

CHART DEVELOPMENT
Spelling Emphasis: q, r or 4 syllables and/or _____
   On the chart, the teacher writes words, word clusters, or sentences (Teacher's Choice) containing the day's letters or number of syllables or _____.

WRITING
On their papers, students write
- their favorite words from the chart
- other words/clusters/sentences that would be appropriate for the chart
Papers are dated and filed.

Lesson 173

Research

LEAD-IN
Teacher introduces the Project Idea.
Theme: Subtopic #1 or _____
Material: Any or _____
Reading Focus: Individual Written Report—Day 2 or _____

SEARCH & RECORD
Project Idea: Students work in teams of 2 or 3 exploring materials looking for information related to the day's subtopic. As they locate information, they raise their hands and tell the teacher what

they have found. The teacher records the information volunteered on a piece of chart paper in notetaking form.
   After 10 to 15 minutes, each student selects what he or she wishes to record in their notetaking packet.

SHARING
Students show and tell about their notes to a group of 4 to 6 students or _____.
   Booklets are dated and filed.

Recreational Reading

CONVERSATIONS
In-Depth: Teacher holds 7- to 10-minute conversations with 3 or 4 students (individually) discussing classification, pronouns and their referents, connotations of the words chosen by the author, and/or _____.

CLIPBOARD NOTES
Teacher notes titles being read or _____.

BOOK SHARING
Each person tells another person something he or she has read about that day.

and Storytime

READ ALOUD
Get to Know an Author/Illustrator Series:
Tomie dePaola
   The Art Lesson or _____
   Discuss different ways to use a crayon: using the side, crayon resist, crayon scratch board, etc. After completing activities, have a "Gallery Talk." Each artist will describe his or her drawing and describe the techniques used.

ACTIVITY (Optional)
Draw a picture using crayons. Try different techniques of using crayons.

Writing

MINI-LESSON
Teacher helps students select a Writing Topic from their personal list or the teacher introduces a topic of his or her choice.

COMPOSING
Each student writes (by drawing or developmental spelling) on
■ the lesson's topic
■ a personally chosen topic
■ a topic begun previously

SHARING
Papers are read to a classmate or the teacher, dated, and filed.

Word Study

CHART DEVELOPMENT
Spelling Emphasis: *s, t* or 4 syllables and/or _____
   On the chart, the teacher writes words, word clusters, or sentences (Teacher's Choice) containing the day's letters or number of syllables or _____.

WRITING
On their papers, students write
■ their favorite words from the chart
■ other words/clusters/sentences that would be appropriate for the chart
Papers are dated and filed.

Research

LEAD-IN
Teacher introduces the Project Idea.
Theme: Subtopic #2 or _____
Material: Any or _____
Reading Focus: Individual Written Report—Day 3 or _____

SEARCH & RECORD
Project Idea: Students work in teams of 2 or 3 exploring materials looking for information related to the day's subtopic. As they locate information, they raise their hands and tell the teacher what they have found. The teacher records the information volunteered on a piece of chart paper in notetaking form.

After 10 to 15 minutes, each student selects what he or she wishes to record in their notetaking packet.

SHARING
Students show and tell about their notes to a group of 4 to 6 students or _____.

Booklets are dated and filed.

Recreational Reading

CONVERSATIONS
In-Depth: Teacher holds 7- to 10-minute conversations with 3 or 4 students (individually) discussing classification, pronouns and their referents, connotations of the words chosen by the author, and/or _____.

CLIPBOARD NOTES
Teacher notes titles being read or _____.

BOOK SHARING
Each person tells another person something he or she has read about that day.

and Storytime

READ ALOUD
Bill and Pete by Tomie dePaola or _____

Discuss ways Bill and Pete helped each other. Teacher may show other books or information about symbiosis. Also, talk about the different emotions in the story.

ACTIVITY (Optional)
Teacher provides a shape of a large toothpaste tube with no writing on it. Each student designs alligator toothpaste for those poor alligators who do not have a bird to clean their teeth.

Writing

MINI-LESSON
Teacher helps students select a Writing Topic from their personal list or the teacher introduces a topic of his or her choice.

COMPOSING
Each student writes (by drawing or developmental spelling) on
■ the lesson's topic
■ a personally chosen topic
■ a topic begun previously

SHARING
Papers are read to a classmate or the teacher, dated, and filed.

Word Study

CHART DEVELOPMENT
Spelling Emphasis: *v, w* or 4 syllables and/or _____
On the chart, the teacher writes words, word clusters, or sentences (Teacher's Choice) containing the day's letters or number of syllables or _____.

WRITING
On their papers, students write
■ their favorite words from the chart
■ other words/clusters/sentences that would be appropriate for the chart
Papers are dated and filed.

Lesson 175

Research

LEAD-IN
Teacher introduces the Project Idea.
Theme: Subtopic #3 or _____
Material: Any or _____
Reading Focus: Individual Written Report—Day 4 or _____

SEARCH & RECORD
Project Idea: Students work in teams of 2 or 3 exploring materials looking for information related to the day's subtopic. As they locate information, they raise their hands and tell the teacher what

they have found. The teacher records the information volunteered on a piece of chart paper in notetaking form.
After 10 to 15 minutes, each student selects what he or she wishes to record in their notetaking packet.

SHARING
Students show and tell about their notes to a group of 4 to 6 students or _____.
Booklets are dated and filed.

Recreational Reading

CONVERSATIONS
In-Depth: Teacher holds 7- to 10-minute conversations with 3 or 4 students (individually) discussing classification, pronouns and their referents, connotations of the words chosen by the author, and/or _____.

CLIPBOARD NOTES
Teacher notes where students choose to read or _____.

BOOK SHARING
Each person tells another person something he or she has read about that day.

Dear Uncle Frank,
Thank you for taking me to the circus.
I love you!
John

and Storytime

READ ALOUD
Now One Foot, Now the Other by Tomie dePaola or _____
Discuss grandparents or older friends. Talk about things students have done with their grandparents or an older friend.

ACTIVITY (Optional)
Students draw a picture of a time they spent with a grandparent or older friend or write a letter to a grandparent or older friend.

Writing

MINI-LESSON
Teacher helps students select a Writing Topic from their personal list or the teacher introduces a topic of his or her choice.

COMPOSING
Each student writes (by drawing or developmental spelling) on
- the lesson's topic
- a personally chosen topic
- a topic begun previously

SHARING
Papers are read to a classmate or the teacher, dated, and filed.

Word Study

CHART DEVELOPMENT
Spelling Emphasis: x, y, z or 4 syllables and/or _____
On the chart, the teacher writes words, word clusters, or sentences (Teacher's Choice) containing the day's letters or number of syllables or _____.

WRITING
On their papers, students write
- their favorite words from the chart
- other words/clusters/sentences that would be appropriate for the chart
Papers are dated and filed.

Research

LEAD-IN
Teacher introduces the Project Idea.
Theme: Subtopic #4 or _____
Material: Any or _____
Reading Focus: Individual Written
Report—Day 5 or _____

SEARCH & RECORD
Project Idea: Students work in teams of 2 or 3 exploring materials looking for information related to the day's subtopic. As they locate information, they raise their hands and tell the teacher what they have found. The teacher records the information volunteered on a piece of chart paper in notetaking form.

After 10 to 15 minutes, each student selects what he or she wishes to record in their notetaking packet.

SHARING
Students show and tell about their notes to a group of 4 to 6 students or _____.

Booklets are dated and filed.

Recreational Reading

CONVERSATIONS
In-Depth: Teacher holds 7- to 10-minute conversations with 3 or 4 students (individually) discussing classification, pronouns and their referents, connotations of the words chosen by the author, and/or _____.

CLIPBOARD NOTES
Teacher notes where students choose to read or _____.

BOOK SHARING
Each person tells another person something he or she has read about that day.

and Storytime

READ ALOUD
The Popcorn Book by Tomie dePaola or _____

Two students or the teacher and a student reread parts of the book as partners. One person reads the larger print. The other reads the smaller print.

ACTIVITY (Optional)
Pop popcorn and have a party. Ask students to talk about their summer plans.

Writing

MINI-LESSON
Teacher helps students select a Writing Topic from their personal list or the teacher introduces a topic of his or her choice.

COMPOSING
Each student writes (by drawing or developmental spelling) on
- the lesson's topic
- a personally chosen topic
- a topic begun previously

SHARING
Papers are read to a classmate or the teacher, dated, and filed.

Word Study

CHART DEVELOPMENT
Spelling Emphasis: *a* or 5 syllables and/or _____
On the chart, the teacher writes words, word clusters, or sentences (Teacher's Choice) containing the day's letters or number of syllables or _____.

WRITING
On their papers, students write
- their favorite words from the chart
- other words/clusters/sentences that would be appropriate for the chart
Papers are dated and filed.

279

Lesson 177

Research

LEAD-IN
Teacher introduces the Project Idea.
Theme: Writing the Report or
_____
Material: Any or _____
Reading Focus: Individual Written
Report—Day 6 or _____

SEARCH & RECORD
Project Idea: Using the notes
gathered over the last four days, students
begin writing their reports. Notes may be
made first about what should be included
in the introduction and conclusion.
Writing may continue during the Writing
module.

SHARING
Students read their rough drafts to a
small group of students and discuss what
else they need to add or _____.
 Booklets and rough drafts are dated
and filed.

Recreational Reading

CONVERSATIONS
In-Depth: Teacher holds 7- to 10-
minute conversations with 3 or 4 students
(individually) discussing classification,
pronouns and their referents,
connotations of the words chosen by the
author, and/or _____.

CLIPBOARD NOTES
Teacher notes where students choose to
read or _____.

BOOK SHARING
Each person tells another person
something he or she has read about that
day.

and Storytime

READ ALOUD
Book Groups Meet
 Students meet in groups of 4 or 5 and
discuss favorite books. Alone or with a
partner, students introduce the rest of the
group to a book other students may enjoy
reading over the summer. Some may
choose to read aloud or act out parts of
their books.

Writing

MINI-LESSON
Teacher helps students select a Writing
Topic from their personal list or the
teacher introduces a topic of his or her
choice.

COMPOSING
Each student writes (by drawing or
developmental spelling) on
■ the lesson's topic
■ a personally chosen topic
■ a topic begun previously

SHARING
Papers are read to a classmate or the
teacher, dated, and filed.

Word Study

CHART DEVELOPMENT
Spelling Emphasis: *e* or 5 syllables
and/or _____
 On the chart, the teacher writes words,
word clusters, or sentences (Teacher's
Choice) containing the day's letters or
number of syllables or _____.

WRITING
On their papers, students write
■ their favorite words from the chart
■ other words/clusters/sentences that
 would be appropriate for the chart
Papers are dated and filed.

Research

LEAD-IN
Teacher introduces the Project Idea.
Theme: Revising and Publishing or
_____

Material: Any or _____
Reading Focus: Individual Written
Report—Day 7 or _____

SEARCH & RECORD
Project Idea: Students complete their
reports and prepare them for publication.

SHARING
Class is divided into three large groups.
Student present their reports to their
groups.
    Reports are displayed in the room for
all to see.

Recreational Reading

CONVERSATIONS
Small Group: For approximately 10 to
15 minutes teacher meets with a small
group of students who have all read the
same story or portion of a book. The other
students read quietly in books of their
choice.

CLIPBOARD NOTES
Teacher notes which students read
audibly or _____.

BOOK SHARING
Each person tells another person
something he or she has read about that
day.

and Storytime

READ ALOUD
Carousel by D. Crews and *Up and Down
on the Merry-Go-Round* by Bill Martin,
Jr., and John Archambault or _____
    Compare the two books. Discuss
students' experiences on merry-go-rounds.

ACTIVITY (Optional)
Teacher provides shapes of horses (or
students draw them). Students decorate

their carousel horses, cut them out, and
attach them to a stick or straw.

Writing

MINI-LESSON
Teacher helps students select a Writing
Topic from their personal list or the
teacher introduces a topic of his or her
choice.

COMPOSING
Each student writes (by drawing or
developmental spelling) on
- the lesson's topic
- a personally chosen topic
- a topic begun previously

SHARING
Papers are read to a classmate or the
teacher, dated, and filed.

Word Study

CHART DEVELOPMENT
Spelling Emphasis: *i* or 5 syllables
and/or _____
    On the chart, the teacher writes words,
word clusters, or sentences (Teacher's
Choice) containing the day's letters or
number of syllables or _____.

WRITING
On their papers, students write
- their favorite words from the chart
- other words/clusters/sentences that
  would be appropriate for the chart
Papers are dated and filed.

Lesson 179

Research

LEAD-IN
Teacher introduces the Project Idea.
Theme: Places to buy cars or
_____

Material: Yellow pages or _____
Reading Focus: Functional reading
or _____

SEARCH & RECORD
Project Idea: In teams of 2 or 3,
students explore the yellow pages of a
telephone book looking for places to
purchase cars. They record the name,
address, phone number, and type of car
for each business on their list.

SHARING
Two or more teams compare their findings
or _____.
    Papers are dated and filed.

Recreational Reading and Storytime

CONVERSATIONS
Small Group: For approximately 10 to
15 minutes teacher meets with a small
group of students who have all read the
same story or portion of a book. The other
students read quietly in books of their
choice.

CLIPBOARD NOTES
Teacher notes which students read
audibly or _____.

BOOK SHARING
Each person tells another person
something he or she has read about that
day.

READ ALOUD
Bored Nothing to Do by Peter Spier or
_____

    Talk about the use of quotation marks
and other punctuation in the text. Why is
it used? What does it tell the reader?

ACTIVITY (Optional)
Teacher provides assorted small items
of junk. Students work in small groups
or alone to create a contraption out of
junk.

Writing

MINI-LESSON
Teacher helps students select a Writing
Topic from their personal list or the
teacher introduces a topic of his or her
choice.

COMPOSING
Each student writes on
■ the lesson's topic
■ a personally chosen topic
■ a topic begun previously

SHARING
Papers are read to a classmate or the
teacher, dated, and filed.

Word Study

CHART DEVELOPMENT
Spelling Emphasis: *o* or 5 syllables
and/or _____
    On the chart, the teacher writes words,
word clusters, or sentences (Teacher's
Choice) containing the day's letters or
number of syllables or _____.

WRITING
On their papers, students write
■ their favorite words from the chart
■ other words/clusters/sentences that
would be appropriate for the chart
Papers are dated and filed.

Lesson 180

Research

LEAD-IN
Teacher introduces the Project Idea.
Theme: Names of schools or
_____

Material: Yellow pages or _____
Reading Focus: Functional reading
or _____

SEARCH & RECORD
Project Idea: In teams of 2 or 3,
students explore the yellow pages of a

telephone book looking for names of
schools. They record the name, address,
phone number, and type of school for each
school on their list.

SHARING
Two or more teams compare their findings
or _____.
   Papers are dated and filed.

Recreational Reading

CONVERSATIONS
Small Group: For approximately 10 to
15 minutes teacher meets with a small
group of students who have all read the
same story or portion of a book. The other
students read quietly in books of their
choice.

CLIPBOARD NOTES
Teacher notes which students read
audibly or _____.

BOOK SHARING
Each person tells another person
something he or she has read about that
day.

and Storytime

READ ALOUD
Do Not Disturb by Nancy Tafuri or
_____
   Discuss ways students cannot disturb
the environment during their summer
vacation.

ACTIVITY (Optional)
Make a "Do Not Disturb" sign.

Writing

MINI-LESSON
Teacher helps students select a Writing
Topic from their personal list or the
teacher introduces a topic of his or her
choice.

COMPOSING
Each student writes (by drawing or
developmental spelling) on
■ the lesson's topic
■ a personally chosen topic
■ a topic begun previously

SHARING
Papers are read to a classmate or the
teacher, dated, and filed.

Word Study

CHART DEVELOPMENT
Spelling Emphasis: *u* or 5 syllables
and/or _____
   On the chart, the teacher writes words,
word clusters, or sentences (Teacher's
Choice) containing the day's letters or
number of syllables or _____.

WRITING
On their papers, students write
■ their favorite words from the chart
■ other words/clusters/sentences that
   would be appropriate for the chart
   Papers are dated and filed.

▶ Appendix

Related Readings

Atwell, Nancie. *In the Middle. Writing, Reading, and Learning with Adoles-cents.* Portsmouth, NH: Boynton/Cook Publishers, 1987.

Calkins, Lucy McCormick. *The Art of Teaching Writing.* Portsmouth, NH: Heinemann, Inc., 1986.

Clay, Marie M. *What Did I Write?* Portsmouth, NH: Heinemann, Inc., 1987.

Gentry, Richard R. *Spel . . . Is Four-Letter Word.* Portsmouth, NH: Heinemann, Inc., 1987.

Graves, Donald. *Writing: Teachers and Children at Work.* Portsmouth, NH: Heinemann, Inc., 1983.

Hansen, Jane, Thomas Newkirk, and Donald Graves (eds.). *Breaking Ground: Teachers Relate Reading and Writing in the Elementary School.* Portsmouth, NH: Heinemann, Inc., 1985.

Newkirk, Thomas, and Nancie Atwell (eds.). *Understanding Writing: Ways of Observing, Learning, and Teaching.* Second Edition. Portsmouth, NH: Heinemann, Inc., 1988.

Newman, Judith. *Whole Language: Theory in Use.* Portmouth, NH: Heinemann, Inc., 1985.

Routman, Regie. *Transitions: From Literature to Literacy.* Portsmouth, NH: Heinemann, Inc., 1988.

Smith, Frank. *Insult to Intelligence.* New York: Arbor House, 1986.

_____. *Reading without Nonsense.* Second Edition. New York: Teachers College Press, 1985.

Temple, Charles A., Ruth G. Nathan, and Nancy A. Burris. *The Beginnings of Writing.* Boston: Allyn & Bacon, 1982.

Turbill, Jan. *Now We Want to Write!* Portsmouth, NH: Heinemann, Inc., 1983.

Themes and Materials in Research Lessons

Lesson	Topic/Focus	Resource	Lesson	Topic/Focus	Resource
1	Newspapers	locate b B	51	Text: math	Words with q r
2	Newspapers	locate c C	52	Text: math	television
3	Text: math	words with b c	53	Magazines	television
4	Text: math	food	54	Magazines	describing words
5	Magazines	food	55	Library books	words describing people
6	Magazines	events			
7	Library books	events	56	Library books	words describing places
8	Library books	events			
9	Newspapers	d D	57	Newspapers	s S
10	Newspapers	f F	58	Newspapers	t T
11	Text: science	words with d f	59	Text: science	words with s t
12	Text: science	seasons	60	Text: science	water
13	Magazines	seasons	61	Magazines	water
14	Magazines	colors	62	Magazines	words for actions
15	Library books	colors	63	Library books	words ending with -ing
16	Library books	colors			
17	Newspapers	g G	64	Library books	words ending with -ed
18	Newspapers	h H			
19	Text: social studies	words with g h	65	Newspapers	v V
20	Text: social studies	jobs	66	Newspapers	w W
21	Magazines	jobs	67	Text: social studies	words with v w
22	Magazines	eyes: character traits	68	Text: social studies	what people are doing
23	Library books	character traits	69	Magazines	what people are doing
24	Library books	character traits			
25	Newspapers	j J	70	Magazines	transportation
26	Newspapers	k K	71	Library books	transportation
27	Text: math	Words with j k	72	Library books	transportation
28	Text: math	math words	73	Newspapers	x X z Z
29	Magazines	math words	74	Newspapers	y Y
30	Magazines	feet; what they are doing	75	Text: math	Words with x y z
			76	Text: math	opposites
31	Library books	feet; what doing now/next	77	Magazines	opposites
			78	Magazines	characters
32	Library books	events; now/next	79	Library books	characters
33	Newspapers	l L	80	Library books	characters
34	Newspapers	m M	81	Newspapers	details in picture
35	Text: science	words with l m	82	Newspapers	details in picture
36	Text: science	science words	83	Text: science	noisy things
37	Magazines	science	84	Text: science	quiet things
38	Magazines	hands; what doing now/before	85	Magazines	noisy and quiet things
39	Library books	events; now/before	86	Magazines	houses
40	Library books	events; now/before	87	Library books	houses
41	Newspapers	n N	88	Library books	houses
42	Newspapers	p P	89	Catalogs	big/little
43	Text: social studies	words with n p	90	Catalogs	expensive/ inexpensive
44	Text: social studies	objects which could be purchased	91	Newspapers	advertisements; places
			92	Newspapers	places
45	Magazines	money: $, ¢	93	Text: social studies	places
46	Magazines	money; relative costs	94	Text: social studies	rural, urban, suburban
47	Library books	places	95	Maps	rivers & lakes
48	Library books	places	96	Maps	big cities & little towns
49	Newspapers	q Q			
50	Newspapers	r R			

Lesson	Topic/Focus	Resource	Lesson	Topic/Focus	Resource
97	Magazines	rural, urban, suburban	137	Telephone yellow page	what is for sale
98	Magazines	real and make-believe	138	Telephone yellow pages	phone numbers
99	Library books	real and make-believe	139	Newspapers	names of businesses
100	Library books	feelings	140	Newspapers	symbols
101	Art prints	feelings	141	Text: math	things made or manufactured
102	Art prints	compare two prints	142	Text: math	things not made or manufactured
103	Newspapers	sports; main idea	143	Forms	writing address
104	Newspapers	advertisements; connotations of words	144	Forms	completing orders
			145	Magazines	main idea
105	Text: math	direction words	146	Magazines	label details in picture
106	Text: math	locate addition & subtraction problems	147	Library books	details in pictures
			148	Newspapers	animal babies
107	Telephone white pages	look up numbers for group	149	Text: science	animal babies
			150	Text: science	symbols
108	Telephone white pages	emergency numbers	151	Maps	symbols
			152	Maps	landmarks
109	Magazines	slithery, slimy things	153	Picture Report—Day 1	birds
			154	Picture Report—Day 2	birds
110	Magazines	soft, furry things	155	Picture Report—Day 3	birds
111	Library books	little things	156	Newspapers	places
112	Library books	big things	157	Magazines	places
113	Catalogs	relative size	158	Magazines	fairy tales; retelling
114	Catalogs	relative cost	159	Library books	fairy tales; characters
115	Newspapers	big and little words	160	Library books	fairy tales; magic
116	Newspapers	changes	161	Table of Contents	textbook
117	Text: science	changes	162	Table of Contents	magazine
118	Text: science	changes	163	ind. Written Report—Day 1	dinosaurs
119	Catalogs	senses: taste, hear	164	ind. Written Report—Day 2	dinosaurs
120	Catalogs	senses: smell, feel	165	ind. Written Report—Day 3	dinosaurs
121	Magazines	shapes	166	ind. Written Report—Day 4	dinosaurs
122	Magazines	comparison	167	ind. Written Report—Day 5	dinosaurs
123	Library books	comparison	168	Text; science	specialized vocabulary
124	Library books	money	169	Text: science	index
125	Menus	cost of items	170	Newspapers	index
126	Menus	colors of food	171	Newspapers	people in the news
127	Newspapers	colors of items	172	ind. Written Report—Day 1	class chooses topic
128	Newspapers	comics; sequence	173	ind. Written Report—Day 2	subtopic 1
129	Text: social studies	sequence of events	174	ind. Written Report—Day 3	subtopic 2
			175	ind. Written Report—Day 4	subtopic 3
130	Text: social studies	clothing	176	ind. Written Report—Day 5	subtopic 4
131	Art prints	clothing	177	ind. Written Report—Day 6	writing the report
132	Art prints	main idea	178	ind. Written Report—Day 7	revising & publishing
133	Magazines	main idea			
134	Magazines	details	179	Telephone yellow pages	places to buy cars
135	Library books	details	180	Telephone yellow pages	names of schools
136	Library books	businesses			

Suggested Book Titles For Storytime

1.	Brown Bear, Brown Bear	B. Martin, Jr.	Holt, 1983
2.	Are You My Mother?	P. D. Eastman	Random House, 1960
3.	Sleepy Book	C. Zolotow	Harper, 1958/1988
4.	In the Forest	M. H. Ets	Viking, 1944
5.	Gregory the Terrible Eater	M. Sharmat	Four Winds, 1980
6.	It's Mine	L. Lionni	Knopf, 1986
7.	Parade	D. Crews	Morrow, 1986
8.	The Biggest Bear	L. Ward	Houghton Mifflin, 1952
9.	Alexander and Terrible…Day	J. Viorst	Macmillan, 1972
10.	Runaway Bunny	M. W. Brown	Harper, 1972
11.	Apples and Pumpkins	A. Rockwell	Macmillan, 1989
	Seasons	B. Wildsmith	Oxford, 1980
	Frog and Toad All Year	A. Lobel	Harper, 1976
12.	Riddles about the Seasons	J. Ball	Silver, 1989
	What Am I? Very First Riddles	S. Calmenson	Harper, 1989
13.	The Tale of Squirrel Nutkin	B. Potter	Warne, 1903
	The Meanest Squirrel I Ever Met	G. Zion	Scribner's, 1962
14.	Color Farm	L. Ehlert	Harper, 1990
	Is It Rough? Is It Smooth?	T. Hoban	Greenwillow, 1984
	Color Zoo	L. Ehlert	Harper, 1989
15.	Planting A Rainbow	L. Ehlert	Harcourt, 1988
	A Rainbow of My Own	D. Freeman	Penguin, 1978
16.	Samuel Todd's Book of Colors	E. L. Konigsburg	Macmillan, 1990
	The Mixed-Up Chameleon	E. Carle	Crowell, 1984
	Rainbow Crow	N. Van Laan	Knopf, 1989
17.	Someday	C. Zolotow	Harper, 1965
18.	How to Hide a Gray Tree Frog	R. Heller	Putnam, 1986
	How to Hide a Polar Bear	R. Heller	Putnam, 1986
19.	Petunia	R. Duvoisin	Knopf, 1952
20.	My Teacher Sleeps at School	L. Weiss	Penguin, 1985
	John Patrick Norman McHennessy, The Boy Who Was Always Late	J. Burningham	Crown, 1987
21.	Owliver	R. Kraus	Dutton, 1974
22.	Eyes	J. Bailey	Doubleday, 1974
	The Eye Book	T. LeSeig	Random House, 1968
	Look At Your Eyes	P. Showers	Harper Jr., 1976
23.	Leo, the Late Bloomer	R. Kraus	Dutton, 1971
24.	Mike Mulligan & His Steam Shovel	V. L. Burton	Houghton Mifflin, 1939
25.	Gorilla	A. Browne	Knopf, 1985
	The Wednesday Surprise	E. Bunting	Clarion, 1989
	The Wall	E. Bunting	Clarion, 1990
26.	Weird Parents	D. & A. Wood	Dial, 1990
	Blueberries for Sal	R. McCloskey	Viking, 1948/1968
	Follow Me	N. Tafuri	Greenwillow, 1990
	River Dream	A. Say	Houghton, Mifflin, 1988
27.	The Baby	J. Burningham	Harper, 1975
	Earthlets	T. Ross	Dutton, 1989
	The Baby's Catalogue	J. & A. Ahlberg	Little, Brown, 1986
	She Come Bringing Me That Little Baby Girl	E. Greenfield	Harper, 1974
28.	Stevie	J. Steptoe	Harper, 1969
	Abby	J. Caines	Harper, 1973
29.	Wilfrid Gordon McD Partridge	M. Fox	Kane/Miller, 1985
	Miss Rumphius	B. Cooney	Penguin, 1985
	Harry & the Lady Next Door	G. Zion	Harper, 1960
30.	Feet	P. Parnall	Macmillan, 1988
	The Foot Book	Dr. Seuss	Random House, 1968
31.	Shoes	E. Winthrop	Harper, 1986
	Making Shoes	N. Tafuri	Greenwillow, 1988
	Big Shoe, Little Shoe	D. Cazet	Bradbury, 1984

32.	Ramona the Pest (one chapter re: school)	B. Cleary	Morrow, 1984
33.	A Tree Is Nice	J. M. Udry	Harper, 1987
34.	Spot's Birthday Party	E. Hill	Random House, 1959
	Clifford's Birthday Party	N. Bridwell	Scholastic, 1988
35.	Birthday Presents	C. Rylant	F. Watts, 1987
	The Birthday Moon	L. Duncan	Penguin, 1989
	June 7!	Allki	Macmillan, 1972
36.	Poems from Celebrations	M. C. Livingston	Holiday House, 1985
	Birthday Poems	M. C. Livingston	Holiday House, 1989
37.	Polar Express	C. Van Allsburg	Houghton Mifflin, 1985
38.	Crictor	T. Ungerer	Harper, 1958
39.	Can I Keep Him?	S. Kellogg	Dial, 1971
40.	Lyle, Lyle Crocodile	B. Waber	Houghton Mifflin, 1965
41.	The Paper Crane	M. Bang	Greenwillow, 1985
42.	Eating the Alphabet	L. Ehlert	Harcourt, 1989
	Growing Vegetable	L. Ehlert	Harcourt, 1987
	Feathers for Lunch	L. Ehlert	Harcourt, 1990
43.	Heckety Peg	D. & A. Wood	Harcourt, 1987
44.	Stone Soup	M. Brown	Macmillan, 1986
45.	Umbrella	T. Yashima	Penguin, 1958
46.	Marge's Diner	G. Gibbons	Harper, 1989
47.	The Mitten	J Brett	Putnam, 1990
	The Mitten	A. Tresselt	Scholastic, 1985
48.	The New Kid on the Block	J. Prelutsky	Greenwillow, 1984
49.	Peanut Butter and Jelly	N. Wescott	Dutton, 1987
	Bread & Jam for Frances	R. Hoban	Harper, 1964
	Bread, Bread, Bread	A. Morris	Lothrop, 1989
50.	A. Lobel Series		
	Frog & Toad Are Friends	A. Lobel	Harper, 1970
	"Lost Buttons"		
51.	Prince Bertram the Bad	A. Lobel	Harper, 1963
52.	Mouse Tales	A. Lobel	Harper, 1972
53.	Uncle Elephant	A. Lobel	Harper, 1981
54.	Oh! Were They Ever Happy	P. Spier	Doubleday, 1978
55.	Weather Words & What They Mean	G. Gibbons	Holiday House, 1990
	Flash, Crash, Rumble, and Roll	F. Branley	Harper, 1985
	Hurricane Watch	F. Branley	Harper, 1985
	Rain & Hail	F. Branley	Harper, 1963/1983
	The Storm Book	C. Zolotow	Harper, 1989
56.	The Little House	V. L. Burton	Houghton Mifflin, 1942/ 1969
57.	Owl Moon	J. Yolen	Philomel, 1987
58.	Airport	B. Barton	Crowell, 1982
	Flying	D. Crews	Greenwillow, 1986
59.	Magic Schoolbus Visits Waterworks	J. Cole	Scholastic, 1988
	Great White Man-Eating Shark	M. Mahy	Dial, 1990
60.	Swimmy	L. Lionni	Pantheon, 1968
61.	Little Tim and Brave Sea Captain	E. Ardizonne	Penguin, 1983
62.	King Bidgood's in the Bathtub	D. & A. Wood	Harcourt, 1985
63.	The Tub People	P. Conrad	Harper, 1989
	Time to Get Out of Bath, Shirley	J. Burningham	Crowell, 1978
64.	Fire! Fire!	G. Gibbons	Harper, 1964
	The Fire Cat	E. Averill	Harper, 1960
65.	Make Way For Ducklings	R. McCloskey	Viking, 1941
66.	Imogene's Antlers	D. Smith	Crown, 1985
	Mother, Mother, I Feel Sick...	R. Charlip	Parents Mag Press, 1966
67.	Arthur's Loose Tooth	L. Hoban	Harper, 1985
	Dr. DeSoto	W. Steig	Scholastic, 1982
68.	Machines at Work	B. Barton	Crowell, 1987
	Machines	A. & H. Rockwell	Harper, 1985
	Building a House	B. Barton	Penguin, 1984
69.	Katy and the Big Snow	V. L. Burton	Houghton Mifflin, 1943/ 1971

70.	Transportation books by B. Barton		
	Airplanes	B. Barton	Harper, 1986
	Boats		Harper, 1986
	Trains		Harper, 1986
	Trucks		Harper, 1986
	Wheels		Harper, 1979
71.	Round Trip	A. Jonas	Greenwillow, 1983
72.	I Want to Be An Astronaut	B. Barton	Crowell, 1988
73.	Shooting Stars	F. Branley	Crowell, 1989
74.	Happy Birthday Moon	F. Asch	Prentice-Hall, 1982
	Moongame	F. Asch	Prentice-Hall, 1984
75.	Moon Man	T. Ungerer	Harper, 1967
76.	Fortunately	R. Charlip	Four Winds, 1964
77.	Madeline's Rescue	L. Bemmelmans	Viking, 1939/1967
78.	Rotten Ralph	J. Gantos	Houghton Mifflin, 1976
79.	Most Wonderful Egg in the World	H. Heine	Macmillan, 1987
80.	Amelia Bedelia	P. Parish	Harper, 1963
81.	The Quilt Story	T. Johnston	Putnam, 1985
	Sam Johnson and the Blue Ribbon Quilt	L. Ernst	Lothrop, 1983
82.	Alexander and Wind-Up Mouse	L. Lionni	Pantheon, 1969
83.	It's Too Noisy!	J. Cole	Harper, 1989
	Too Much Noise	A. McGovern	Houghton Mifflin, 1967
	Noisy Nora	R. Wells	Dial, 1973
	The Quiet Mother and the Noisy Boy	C. Zolotow	Harper, 1989
84.	The City Noisy Book	M. W. Brown	Harper, 1939
	The Indoor Noisy Book	M. W. Brown	Harper, 1942
85.	Ben's Trumpet	R. Isadora	Greenwillow, 1979
86.	Ira Sleeps Over	B. Waber	Houghton Mifflin, 1972
	The Red Wool Blanket	B. Graham	Little, Brown, 1987
87.	A House Is a House For Me	M. A. Hoberman	Penguin, 1978
	The Big Orange Spot	D. Pinkwater	Hastings House, 1977
88.	Napping House	D. & A. Wood	Harcourt, 1984
	The Bed Book	S. Piath	Harper, 1976
89.	Night in the Country	C. Rylant	Bradbury, 1986
	Wait Till the Moon Is Full	M. W. Brown	Harper, 1948
	Nighttime Animals	J. Cole	Knopf, 1985
90.	One Fine Day	N. Hogrogian	Macmillan, 1971
	Flossie and the Fox	P. McKissack	Dial, 1986
91.	The Relative Came	C. Rylant	Bradbury, 1985
92.	Time of Wonder	R. McCloskey	Viking, 1957
93.	Guess Who My Favorite Person Is	B. Baylor	Atheneum, 1977
94.	Harold & the Purple Crayon	C. Johnson	Harper, 1955
	Blackboard Bear	M. Alexander	Dial, 1972
95.	Alphabet Puzzle	J. Downie	Lothrop, 1988
	Anno's Alphabet	M. Anno	Crowell, 1975
96.	Where the Wild Things Are	M. Sendak	Harper, 1963/1988
97.	A Dark, Dark Tale	R. Brown	Dial, 1984
98.	Arrow to the Sun	G. McDermott	Viking, 1974
99.	Space Case	E. Marshall	Dial, 1982
100.	Many Moons	J. Thurber	Harcourt, 1943
101.	Any in either series: Getting to Know		
	World's Greatest Artist	M. Venezia	Childrens Press, 1988
	Art For Children	E. Raboff	Harper Trophy, 1987
102.	Any In series—same as above		
103.	Dallas Titans Get Ready for Bed	K. Kuskin	Harper, 1986
104.	Rain Makes Applesauce	J. Scheer	Holiday House, 1964
105.	Let's Be Enemies	J. M. Udry	Harper, 1988
106.	Anno's Counting House	M. Anno	Philomel, 1982
	Anno's Counting Book	M. Anno	Crowell, 1977
	Arthur's Funny Money	L. Hoban	Harper, 1981
107.	Snakes Are Hunters	P. Lauber	Harper, 1988
	A Snake's Body	J. Cole	Morrow, 1981
108.	Curious George Rides a Bike	H. A. Rey	Houghton Mifflin, 1952
109.	Crocodile Beat	G. Jorgensen	Bradbury, 1989

	Thump, Thump, Rat-a-Tat	G. Baer	Harper, 1989
110.	Millions of Cats	W. Gág	Geoghegan, 1928
111.	Anansi the Spider	G. McDermott	Holt, 1972
	The Grouchy Ladybug	E. Carle	Crowell, 1977
112.	Dinosaur Bones	Aliki	Harper, 1988
	Bones, Bones, Dinosaur Bones	B. Barton	Crowell, 1990
113.	Bugs!	P. & F. McKissack	Childrens Press, 1988
	When It Comes to Bugs	A. Fisher	Harper, 1986
	Big on Bugs	E. Fine & J. Josephson	Learning Works, 1982
	My First Insects, Spiders & Crawlers	C. Fitzsimons	Harper, 1987
114.	Andy and the Lion	J. Daugherty	Penguin, 1989
	Androcles and the Lion	J. Stevens	Holiday, 1989
115.	Corduroy	D. Freeman	Viking, 1968
116.	Little Blue & Little Yellow	L. Lionni	Astor-Honor, 1959
	The Great Blueness	A. Lobel	Harper, 1968
	Mouse Paint	E. Walsh	Harcourt, 1989
117.	The Three Bears	P. Galdone	Ticknor/Fields, 1985
118.	Goldilocks & the Three Bears	J. Marshall	Dial, 1988
119.	The Jolly Postman	J. & A. Ahlberg	Little, Brown, 1986
120.	City Sounds	R. Emberly	Little, Brown, 1989
121.	Playing Marbles	J. Brinckloe	Morrow, 1988
	The Klutz Book of Marbles	Eds. of Klutz Bks	Klutz, 1989
	Games (and How to Play Them)	A. Rockwell	Harper, 1973
	1 2 3 Play With Me	K. Gundersheimer	Harper, 1984
122.	Will's Mammoth	R. Martin	Putnam, 1989
	I Want a Dog	D. Khaisa	C. N. Potter, 1987
123.	Ghost-Eye Tree	B. Martin, Jr. & J. Archambault	Holt, 1988
124.	Everybody Needs a Rock	B. Baylor	Atheneum, 1974
125.	Jumanji	C. Van Allsburg	Houghton Mifflin, 1981
	Cat in the Hat	Dr. Seuss	Random House, 1987
126.	Tana Hoban Day—assorted books	T. Hoban	
	26 Letters and 99 Cents		Greenwillow, 1987
	Of Colors and Things		Greenwillow, 1989
	I Read Symbols		Greenwillow, 1983
	Take Another Look		Greenwillow, 1981
	Is It Larger? Is It Smaller?		Greenwillow, 1985
	Shapes, Shapes, Shapes		Greenwillow, 1986
	Shapes and Things		Greenwillow, 1970
127.	Two Bad Ants	C. Van Allsburg	Houghton Mifflin, 1988
	George Shrinks	W. Joyce	Harper, 1985
128.	Chair for My Mother	V. Williams	Greenwillow, 1982
129.	A variety of ABC books		
	Alphabatics	S. MacDonald	Bradbury, 1986
	The Museum of Modern Art New York ABC	F. C. Mayers	Abrams, 1986
	ABCing	J. Beller	Crown, 1984
	Arlene Alda's ABC Book	A. Alda	Celestial Arts, 1981
	A, My Name is Alice	J. Bayer	Dial, 1984
130.	Thomas' Snow Suit	R. Munsch	Firefly, 1985
	Pelle's New Suit	E. Beskow	Harper, 1929
131.	Going Up	P. Sis	Greenwillow, 1989
132.	Drummer Hoff	B. Emberley	Prentice-Hall, 1967
133.	Philharmonic Gets Dressed	K. Kuskin	Harper, 1982
134.	Getting Dressed	V. Cole	Harper, 1989
135.	Do You Want to Be My Friend?	E. Carle	Harper, 1971
136.	The Josephine Story Quilt	E. Coerr	Harper, 1986
	The Quilt	A. Jonas	Greenwillow, 1984
	The Keeping Quilt	P. Polocco	Simon/Schuster, 1988
137.	Delpine	M. Bang	Morrow, 1988
138.	May I Bring a Friend?	B. Schenk de Regniers	Macmillan, 1964
	Little Bear's Friend	E. Minarik	Harper, 1960
139.	"Eeyore Has A Birthday Party and Gets Two Presents" in Winnie-the-Pooh	A. A. Milne	Dutton, 1926

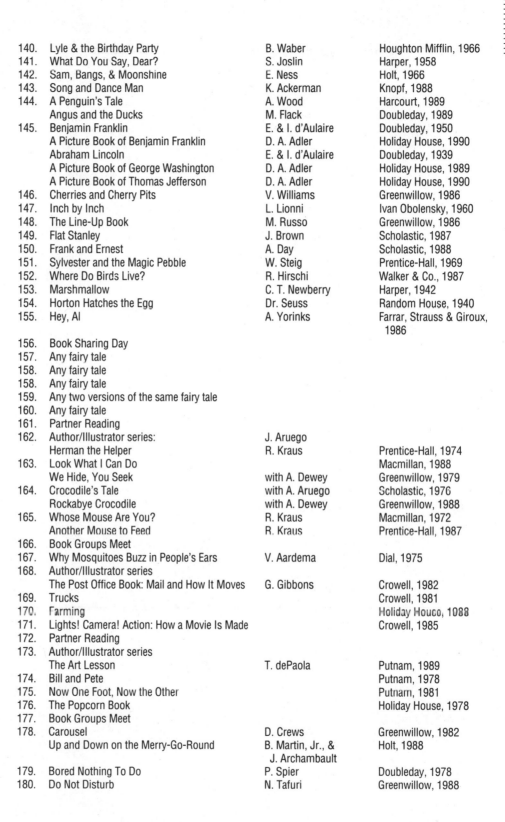

140.	Lyle & the Birthday Party	B. Waber	Houghton Mifflin, 1966
141.	What Do You Say, Dear?	S. Joslin	Harper, 1958
142.	Sam, Bangs, & Moonshine	E. Ness	Holt, 1966
143.	Song and Dance Man	K. Ackerman	Knopf, 1988
144.	A Penguin's Tale	A. Wood	Harcourt, 1989
	Angus and the Ducks	M. Flack	Doubleday, 1989
145.	Benjamin Franklin	E. & I. d'Aulaire	Doubleday, 1950
	A Picture Book of Benjamin Franklin	D. A. Adler	Holiday House, 1990
	Abraham Lincoln	E. & I. d'Aulaire	Doubleday, 1939
	A Picture Book of George Washington	D. A. Adler	Holiday House, 1989
	A Picture Book of Thomas Jefferson	D. A. Adler	Holiday House, 1990
146.	Cherries and Cherry Pits	V. Williams	Greenwillow, 1986
147.	Inch by Inch	L. Lionni	Ivan Obolensky, 1960
148.	The Line-Up Book	M. Russo	Greenwillow, 1986
149.	Flat Stanley	J. Brown	Scholastic, 1987
150.	Frank and Ernest	A. Day	Scholastic, 1988
151.	Sylvester and the Magic Pebble	W. Steig	Prentice-Hall, 1969
152.	Where Do Birds Live?	R. Hirschi	Walker & Co., 1987
153.	Marshmallow	C. T. Newberry	Harper, 1942
154.	Horton Hatches the Egg	Dr. Seuss	Random House, 1940
155.	Hey, Al	A. Yorinks	Farrar, Strauss & Giroux, 1986
156.	Book Sharing Day		
157.	Any fairy tale		
158.	Any fairy tale		
158.	Any fairy tale		
159.	Any two versions of the same fairy tale		
160.	Any fairy tale		
161.	Partner Reading		
162.	Author/Illustrator series:	J. Aruego	
	Herman the Helper	R. Kraus	Prentice-Hall, 1974
163.	Look What I Can Do		Macmillan, 1988
	We Hide, You Seek	with A. Dewey	Greenwillow, 1979
164.	Crocodile's Tale	with A. Aruego	Scholastic, 1976
	Rockabye Crocodile	with A. Dewey	Greenwillow, 1988
165.	Whose Mouse Are You?	R. Kraus	Macmillan, 1972
	Another Mouse to Feed	R. Kraus	Prentice-Hall, 1987
166.	Book Groups Meet		
167.	Why Mosquitoes Buzz in People's Ears	V. Aardema	Dial, 1975
168.	Author/Illustrator series		
	The Post Office Book: Mail and How It Moves	G. Gibbons	Crowell, 1982
169.	Trucks		Crowell, 1981
170.	Farming		Holiday House, 1988
171.	Lights! Camera! Action: How a Movie Is Made		Crowell, 1985
172.	Partner Reading		
173.	Author/Illustrator series		
	The Art Lesson	T. dePaola	Putnam, 1989
174.	Bill and Pete		Putnam, 1978
175.	Now One Foot, Now the Other		Putnam, 1981
176.	The Popcorn Book		Holiday House, 1978
177.	Book Groups Meet		
178.	Carousel	D. Crews	Greenwillow, 1982
	Up and Down on the Merry-Go-Round	B. Martin, Jr., & J. Archambault	Holt, 1988
179.	Bored Nothing To Do	P. Spier	Doubleday, 1978
180.	Do Not Disturb	N. Tafuri	Greenwillow, 1988

Spelling Emphases Suggested in the Word Study Lessons

1. b	46. L	91. oo	136. h
2. c	47. M	92. ew	137. j
3. d	48. N	93. ss	138. k
4. f	49. O	94. oi	139. l
5. *b, c	50, *x, y	95. oy	140. m
6. g	51. P	96. ll	141. n
7. h	52. Q R	97. al	142. p
8. j	53. S	98. au	143. q
9. k	54. T	99. aw	144. r
10. *d, f	55. *z, a	100 un	145. s
11. l	56. U V	101. ou	146. t
12. m	57. W X	102. ow	147. v
13. n	58. Y Z	103. pp	148. w x
14. p	59. br	104. en	149. y z
15. *g, h	60. *e, i	105. ed	150. th
16. q	61. bl	106. ar	151. er
17. r	62. cr	107. kn	152. tr
18. s	63. dr	108. ly	153. ing
19. t	64. fl	109. n't	154. ch
20. *j, k	65. *o, u	110. tion	155. on
21. v	66. fr	111. ing	156. ly
22. w	67. gr	112. ble	157. ba
23. x	68. pr	113. ee	158. bl
24. y	69. sl	114. gh	159. gr
25. *l, m	70. sk	115. ei	160. dy
26. z	71. sc	116. ld	161. bi
27. a	72. sp	117. ry	162. tion
28. e	73. st	118. bb	163. ble
29. I	74. sh	119. rr	164. ed
30. *n, p	75. ch	120. dge	165. or
31. o	76. al	121. al	166. b c
32. u	77. qu	122. le	167. d f
33. A	78. wh	123. al	168. g h
34. B	79. ph	124, ea	169. j k
35. *q, r	80. wr	125. te	170. l m
36. C	81. nd	126. nt	171. n p
37. D	82. mp	127. igh	172. q r
38. E	83. ng	128. ad	173. s t
39. F	84. sw	129. ck	174. v w
40. *s, t	85. cl	130. ow	175. x y z
41. G	86. er	131. b	176. a
42. H	87. ir	132. c	177. e
43. I	88. ur	133. d	178. i
44. J K	89. or	134. f	179. o
45. *v, w	90. dy	135. g	180 u

*Review Lessons

Index

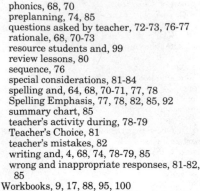

SuccesSuccesSuccesSuccesSuccesSuccesSuccesS

phonics, 68, 70
preplanning, 74, 85
questions asked by teacher, 72-73, 76-77
rationale, 68, 70-73
resource students and, 99
review lessons, 80
sequence, 76
special considerations, 81-84
spelling and, 64, 68, 70-71, 77, 78
Spelling Emphasis, 77, 78, 82, 85, 92
summary chart, 85
teacher's activity during, 78-79
Teacher's Choice, 81
teacher's mistakes, 82
writing and, 4, 68, 74, 78-79, 85
wrong and inappropriate responses, 81-82, 85
Workbooks, 9, 17, 88, 95, 100
Worksheets, 12, 30, 89, 94, 100
Writer's workshop, 66
Writing, 2. *See also* Writing module
to communicate, 13
literature as model for, 52
patterns and conventions of, 71
process, 11

Recreational Reading and Storytime and, 52
skills, 5, 18, 57
Storytime discussion and, 49
time for, 9
Word Study module and, 4, 68, 74, 78-79, 85
Writing module, 4, 54-67
audience and, 54, 58, 64
basic principles, 54-59
classroom arrangement/atmosphere and, 102
clipboard notes for, 90
composing time, 57, 59, 62-64, 67
content and form, 57
content areas integrated in, 60, 66, 67
conversations, teacher-student, 57, 61, 62-63, 64, 67, 91
conversations, student-student, 102
decision making by teacher, 59, 60-61, 67
discussion, 56, 59, 60, 61, 62, 67
evaluating students, 59, 64, 65
folder for. 54, 59, 62, 64-65, 66, 79, 86
mini-lesson and, 4, 11, 56, 60, 61-62, 66, 67

models for, 58-59
modifying, 59-60, 66-67
parents and, 89
preplanning, 59-60, 67
procedures, 59-66
publishing/editing, 54-55, 56, 58, 59, 64, 65-66, 67
Recreational Reading and Storytime module and, 58-59, 61
reports, 27
Research module and, 61
resource teachers and, 99
schedules, 59
sharing and, 4, 11, 54, 59, 64-65, 67
spelling and, 56, 57, 62, 64, 71, 88
students' decision making, 59, 60, 67, 66
substituting class book for, 49
substitutions, 59-60
summary chart, 67
taking home, 64-65
time/schedule for, 54, 59
topics, 4, 9, 54, 56, 59, 60-61, 66, 96
topics, students' list of, 62
Word Study charts and, 84
Word Study module and, 72

296 ▶ Index